W9-AUJ-947

The
Social Origins
of the
Iran-Iraq War

The
Social Origins
of the
Iran-Iraq War

W. Thom Workman

LYNNE
RIENNER
PUBLISHERS

BOULDER
LONDON

DS
79.719
W67
1994

c. 1

28966030
DLC

2-10-95

Published in the United States of America in 1994 by
Lynne Rienner Publishers, Inc.
1800 30th Street, Boulder, Colorado 80301

and in the United Kingdom by
Lynne Rienner Publishers, Inc.
3 Henrietta Street, Covent Garden, London WC2E 8LU

© 1994 by Lynne Rienner Publishers, Inc. All rights reserved

Library of Congress Cataloging-in-Publication Data
Workman, W. Thom.
    The social origins of the Iran-Iraq War / W. Thom Workman.
    Includes bibliographical references and index.
    ISBN 1-55587-460-6 (alk. paper)
    1. Iran-Iraq War, 1980–1988—Causes. 2. Iran-Iraq War, 1980–1988—
Social aspects—Iran. 3. Iran-Iraq War, 1980–1988—Social aspects—
Iraq. 4. Iran—Politics and government—1979– 5. Iraq—Politics
and government.
    DS79.719.W67 1994
    955.05'4—dc20   93-29380
                                                      CIP

British Cataloguing in Publication Data
A Cataloguing in Publication record for this book
is available from the British Library.

Printed and bound in the United States of America

 The paper used in this publication meets the requirements
of the American National Standard for Permanence of
Paper for Printed Library Materials Z39.48-1984.

To Beverly with love

Contents

Acknowledgments

This study is a substantially revised version of my doctoral thesis, written in Toronto and submitted to the Department of Political Science at York University during the summer of 1991. I wish to express my deep gratitude to David Dewitt, my academic supervisor, who afforded me the intellectual trust and freedom to "go off on my own." My thanks are also due to David Bell and David Leyton-Brown, the two remaining members of "David[3]," whose constant support and encouragement provided me with the scholarly stamina to see this study through to completion. I would also like to thank Gabriel Ben-Dor of Haifa University for his encouragement and guidance.

Along the way I have benefited immensely from the friendly contributions of a number of people, especially the weary but patient participants in the Donner Workshop on Security and Conflict Resolution at York University. Many of the ideas presented in this book had a long period of germination at those semiformal gatherings.

I have profited most deeply from the constant friendship of Mike Burke, who, in addition to scrupulously examining parts of this study, helped me to cope with the tribulations of academic life and to understand the "whys" of such an endeavor. My debt to him is inexpressible.

I also wish to acknowledge the support of the York Centre for International and Strategic Studies. In particular, I would like to thank Heather Chestnutt for her kind assistance in the preparation of the manuscript. This study was partly researched using the facilities of the Dayan Centre for Middle Eastern and African Studies at Tel Aviv University and the Kurdish Cultural Library in New York.

I am indebted to the Canadian Institute for International Peace and Security and the Social Sciences and Humanities Research Council of Canada, whose financial support made this study possible.

Finally, I wish to express my admiration to Beverly for making it through the long haul and to thank Meredith for getting here in time to prove that there is more to life than research and writing—19 February 1991 was probably the lesser challenge for all of us.

W. Thom Workman

1

Introduction: Toward the Critical Contemplation of the Iran-Iraq War

The first Gulf war—better known as the Iran-Iraq War—was tragic by any account. When one considers its economic costs, physical destruction, and human toll, there is merit in the claim that the Iran-Iraq War was the Third World's first "Great War."[1] Indeed, it was the longest conventional war of the twentieth century.[2] Estimates suggest that upwards of one million lives were lost: a further two million people were wounded. Almost 40 percent of the adult male population in the two countries took part in the war. Material damage has been estimated at upwards of $350 billion; and the overall costs of the war have been estimated at $1,190 billion. More than one million people were uprooted in the course of the fighting; at least 157 Iranian towns with populations of more than five thousand were damaged or wholly destroyed; and some 1,800 border villages were virtually wiped off the map.[3] The Iranian and Iraqi economies suffered steep declines in oil revenues and economic productivity.[4] And the belligerents flirted with the nadir of humanity, using chemical weapons and employing teenaged boys on the battlefield.

This listing of the devastation and carnage of the Iran-Iraq War suffices in decrying the fact that it ever transpired. Indeed, the war is a precise example of the kind of destruction that has impelled traditional research into contemporary warfare. The *traditional science of war* may be broadly summarized as the study of war with the view, in the spirit of Immanuel Kant, to engineering a *permanent or perpetual* peace. It is poignantly inherent in Herodotus's lament at the outset of *The Histories:* "In peace, sons bury their fathers, but in war fathers bury their sons." The traditional approach, moreover, rests upon well-elaborated scientific foundations generally consistent with the positivist temper of North American social science: i.e., traditional war science seeks to establish objective theories of warfare that will ultimately help to guide the world in peaceful directions. When one considers the sheer number of researchers that have explicitly or implicitly employed the traditional framework in their studies on war, the

1

number of scholarly periodicals and edited volumes informed by its ethical and intellectual premises, as well as its salience across many academic fields—anthropology, history, sociology, psychology, political science—it is apparent that the traditional framework became the prevailing scientific narrative of post–World War II scholarship.

There are, however, other costly dimensions to the Iran-Iraq War— costs that tend to be overlooked, downplayed, or ignored altogether by the traditional intellectual framework. The Iran-Iraq War profoundly affected the balance of social forces in both countries. By further eroding the social power of oppressed groups and classes, it worked to the near exclusive advantage of the ruling regimes. The Iran-Iraq War, to state it baldly, had two victors: the Ba'th regime in Baghdad and the Theocratic regime in Tehran.

In Iran, the prosecution of the war allowed the radical clerics to consolidate the Islamic Revolution. It did this in a number of ways: by delegitimizing political opposition, by providing a pretext for extensive political repression, by providing a "natural" context for the *theocratic-populist* strategy of the clerics (an approach that inter alia helped to keep the population politically mobilized), by maintaining a coherence and common focus among the clerics in power, by necessitating the expansion of revolutionary institutions under clerical control, and by providing a permanent excuse as to why the revolution had failed to deliver on its promises to the poor.

In Iraq, the war created similar opportunities for the Ba'th regime. It allowed the Baghdad regime to enhance its political power by engaging in its own "war populism" (a strategy that partially overcame the fissured character of Iraqi society and enhanced the regime's image as "defender of the Arab nation"), by providing the regime with a forum to raise the profile and image of Saddam Hussein, by allowing the Ba'th regime to continue to carve out a modest social base among Iraq's rapidly expanding capitalist class, by encouraging the expansion of the military, by providing a "wartime exigencies" foil for the repression of internal political opposition, and by weakening the cohesion and domestic image of Iraq's opposition forces. Both regimes, in short, were able to parlay the protracted military stalemate into concrete political gains.

The social corollary of these dynamics allows us to identify the real losers of the eight-year Iran-Iraq War. The strengthening of the regimes in Baghdad and Tehran translated into the increasing marginalization of subaltern groups in both countries—especially women, the urban poor, the working classes, and the Kurdish peoples. More specifically, the deleterious effect of the war on the underprivileged was both direct and indirect. In an immediate sense, each regime often used the war directly to rationalize and justify policies targeted at many of its disempowered constituencies. At the same time, by helping to entrench regimes with narrowly defined political projects—projects that generally refused to countenance meaningfully the political aspirations of disempowered social groups—the war indirectly contributed to an intensification of their subordinate social standing. It is a cruel irony that the vast majority of those who suffered the burdens of the war came from groups whose prospects for social advancement were severely thwarted by the war itself.

The task of identifying the steep social costs of the Iran-Iraq War compel us to take a different orientation in the study of war. The *critical science of warfare* could be broadly summarized as the contemplation of warfare in terms of the prevailing constellations of social power within societies. It seeks to reveal the relationship between countervailing social forces on the one hand and the outbreak and prosecution of warfare on the other. In addition to drawing attention to the deplorable waste and carnage of contemporary warfare, the critical study of war necessarily emphasizes its social costs, understood in terms of the maintenance or intensification of oppressive social relations in any given society. The ultimate aim of this development of theoretical knowledge is to transform society in less oppressive directions.

The conventional and critical approaches to the scholarly study of war form two radically contrasting intellectual axes. With the traditional science of war holding a hegemonic position in Western scholarship, the critical grouping has remained on the margins. But the body of impressive works that easily fall within the emerging critical tradition is growing. In order to appreciate fully the intellectual footings of the present study it is necessary briefly to compare and contrast the two scholarly approaches. Accordingly, the essential elements of the traditional science of war are identified. This should help to establish the fundamental features of the critical science of war.

The Traditional Science of War

The traditional science of war receives a woolly and inconsistent assortment of working appellations—causes of war research, peace research, and conflict management/resolution research among others. It has been the hegemonic intellectual discourse around research on war for most of the post–World War II period, although its status in the post–Cold War era is less certain. The following outline is geared specifically toward the provision of intellectual oppositions with a more critical social scientific strategy. The ease with which the schematic character of the following polarizations can lead to facile or forced generalizations must be borne in mind. In particular, individual scholars falling under the rubric of either scholarly approach may vary considerably along any of the categorical oppositions. Nonetheless, the schematic does provide invaluable insight into differing intellectual and political tendencies associated with the study of war, and is an indispensable step in the calibration of war research with a genuinely emancipatory social science.

To begin outlining the *traditional science of war,* attention must be drawn to the fact that warfare has forever been imbued with moral content. As Michael Walzer affirms, "For as long as men and women have talked about war, they have talked about it in terms of right and wrong."[5] The disdain that different ages have shown for war, furthermore, appears to be linked directly to its prosecution. F. H. Hinsley writes: "We cannot say who first devised a plan for perpetual peace: the aim cannot be much less old than the practice of war. The interest men have shown in this aim—the concern they have felt at the absence of peace or for the maintenance of peace—has fluctuated throughout history. It has been most intense during and immediately after periods of especially frequent, especially extensive or especially destructive war."[6] These tendencies are true equally of the contemporary era. *War* has come to be contrasted with *peace* in the manner that Saint Augustine would have pitted *evil* against *good.* And as Hinsley's speculations suggest, the current view that war is "pathological and abnormal" has been traced directly to the liberal reaction against World War I.[7] The salience of this view is now beyond question, and at times even has been celebrated. "The present trend," stressed one researcher in the early 1970s, "seems to be toward a great popular uprising against war, in which the masses of the people will issue an ultimatum to their leaders and rulers against all wars."[8] This prevailing assessment has undoubtedly been impelled by the totalizing wars of the twentieth century, by the vivid images of war captured through the media, and by the prospect of nuclear annihilation. As is elegantly revealed in Hans Morgenthau's *Death in the Nuclear Age* and Wilfred Owen's *The Old Lie,* the utter horror of war in the twentieth century has inspired scholarly and poetic imaginations alike.

This pervasive view of warfare as one of humanity's most pressing problems constitutes the fundamental point of departure for the traditional science of war.[9] As the following twist on the popular shibboleth from academia reveals, the research community often is driven self-consciously by a sense of urgency:

> Students of war are under a special injunction to "publish or perish." War is one of the most intractable human problems. The fear of war, and the threat of global cataclysm, is always with us. Perhaps many people would name some other horseman—hunger or disease—as the most fearsome; each of us has different private fears. Others would place the quest for human dignity and equality above that for peace. But the danger of war is so great, and so immediate, that without reliable peace it hardly seems possible to pursue other goals effectively. Contemporary wars, military preparations, and continued payment of the cost of past war amount, in the United States, to more than all public expenditure for health and

education combined. True, war has been so universally part of the human condition that the prospects for understanding how to avoid it, especially under the pressures modern technology puts upon us, do not seem very good. But the need to try is certainly there.[10]

With war widely regarded as the fetter of human dignity, as something that can choke meaningful human progress, and ultimately as something that could destroy modern civilization itself, social scientists turning their attention to war are encouraged to be fully cognizant of the potential significance of their research findings.

The goal of eradicating war is ingrained firmly across the scientific community. As one researcher typically emphasizes: "The problem that most concerns sociologists working on peace promotion is how to prevent warfare. This concern focuses particularly on the prevention of nuclear war. . . . At the same time, widespread persistence of non-nuclear limited wars has revived social science's interest in so-called conventional warfare."[11] Although these sentiments were cultivated in an atmosphere of superpower conflict and protracted regional conflicts, they are unlikely to be dampened significantly in view of the presence of large weapons stockpiles, the continuing likelihood of nuclear proliferation, and the sustained presence of regional conflicts across the globe. Indeed, one of the first tests of the post–Cold War era led to war in the Middle East.

The goal of eradicating warfare is coupled with the belief that it can be achieved through careful scientific research and the refinement of theoretical understanding. A new faith gradually emerged that to know war is to conquer war. The classical axiom, *si vis pacem para bellum* (if you wish for peace prepare for war), has been supplanted with Liddell Hart's dictum, "If you wish for peace, *understand* war." In order to achieve this level of theoretical understanding, the research community has commissioned a model of science initially developed and honed in the natural sciences. That is, the war research community, in a manner consistent with the broader social scientific college, appropriated the methods and rationales of natural science in the study of war. This particular understanding of the social sciences has been summarized lucidly by Richard J. Bernstein:

> At the core of the naturalistic understanding of social and political inquiry is the demand for empirical explanatory theories of human behaviour. When this idea of empirical theory is fully articulated, it requires that we discover basic invariants, structures, or laws that can serve as the foundation for theoretical explanations—explanations which will take a deductive form, and from which we can derive counterfactual claims about the relations of independent and dependent variables. It has been projected that the social sciences, as they mature, will discover well-tested bodies of empirical theory which will eventually coalesce in ever more adequate and comprehensive theories.[12]

The research community seeks to generate a theoretical portrait of war, a nomological body of theory capable of easily articulating war's etiological calendar. Expressed in terms more in line with current methodological parlance, war is assigned the status of *dependent variable:* it is the thing requiring explanation. War is explicated successfully by identifying those *independent variables* responsible for its outbreak and course. This prevailing view of the scientific task of war research received one of its clearest accounts in Luther Bernard's study:

> Like all other forms of social behaviour, [war] has its natural causes, some of which exist in the social and physical environments and others in the human nature of men. These causes of war are neither mysterious nor extraordinarily obscure. They are discoverable by means of patient orderly research and they are removable by ordinary means of human diligence and cooperative endeavour. Otherwise, the study of war would not be amenable to scientific organization and a social science of war could not be produced. Such a science can be constructed; and when it is established as a pure science, an applied social science or technology presumably can be developed as a means to the abolition or prevention of war. It is not possible to abolish war until its social phenomena have been reduced to a science and its causes have been isolated and rendered susceptible of intellectual definition.[13]

Anatol Rapoport, in the inaugural edition of the *Journal of Conflict Resolution,* wrote: "The idea of turning the cold and brilliant light of mathematics on a subject where passions obscure reason is in itself the embodiment of the best in scientific ethics." This model of science reached its apogee in the *Correlates of War* project housed at the University of Michigan.[14]

The difficulties of achieving the necessary rigor required by the naturalistic model of science have been noted frequently. David Wilkinson's appraisal of Lewis Fry Richardson's *Statistics of Deadly Quarrels* drew attention to the fact that his work contained no controlled or uncontrolled experimentation, no experimental intervention or experimental manipulation, no replication, no examination of random samples from sample populations, and a minimum of direct observation. But in his assessment of these gaps, Wilkinson tersely wrote: "Shortcomings that are inescapable simply have to be recognized and accepted."[15] In other words, researchers must recognize that the research methods of natural science are not entirely imitable in the study of war. Other doubts have been expressed about the purely scientific possibilities of the research enterprise pertaining to war, pointing inter alia to the lack of agreement about the facts to be selected, to the interpretation of those facts, and to the tendency to relegate nonquantifiable aspects of war to secondary importance.[16] Still, the conclusion that the naturalistic scientific model is appropriately archetypical is invariably sustained, even if it cannot be transported to the study of war in its pristine form. Such difficulties, in essence, do not preclude the possibility of developing a scientific corpus of knowledge about war, as the following defense of the prevailing scientific sentiments illuminatingly reveals:

> No two animals are exactly alike, and certainly not the flea and the elephant. Hence, one might argue that no valid generalizations can be stated that embrace both species. Yet the scientific disciplines of physiology, biochemistry, and genetics have proven this wrong. Science does not say that the flea and the elephant are the same thing but only that they are similar in certain ways, e.g., both are produced from the union of an egg and a sperm. Concomitantly, two wars, though not exactly the same, may have enough in common to permit the development of valid generalization, e.g., both may have developed out of an arms race precipitated by one state's misperception of another's intentions.[17]

Although an unblemished model of natural science cannot be carried over into the study of war, the model is the measure of good science. Analysts must accept the unique difficulties facing the field. Therefore, occasional skepticism about the potential harvests of the science of war does not create a lack of faith in the scientific method itself: "Science may not save us, but we are unlikely to be saved without it."[18]

When we probe a little deeper, we also see that the traditional science of war rests upon a rather strict separation of the *observer* and the *observed.* It subscribes to a conception of social science as *wertfrei,* that is, a conception of science that aspires to study dispassionately the *facts* of social life independently of *normative speculation.* The *facts* (of war) can be ascertained apart from the *values* of the researcher or the cultural predilections of his or her society. The theory of war describes the world the way it *is;* not the way it *ought* to be. The oft repeated disciplinary injunction is that investigators must "search for overarching explanatory theories based upon the *organized and dispassionate collection of data.*"[19] Researchers must take care to preserve scientific neutrality. To fashion research on anything other than uncontaminated raw data invites the unfortunate spectre of ideologically tainted theories of war.

The conviction that the theory of war can and should be *objective* (understood as theoretical knowledge that is unsullied by the values and biases of the research community) can be observed in the scholarly rationale that accompanied the development of the discipline of peace research. The original appellation arose from the concern that analysts of war were not explicit enough in their condemnation of war. It was felt that professional dispassion might be extending too far. While this fear of ethical flinching was overstated terribly, the debate nonetheless helps to reveal the basic position of traditional science. In response to the challenge of *Peace Research,* the editors of *War, Its Causes and Correlates* stressed the need for an "applied science of war" to be functionally cast astride the "basic science of war":

> It is difficult to beg for patience in the face of urgent problems but applied science is impossible without a basic science and it is false to criticize the physician who remains in his laboratory to provide the explanations which will allow his fellow at the bedside to save the patient. Conversely, there are times, and now is one of them, when the scientist in basic research must invite the applied scientist to join him in the laboratory so their combined skills, access to data, and approaches to problems which hold the only hope of survival for the patient and themselves may be utilized.[20]

Other commentators rationalized the challenge of *Peace Research* in a similar manner. Anatol Rapoport wrote that the concern with the "purity" of war science reflected a confusion between *objectivity* and *neutrality*. He stressed that science always has been motivated by specific goals: "Individual scientists may have been motivated by nothing but their personal curiosity, but the scientific enterprise as a whole was driven throughout history by needs and aspirations both good and evil."[21] Rapoport's concern, in a manner consistent with the broader justification for peace research, did not lie in challenging the possibility of an *objective* science of war but rather in calling attention to the need to be more explicit about the goal of the research enterprise, that is, the elimination of war. "There is no need," Rapoport therefore concluded, "for the peace researcher to assume the posture of political or moral neutrality in the interest of preserving the credibility accorded to scientific objectivity."[22] This position received its clearest articulation in the preface to a multidisciplinary study of war:

> These writings characteristically show social scientists trying to grapple with what is commonly recognized as the greatest dilemma of the modern age. For most of them a detached objectivity is a condition of their craft, yet here they emerge as sufficiently involved and committed to focus on a historic issue. This effort illustrates an inconsistency in social science itself. Although they generally view themselves as naturalists in the positivist tradition, these thinkers are also morally sensitive men whose interest in war has stemmed from a desire to improve the lot of humanity. Their self-image as impartial and detached observers is maintained in spite of the fact that the quality of their involvement with the subject matter is different from the involvement of, say, the chemist in his laboratory with the compounds in his test tubes. But this charming inconsistency is not damaging to their work; rather, their moral concern has served to channel their scientific energies. They have mustered the utmost detachment of which they are capable in the service of their moral commitment.[23]

The challenge of *Peace Research* reinforced the fundamental motivation of the research enterprise and underscored the widely accepted belief in scientific objectivity.

As we continue to unpack the traditional science of war, we must call attention to its understanding concerning *theoretical knowledge* on the one hand and its *application* or *usage* on the other. *Knowledge-claims,* in short, are intended to form the raw materials out of which peace can be fashioned. As one significant contribution to the field revealed: "With such understanding [of war] comes the first meaningful possibility of controlling it, eliminating it, or finding less reprehensible substitutes for it."[24] Knowledge of the independent variables responsible for war, in line with the more conventional methodological language, will allow researchers to intervene and eliminate war. An understanding of the causal register of war will allow the practitioners of peace to enter the outside world, with a kind of toolchest of knowledge, to manipulate, induce, suppress, modify, restrain, gently coax, subdue, countervail, or persuade those factors responsible for war. It is an orientation entirely consistent with Karl Popper's widely popular notion of "piece-meal [perhaps peace-meal] engineering." The traditional science of war, therefore, fully accords with an *instrumentalist* account of the relationship between theory and practice. It is valuable to reflect upon Brian Fay's summary of *instrumentalism:*

> The form of characteristically scientific knowledge in the modern period thus lends itself to a particular sort of instrumental use. Scientific theory provides knowledge of basic causal patterns such that precise determinations of likely outcomes are made possible, and the variables needed to be manipulated in order to produce a desired outcome or prevent an undesired one are revealed. This use of scientific knowledge has been most successful in controlling material processes, with space exploration and medicine probably offering the most dramatic instances of it. But it is a use of knowledge not confined to material processes, at least in aspiration. In the use of economic theory by governments in their attempt to control the economy, in the employment of behaviour modification techniques in psychiatric wards and prisons, in the application of psychological theories of motivation to questions of business management—to cite but a few instances—social scientific theory is conceived as useful in so far as it provides the basis for the engineering of social life.[25]

Fay's summary faithfully depicts the understanding of theory and practice informing the traditional science of war. With science comes objective scientific knowledge; with objective scientific knowledge comes a well-guided interventionist enterprise capable of effacing war from human history. The theoretical knowledge of war, in essence, establishes the real possibility of achieving the Kantian ideal of *perpetual peace.*

It is evident, therefore, that the traditional science of war rests upon one of the most fundamental precepts of the modern age; namely, that the social world can be subjected to human control through the careful gathering and application of scientific knowledge. This distinctive program of the Enlightenment views the harvests of science as something to be enlisted to benefit the condition of humankind. The successes of the natural sciences have bolstered this optimism. The traditional science of war shares with its sibling social sciences the belief that the social world (like its material counterpart in the natural sciences) can be harnessed and manipulated in directions more consonant with contemporary human aspirations. If peace is desired, then modern science brings us one step closer to its realization. One researcher has remarked, in fact, that the pervasive desire to see war eliminated is itself encouraged by the belief in the possibilities of manipulating and controlling human life. He writes: "Perhaps more important is our greater belief in the prospects of controlling society. War at one time was regarded as inevitable. However, so was slavery, which is now an almost defunct institution. If war is not seen to be an inevitable feature of human life, dislike of it will make people work to stop it rather than make the best of a bad job."[26]

Not surprisingly, the aforementioned disdain for war and the particular sense of (scientific) task has meant that the traditional science of war often has compared itself to epidemiology.[27] Epidemiology forms the analogical cornerstone for the traditional science of war. "War is like a disease," one recent inquiry begins, "for example, cancer or heart disease."[28] "An analogy with medicine," writes Robin Clarke in *The Science of War and Peace,*

> is instructive. Until 1848 no one knew what caused cholera. But in that year a Dr. John Snow looked up from his individual patients and sought a social pattern for the disease. On a map he plotted the addresses of 500 people who had died from cholera in Soho in a period of 10 days. All the deaths were clustered around a central spot which, investigation proved, was the site of a water pump. When its handle was removed, the epidemic died out and Dr. Snow had proved that cholera was caused by contaminated water. Why the world had to wait another hundred years before anyone applied the same principle to the study of war is inexplicable.[29]

The task of those who study war, as with researchers in pathology and the medical sciences, is to identify the factors responsible for this social affliction. Only then can researchers develop the appropriate antidote for war. Jean-Jacques Rousseau, in the *Abstract of the Abbé de Saint-Pierre's Project for Perpetual Peace,* established that "the cause of the disease, once known, suffices to indicate the remedy, if indeed there is one to be found." As Kenneth Waltz wrote at the outset to his monumental study on the causes of war:

> A prescription based on faulty analysis would be unlikely to produce the desired consequences. . . . A prescription would be unacceptable if it were not logically related to its analysis. *One who suffers from infected tonsils profits little from a skillfully performed appendectomy.* If violence among states is caused by the evilness of man, to aim at the internal reform of states will not do much good. And if violence among states is the product of international anarchy, to aim at the conversion of individuals can accomplish little. One man's prognosis confounds the other man's prescription.[30]

With respect to the above mentioned distinction between scientific objectivity and scientific neutrality, Anatol Rapoport later restated this distinction through the epidemiological analogy: "The physician does not pretend to be neutral with regard to the life-and-death struggle between the patient and the disease. He is unequivocally on the side of the patient."[31]

This completes our outline of the traditional science of war. Twenty-five centuries after Herodotus, the sentiments that informed his lament are entirely intact. For the traditional scientist, the disdain for war as a recurring historical practice is marked, a conviction distinguishing this community of scholars from their brethren in strategic studies. Research is undertaken in order to rid humanity of war. The naturalistic model of science is employed to this end. Primary stress is placed upon the importance of discovering the immutable laws of war. When these laws have been established, the world may be guided in more peaceful directions. Ultimately, the task of the traditional science of war is to inoculate humankind against this costly and enduring social plague.

The Critical Science of War

Science, like Art, is fun, a playing with truths, and no game
should even pretend to slay the heavy-lidded riddle
What is the Good Life?
W. H. Auden's "Unpredictable but providential"

The conventional study of war embodies a moral elegance and rational allure that commands intellectual mindfulness and respect. As reasonably compelling and as morally seductive as the traditional science of war at first appears to be, however, analytical enterprises can be motivated by a different set of social concerns and proceed from a fundamentally different cluster of premises regarding the nature of science and the appropriate relationship between theory and practice. Regardless of the fact that war is a terrible and costly venture, I suggest that it can be viewed with even greater cynicism and suspicion.

The approach outlined here is labelled appropriately as the *critical science of war,* an intellectual enterprise crystallizing within a wider critical theoretical tradition. It is helpful to speak briefly about the broader intellectual tradition.[32] Critical analysis could be defined as the process of offering "insight into what has happened, and into what we have become, which at the same time offers a critique, and hence some notion of a good unrealized or repressed in history, which we therefore understand better how to rescue."[33] The social ontology privileged by critical science stresses existing modes of domination within contemporary society, domination woven into and inextricably bound up with prevailing constellations of social power.

These configurations of social power are unlikely to have identifiable nodal points or centers of gravity, and are more likely to be suffused throughout society's hegemonic ideological and cultural practices.[34] Individuals interiorize cultural understandings and thereby reproduce prevailing relations of power. Critical social science thus expresses an immediate concern with social oppression, a condition that obtains when human potential is frustrated by sociostructural blockages.[35] It is a condition frequently faced by lower socioeconomic classes, women, minority racial groups, and homosexuals. Members of these social groups tend to find most life-paths effectively closed off, and rudimentary life-skills often remain underdeveloped. Their lives tend to be difficult, if not utterly burdensome. Members of oppressed social groups often face day-to-day hardship, uncertainty, and fear. Society, in other words, is thoroughly coercive, although the complex web of naturalized understandings and the rituals of daily life help to mask these coercions. This mystifying tendency can persist despite the fact that these *oppressive* social conditions are frequently accompanied by outright *repressive* practices by the dominant social groups.

Furthermore, social oppression is viewed as a historically fabricated condition. People create and continually re-create oppression through their self-understandings and practices. A socially oppressive world is not a divinely driven phenomenon. Cynthia Enloe writes that in this regard a feminist bumper sticker would read, "Nothing is natural—well, almost nothing."[36] The critical theoretical enterprise is motivated by the belief that as surely as humans brought about the world, they can unmake it. A socially oppressive society is not insuperable. The subordination of women, of different classes linked to working life and production, or of innumerable racial groups is not an insoluble feature of humanity. Society can be transformed; humans can be emancipated from domination. The task of critical social science—its "emphatic normative dimension"—thus lies in guiding society in less oppressive directions.[37]

With this brief outline of the broader critical task, we can turn now to a specific discussion of a critical study of warfare. Initial steps have been taken to establish theoretical and conceptual compasses capable of walking us critically through specific subject domains or instances of social life.[38] Some scattered efforts to link the study of war with a critical posture have arisen in the past, but the need for a clearer outline is long overdue.[39] The critical science of war can be summarized broadly as the contemplation of war in terms of dialectical *critiques* of social power;[40] i.e., militarism and warfare are empirically analyzed in terms of the dominant constellations of power within society. In a complementary terminological angle, critical analysis explores the relationship between warfare on the one hand and the configuration of countervailing social forces on the other. More directly, the critical science of war asks: What has war to do with immanent social crises? It submits, in the end, a scientific *commentary* upon militarism and warfare from the vantage point of society's inherently conflictual process-es.[41]

It must be emphasized that the critical study of war does not aspire merely to resurrect so-called second image or state/society accounts of war. If this were the case, it simply could be argued that the critical study of war draws out and emphasizes ideas that have been dormant or underexamined by previous work, and thus a strong case could be made that the critical science of war is overdrawing its theoretical or empirical uniqueness. Researchers could contend, quite correctly, that numerous investigations have drawn attention to state/society factors in their examination of war and would easily admit that such factors play a crucial role in the outbreak of war. Indeed, Kenneth Waltz's original contribution to the study of warfare distinguished between the "efficient" and "permissive" causes of war, and associated state-level factors with the former. Waltz wrote: "The structure of the state system does not directly cause state A to attack state B. Whether or not that attack occurs will depend on a number of special circumstances—location, size, power, interest, type of government, past history and tradition—each of which will influence the actions of both states."[42] Waltz held that the relationship between states is not an independent deterministic force in any sense but rather a permissive cause of war, a sort of catalyzing condition or situation. The explanatory power of the *third image* or state system by itself, Waltz contended, is nominal.

What is at issue between the traditional and critical approaches to warfare, however, is not the degree to which state/society issues can be implicated in warfare but rather the very conceptualization of society itself (and thus of the practice of war as well). More specifically, traditional war research customarily has been hampered by a very constricted conception of society. Notably, society has often been conceptualized as a static entity, as in the idea of modern versus feudal or industrial verses agrarian, and thus researchers entirely fail to consider intrasocietal class and communal dynamics. Raymond Aron's eminent consideration of the bellicosity of industrial society over preindustrial society, a study that identified industrial society in terms of its factories and machinery rather than in terms of any class cleavages associated with industrial production, exemplifies such an approach.[43] A second limitation involves a failure to consider societal fractures and cleavages even though a dynamic or evolutionary conception of society is adopted. Choucri and North's examination of war in terms of its population growth and advances in technology (which engenders *lateral pressure* and thus interstate conflict) in *Nations in Conflict* typifies this problem.[44] Choucri and North draw valuable attention to levels of population and technological development but entirely ignore basic cleavages within society, suggesting strongly that society is an unproblematic monolithic entity. A third problem draws attention to divisions within society but then completely fails to explore the dynamic and evolving relations within and between such groups. The contribution by Midlarsky and Thomas comparing the effect of primitive political systems, patrimonial empires, nomad or conquest empires, city-states, feudal systems, centralized historical bureaucratic empires, and modern preindustrial societies upon the incidence and duration of war illustrates this problem.[45] Although their comparative analysis was based on criteria that involved a consideration of social structure understood in terms of economic sectors and social groups, they did not attempt to consider the dynamics or interactions among these groups. Merely drawing attention to what might be termed as a social class is far different from attempting to assess the specific dynamics among social classes and constituencies.

In sharp contrast, the critical science of war conceptualizes society in terms of the evolutionary and dynamic struggle between social groups relationally identified as dominant and subaltern, as more powerful and less powerful, or between groups with considerable social latitude and groups that are relatively oppressed. This understanding of society is the conceptual screen through which the analysis of war must be filtered. The relationship between warfare and the dynamic relations among social classes and groups, in other words, is the principal concern. It must also be noted that such social constituencies can extend easily beyond any national boundaries or divisions, a fact greatly limiting the value of the original threefold division of Waltz. That is, social relations within the state must be contemplated especially in terms of the progressively internationalizing tendencies characteristic of late capitalism.[46]

And thus the very notion of warfare itself changes. War is not pondered, that is, as a *thing* to be manipulated or controlled but rather as part of an elaborate and complex sociopolitical dynamic.[47] The critical science of war stubbornly refuses to reify warfare by cutting it adrift from society at the moment of theoretical inception. In this sense the critical science of war is impelled by the preliminary observation that war is never prosecuted for politically innocent reasons. War is seldom undertaken on behalf of "the people" or "the nation" as if society were some undifferentiated mass. War is organically linked to the rudimentary social and political struggles of society. Observations of this sort have certainly arisen before. Thomas Paine declared more than two centuries ago:

> War is the common harvest of all those who participate in the division and expenditure of public money, in all countries. It is the art of conquering at home: the object of it is an increase of revenue; and as revenue cannot be increased without taxes, a pretence must be made for expenditures. In reviewing the history of the English Government, its wars and its taxes, a bystander, not blinded by prejudice, not warped by interest, would declare, that taxes were not raised to carry on wars, but that wars were raised to carry on taxes.[48]

War enters into rudimentary social struggles, confirms and reflects them, and at the same time reconfigures them. At one and the same moment, war is conditioned by and thrusts back upon the fundamental array of social forces within society. "Does not the threat of an atomic catastrophe which could wipe out the human race," queries Herbert Marcuse in an exemplary manner, "also serve to protect the very forces which perpetuate this danger?"[49]

According to the critical approach, war must be studied in order to draw attention to its links with different modes of socially oppressive relations in society. The orientation and stress of the critical science of war can be considered from another angle. In keeping with the idea that war is not a thing but rather part of a dynamic social process, our primary concern, in contrast to the traditional science of war, does not lie with the prosecution of war itself. Stated baldly, the critical study of war is not singularly motivated by the explicit wish to see war end. This point will likely violate well-honed professional sensibilities, and invite the obligatory basket of pejorative labels. The difference, nonetheless, must be stressed. To be clear, the critical science of war in no way trivializes the utter brutality of war, especially as technological developments have yielded stunning capacities for destruction and annihilation. Warfare breeds intense human suffering and this forever commands us to surrender ourselves to the spirit of Wilfred Owen's remonstrative poem:

> If in some smothering dreams you too could pace
> Behind the wagon that we flung him in,
> And watch the white eyes writhing in his face,
> His hanging face, like a devil's sick of sin;
> If you could hear, at every jolt, the blood
> come gargling from the froth-corrupted lungs,
> Obscene as cancer, bitter as the cud
> Of vile, incurable sores on innocent tongues—
> My friend, you would not tell with such high zest
> To children ardent for some desperate glory,
> The old Lie: *Dulce et decorum est*
> *Pro patria mori.*

But our shared concern with the undeniable horrors of warfare and a deontological claim that war is simply wrong are, of course, entirely different matters. The emphasis and guiding set of concerns of the critical study of war call attention to this difference. It begins with an empirically oriented question: How does war affect the oppressed and disadvantaged groups in society? The particular social effect of war is a matter of empirical investigation, and ethical assessments of war must be held in logical suspension.

Our abandonment of the Kantian ceiling, however, does not mean that we fall helplessly toward the Hobbesian floor. We have simply retired to consequentialist quarters. There is a possibility, perhaps a slim one, that any given war might be fought on behalf of disempowered social constituencies. The possibility of a revolutionary Nicaragua, for example, distributing arms or fighting on behalf of oppressed peasant classes in El Salvador, Honduras, or Guatemala must be taken seriously. While such scenarios are less common, perhaps even rare, the emphasis nonetheless leaves the door wide open for a *just war* (understood, that is, as a war fought to dismantle oppressive social relations).[50] Although it must be realistically acknowledged that most wars will tend toward the preservation of oppressive social relations, the discussion assists in drawing attention to the alternative emphasis of the critical intellectual project.

The critical science of war, as implied in the preceding discussion, will necessarily calculate the costs of war in terms of social gains and losses of oppressed communities, especially with respect to the effect of war upon disempowered socioeconomic classes, women, racial minorities, and homosexuals. The more common tendency associated with the traditional science of war has been to focus upon declining economic productivity, especially falling gross national product (GNP) or sectoral outputs, and upon the destruction of transportation, communication, or power infrastructures. At other times we see attention drawn to military losses and related fighting casualties. Similarly, we also see accounts of physical damage, as in the destruction of towns and cities. And to a lesser extent we see attention drawn to civilian deaths and injuries, and to other human tragedies such as war refugees. The attention to these quantifiable costs understandably reinforces the underlying conviction of the traditional science of war. Warfare is a costly and wasteful venture and humanity would be much better off without it. The near exclusive concern with such costs, however, tends to occlude awareness of the *social effects* of war. What is the relationship, analysts must begin systematically to ask, between warfare and the condition of subordinated social constituencies? Warfare, as we have suggested, often tips the balance of social forces in favor of dominant social groups. Warfare more often than not reinforces existing asymmetries of social power; that is, it tends to the maintenance of socially oppressive relations. While these *effects* of war are certainly less palpable, they are nonetheless real. Societies and nations seldom lose wars: oppressed social classes and groups frequently lose *through* war.

The difficulties of determining the effects of warfare upon subordinate groups cannot be overestimated easily. At least one crucial clarification must be made in order to encourage a more nuanced assessment of the social costs of war—a clarification pointing to a fundamental distinction between sociopolitical actors and social oppression and reaffirming the idea that the concern with the critical science of war lies squarely with the latter. Analysts, to begin, must take care to avoid measuring the effects of war by exclusive reference to political representatives and political groups. Any political group will usually reflect a complex underbelly of social forces and constituencies that nullifies any tidy or straightforward reference to one oppressed social level. A socialist or communist political party, for example, will usually be driven by a bevy of middle-class intellectuals while partially defining and promoting the interests of the working class. Similarly, insurgent or revolutionary forces often have a multi-class core while expressing solidarity with and drawing support from the working classes and peasants. And the political composition and discourse of nationalist political groups often glosses over stunning sociopolitical differences among its factions and wings. Consequently, the successes or setbacks for political actors provides a poor indication about the changing conditions for oppressed social constituencies. Should a political group be a relatively clean expression of a subordinate social base, its gains or losses might still prove to be a poor barometer of the conditions within the oppressed strata, corresponding remarkably little to changes in oppressive social conditions. In fact, by frequently operating in a strategic, cooptive, opportunistic, and short-term environment, these groups often confirm and intensify the gaseous consensus that undergirds any society. These groups, in other terms, often will be forced to operate according to the restrictive social hegemony that is purportedly antithetical to their long-term agenda. They are, so to speak, free only to be encaged; that is, free to maneuver without challenging the unwritten social canons. In effect, overt political success can correspond with the reproduction of ideological understandings that undergird socially oppressive relations within any society. During the stress of war, for example, labor parties may fully support state policies at the same time as the exigencies of warfare are creating a drastic deterioration in working conditions within wartime industries.

The 1991 Gulf War provides an opportunity to illustrate this contrasting emphasis between the traditional and critical sciences of war. The war was devastating for Iraq. The civilian infrastructure was ravaged. In addition to the carnage within the Iraqi military, a large number of civilians died or faced severe hardship. Subsequent civil wars in the north and the south of the country intensified these trends. Shortages of basic necessities, rapidly rising prices, and continuing sanctions exacerbated the war-torn conditions. Infant mortality, one manifestation of the devastation of the civilian infrastructure, has risen dramatically.[51] It is certainly indisputable that the toll of the war and its aftermath has been remarkable, especially when contrasted with the clinical image of the aerial war cultivated by the media. But there is another costly sphere to the war, a dimension that the critical science of war flushes out and emphasizes. The critical approach calls attention to the fact that the Gulf War also bore a profound relationship to the prevailing constellations of social power in Iraq, the Persian

Gulf region, and the allied countries. A brief discussion of the condition of women in Iraq will highlight this point. As a direct result of the war, Iraqi women have been forced to travel long distances for clean water; they have struggled to provide elementary childcare under austere conditions; and they have generally faced immeasurable difficulties trying to organize their households when many basic goods have been inaccessible. At another level, appeals to traditional conceptions of womanhood and motherhood have been recharged in the aftermath of the war—a process unlikely to encourage the meaningful advancement of Iraqi women. The Gulf War has simultaneously worked to cement traditional gender relations in Iraq and manifestly increased the burdens upon Iraqi women immured by strictly defined social codes and practices. In short, the war has done nothing to further the emancipation of Iraqi women, and has likely made their struggle much more difficult. The Gulf War has indeed been a costly war, and the tolls extend well beyond civilian deaths, infrastructural destruction, and military casualties. To overlook its other effects, whether unconsciously or by choice, has towering political ramifications, especially to the extent that such oversight or neglect exacerbates the oppressed condition of society's dominated classes and groups.

The critical science of war, therefore, is vigilant with respect to the political effects of war and the implications of the theoretical knowledge surrounding it. The critical approach is partly motivated by the healthy suspicion that the complacent appropriation and adoption of certain analytical categories, paradigms, and disciplinary writs characteristic of the traditional science of war may have had profoundly negative political consequences; negative in the sense that they have done little to ameliorate oppressive social relations in the post–World War II period. Critics of peace research have certainly raised this issue in the past. Johan Galtung argued strenuously that the focus on the reduction of violence in peace research results in a sort of "negative peace" wherein the preoccupation is with "the conditions of maintaining power, of freezing the status quo, of manipulating the underdog so that he does not take up arms against the topdog." Galtung continued: "This concept of peace will obviously be in the interest of the status-quo powers at the national or international levels, and may easily become a conservative force in politics." In a germinal article written in the late 1960s, Herman Schmidt argued that the ideological emphasis upon "order" constitutes the essence of conflict management thinking and has led to "an identification with the interests of the existing international system, that is, the interests of those who have power in the international system." As a result, Schmidt concluded, "peace research becomes a factor supporting the status quo of the international power structure, providing the decision-makers of the system with knowledge for control, manipulation and integration of the system."[52]

This last observation helps to turn our attention to the nature of the scientific enterprise informing the critical science of war. Recall that the traditional science of war proceeded with an epistemological orientation borrowed directly from the natural sciences. According to this view, the path to true theoretical knowledge in the social sciences is constructed from the ground up; that is, with careful reference to the raw data of social life—data to be collected and deciphered by the *neutral* scientific investigator. The values of the researcher must be shunted to the side for the sake of science. Good theoretical knowledge is necessarily objective. Critical social science, in stark contrast, rejects the conception of social science as *wertfrei*. The human sciences cannot proceed by simply gathering and compiling the "brutish data" of social life.[53] Analysis necessarily involves interpretation. The facts of social life seldom, if ever, deliver unambiguous messages to analytical intruders. Patterns of social life must be decoded by researchers, a process that unavoidably contaminates the analytical process with the worldview of the researcher. Empirical analysis and theoretical formulation cannot proceed in any other manner.

The sciences of war, to employ the widely accepted methodological vernacular, are inescapably value-laden. The conviction that society is oppressive, and that this condition is open to alteration, colors the interpretation of social and political facts. The critical science of war is openly and unapologetically politically explicit in its critique of the oppressive nature of existing social orders and in the desire to see these social orders thoroughly and radically transformed. This is the political baggage that it necessarily brings to its investigations. There is no other route to knowledge. This is not to be read as a license for rampant and undisciplined interrogation of the social world. Careful empirical analysis cannot be jettisoned in the service of naked political aspirations. To say that the sciences of war are value-laden is not to say that they are bald-facedly ideological, deceitful, or manipulative. To contend that theories of war necessarily secrete a political agenda is not to intimate that accounts of warfare are infinitely pliable. It is just to say that the worldview of the researcher, simply put, cannot be held in a state of suspended animation once the process of science ventures forth.[54]

We can extend our discussion of the critical science of war by stressing that it is informed by an alternative view of the appropriate relationship between theory and practice. Indeed, part of the distance between positivist and critical science surrounds the position of the latter tradition, which holds that the very propounding of social theory alters the object of investigation, and that this thereby renders the study of the social world wholly different from the study of the physical world. This basic view informs the relationship between theory and practice envisioned in the critical science of war. The critical approach embraces the *educative* notion of social theory; that is, a conception of social theory "as a means by which people can achieve a much clearer picture of who they are, and of what the real meaning of their social practices is, as a first step in becoming different sorts of people with different sorts of social arrangements."[55] The stress is placed upon learning and empowerment with a view to transforming oppressive social orders. The educative view of social theory proceeds on the assumption that there is a dialectical relationship between peoples' views of the world and more basic patterns of social practices (structural conditions). By molding and pressuring their world views, an alternative, less oppressive set of practices will emerge. As Fay points out:

> The educative conception is rooted in the belief that people's ignorance of themselves is responsible for the situation in which, in a certain sense (i.e. unconsciously), they permit certain conditions to make them feel and act in ways that are self-destructive, and yet, in another sense (i.e. consciously), they are victims of these conditions and their causal force just because they do not know how to relieve themselves of their suffering. In other words, certain external conditions that produce suffering in people can have the causal force they do because these people are unaware that it is in part their conceptions of themselves which give these conditions their causal powers.[56]

It is clear that this view rests upon a dyadic conception of social power "in the sense that all of its many forms invoke the self-understandings of the powerless as well as the powerful." Through enlightening theory people will be free to lead a different sort of life: a more fulfilling and rewarding one; a life less confined by oppressive structural blockages. The process of social enlightenment, therefore, will simultaneously enhance the social power of disadvantaged or oppressed groups within society and contribute to social restructuration.

The critical study of war proceeds upon the assumption that insofar as social theory is "useful" it must assist oppressed groups in transforming their oppressive social conditions: it must enlighten and educate them. The study of war must help people to comprehend themselves and society more incisively; specifically, the relationship between warfare and the conditions of their existence. Consequently, we can see more clearly that the goal of this study stands in blunt contrast with the conventional concern of exploring the causes and course of war primarily for the sake of eliminating it. Rather, the critical approach problematizes war in terms of oppressed social groups with a view to catalyzing fundamental social change. Although the explicit link drawn between the study of war on the one hand and extensive social transformation on the other may appear Panglossian to some, a modest enlightenment curve is detectable in the frequent opposition of labor organizations and women's groups to war (partly due to a growing awareness of the disproportionate burdens of war absorbed by the working classes in the former case and the increasing appreciation of the relationship between patriarchy and war in the latter). Nonetheless, critical expositions on war must work in conjunction with a broader critical project and long-term strategies of social change.

The critical science of war approaches its subject matter as a culturally soiled and politically contaminated affair. The research agenda is virtually without limits. In very fundamental terms, warfare should be addressed according to its relationship to the cultural metanarratives of modernity; that is, the intersubjective sphere of human life that cradles shared understanding and identities. To what extent, for example, has warfare contributed to the conception of society in communal/collective terms; i.e., communal/collective over individualistic/atomistic terms? How does warfare inflect discursive practices that are constitutive of our social relations of power? More specifically, how does the practice of war promote the rapid reshaping of conventional understandings and practices—as in the case of Rosie the Riveter during World War II? Or how does it reinforce conventional understanding and practices—as in the exhortation that women should give birth and nurture families for the war effort? In what manner does the naked drama of war fuse divergent social groups by creating an environment that renders political appeals to shared characteristics—historical, religious, ethnic, and so on—inherently meaningful? Does the rhetoric of warfare tend to blur and mystify oppressive social relations? How do the exigencies of warfare weaken resistant political practices or, alternatively, create tactical or political openings for marginalized social forces?

With a more direct reference to the relationship between warfare and the politics of race, class, gender, and sexual orientation, a number of specific questions can be posed. First, take race: In what manner has the prosecution of warfare reinforced racially premised motifs that sustain racial oppression?[57] What is the relationship between the prosecution of war and the condition of aboriginal peoples? Have racial minorities suffered disproportionate burdens during the prosecution of war? Second, in terms of class: How does war reinforce cultural themes that undergird class relations in society?[58] In what manner has warfare assisted or impaired the emancipatory struggles of the working class? Has the historical support for war tended to vary among different social classes? What are the relative roles of social classes in the origins of warfare? Does the prosecution of war disproportionately benefit narrow class interests by securing their specific needs? How does the development of armed forces and other institutions of warfare further the hegemony of any particular class? Third, with respect to gender: How has modern warfare contributed to the social construction of gender and the oppression of women?[59] How is warfare related to patriarchal society? Have the liberating effects of war with respect to women been sustained into postwar periods? Finally, in terms of sexual orientation: How is warfare related to heterosexual constructs in society?[60] Has the prosecution of war tended to promoted or discourage the marginalization of gays and lesbians? What does the historical refusal of militaries to admit homosexuals openly reveal about war itself?

Why study war? As summarized in Table 1.1, the traditional science of war is primarily concerned with the costs of contemporary warfare; it thus sets the elimination of war as its primary goal. To this end the traditional science enlists the naturalistic model of social science and seeks to develop a nomological theory of war through careful empirical research conducted by neutral investigators. This theoretical knowledge of war will reveal the independent forces that lead to war, thereby allowing the practitioners of peace to craft a more peaceful world. In contrast, the critical science of war is most immediately concerned with transforming society in less oppressive directions. It undertakes research for the sake of exploring the relationship between war and the different modes of social oppression, rejecting positivist claims that social science can be objective. Theoretical knowledge garnered through the critical enterprise is useful to the extent that it is *educative* and *enlightening* and contributes, ultimately, to progressive social change.

Table 1.1   Comparison of Traditional and Critical Sciences of War

Criteria	Traditional Science of War	Critical Science of War
Most basic concern of researcher	War and its destructive potential	Oppressive social relations that may be transformed
View of war within research community	Destructive: should be removed from human practice	War will likely bear a profound relationship to social oppression, especially class, gender, and racial oppression
Costs of war receiving emphasis	Death, physical destruction, economic losses	Social costs—especially the deteriorating social position of subordinate groups
Primary goal of research into warfare	Ending war	Mitigating and removing modes of social oppression
Tasks of scientific enterprise as it relates to the study of warfare	Development of a nomological theory of war	Explication of relationship between war and modes of social oppression
Nature of scientific task	Objective; descriptive; value-free	Value-laden; interpretive
Relationship between theoretical knowledge of war and human practice	Instrumental: knowledge is like a toolchest for practitioners of peace	Educative: knowledge enlightens oppressed communities and informs emancipatory political projects

A Critical Account of the Iran-Iraq War

At least five different explanations for the Iran-Iraq War regularly appear in academic and journalistic commentary. Rarely does a commentator settle for an exclusive casus belli. Rather, there is widespread recognition that a plurality of forces were at work when war broke out in 1980. The first account draws attention to the deeply rooted cultural enmities between Iran and Iraq. It invariably is premised upon a sense of incompatible and immanently hostile societies characterized in racial, sectarian, or religious terms—Aryan/Persian v. Semite/Arab; Shi'i v. Sunni; and secular v. fundamentalist. The outbreak of war was thus the latest conflict between two societies destined to collide.[61] A second explanation calls attention to the megalomaniacal tendencies of Saddam Hussein. Hussein's exaggerated notions of historical destiny led him to invade Iran when the opportunity presented itself. "I think the whole question of how this war began," Samir al-Khalil writes, "resolves itself into what was passing through Saddam Hussein's mind."[62] This explanation finds confirmation in the fact that Iraq named the war *Qadisiyyat Saddam,* after its leader. A third reason for the war emphasizes Iraq's regional aspirations in the face of Iran's postrevolutionary turmoil. Iran's troubles, so this argument runs, interrupted a longstanding balance of power between the two countries. Iraq simply sought to fill this regional vacuum.[63] A fourth argument addresses Iran's attempts to foment a Shi'i uprising in Iraq. Baghdad thus moved against Iran in order to neutralize this source of external agitation.[64] A fifth explanation focuses on the border dispute along the *Shatt al-Arab* waterway. Iraq preferred to see the boundary drawn along the eastern shoreline, thereby giving it full sovereignty over the waterway. In contrast, Iran preferred to see the boundary drawn according to the *thalweg,* or midchannel principle. From this perspective, the war was the result of an intractable territorial conflict. "Even if Iraq and Iran were homogeneous, even if Iraq had no Shi'i problem," writes Daniel Pipes, "the Shatt al-Arab issue would have sufficed to cause war to break out in 1980."[65]

Although each of these accounts contains a kernel of truth, they remain woefully inadequate in that they fail to contextualize socially the Iran-Iraq War.[66] They afford little attention to the complex sociopolitical dynamics at work within each country. Accounts that draw attention to the "ancient animosities" between Iran and Iraq, for example, usually entirely overlook the complex array of social forces that are at play in both republics. Each society is conceptualized in monolithic terms. There is a general failure to address the Iraqi and Iranian societies as dynamic and diverse entities. Similarly, when attention *is* given to social divisions, little additional effort is made to relate these cleavages to other societal dynamics. This is most conspicuous in explanations emphasizing the Shi'i struggle in Iraq. The Shi'i threat to the Ba'th regime is not linked to other developments within

Iraqi society, especially the evolving class structure, urban migration, and the secularizing trends of the twentieth century. Again, explanations calling attention to the *Shatt al-Arab* boundary dispute, or to Iraq's hegemonic aspirations in the Gulf region, generally overlook the relationship of these factors to dynamic state, class, and communal shifts within the two societies.

This is the commentators' primary failing: most accounts tend to separate the war from the broader social canvases. In other words, as real as the war may be, it is not understood as a thoroughly *social* reality. The undulating struggle among contending social groups is omitted. The war, in short, is carelessly reified. It is treated as a self-contained episode suspended above society rather than as an event intimately bound up with it. Understandably, there is a general failure to sense or appreciate the social costs of the war, especially in terms of the intensification of socially oppressive relations in both countries. These conventional accounts of the war are, at best, partial and incomplete; at worst, such analytical parturitions, failing to appreciate the social realities underlying the Iran-Iraq War, may be politically disastrous for many of the oppressed communities in these two societies.

Analysts have been misguided in their efforts to provide a scalar model of the war. Researchers uncover remarkably little when seeking to establish the weightier factor behind the conflict. The central issue concerns the war's relationship to underlying social forces. In its abstract formulation, factor A (for example, the Shi'i struggle in Iraq) and factor B (for example, Iraq's struggle for regional hegemony) are equally important by virtue of their links to class and communal struggles in both states. The pallid quest for *degree* must be supplanted by the discovery of *relationship*. In any analysis, the Iran-Iraq War must be embedded in the webs of society, regardless of how tenuous such connections might appear at first glance.

What would a critical account of the Iran-Iraq War look like? Such an account must expose the relationship between the sweeping socio-structural transformations in both countries and the outbreak of the war in 1980. In the broadest possible terms, we begin to unearth the social character of the war by charting the profound upheaval of both societies as they were gradually drawn into the global economic fold over the last century. To the extent that the opening of the Suez Canal accelerated these trends, we could claim that the slide to war began in 1869. The Iran-Iraq War capped a century of far-reaching social transformation. The undoing of traditional life exacerbated older social fault lines and produced new ones of its own, and eventually generated a political earthquake of unprecedented magnitude. The heinous violence of the war must be superimposed upon this fundamental rupture in the social fabric of the Gulf peoples. From one perspective, the war was a perfectly natural expression of the bloodbathed currents of change that enveloped the region. From another, it emerged somewhat incongruously out of the twin pillars of *development* and *modernization.* The war thus embodied a transplanted European experience, compressed in time and space to be sure, but evincing parallel lapses into wanton barbarism.

Uncovering the social origins of the Iran-Iraq War requires analysts to repair to a largely unexplored theoretical terrain in the study of Middle Eastern politics. Analysis must self-consciously dispense with the "paradigms of social structure and social change" that have accompanied "Western economic, political, military, and ideological penetration" of the region.[67] It is necessary to emphasize the rich socioeconomic and sociopolitical tapestry of the Middle East against more conventional assessments impelled by Western models of *progress* and *development.* Analysts must begin to investigate systematically the region's complex social web. Middle Eastern politics, in complementary terms, necessarily must be redefined to include the complicated interpositions of gender, class, family, tribe, race, state, and so forth. In short, there is a need to adopt a more inclusive intellectual posture with respect to the region, to examine the specificities of everyday life as an integral and indispensable subtext to somewhat more salient trends and events.[68]

This study of the Iran-Iraq War draws directly upon those works that address the evolutionary social fabric of Iran and Iraq.[69] It submits the following thesis: The socioeconomic transformations of the twentieth century set in motion distinct sociopolitical struggles that culminated in the three dynamics most closely associated with the outbreak of the war:

1. Iranian efforts to foment a revolution in Iraq
2. The alarm this created in Baghdad in the face of a possible Shi'i uprising
3. The Ba'th regime's attempts to secure and stabilize oil export revenues.

Expressed differently, the political aspirations and vulnerabilities that impelled both countries to war for almost eight years were stained by the social and political rifts characteristic of estranged regimes—rifts that in turn were signatured fundamentally by the class and communal struggles engendered by the broad transformation of these societies over the last century. *It was a war of two crisis-ridden societies.*

The Islamic Revolution was the pivotal event behind the outbreak of the Iran-Iraq War. And so the analysis begins there. Chapter 2 traces the social transformations in contemporary Iran that culminated in the collapse of the Pahlavi monarchy in 1979. Chapter 3 addresses the social changes in Iraq that began in the midnineteenth century and concludes by calling attention to the growing alienation of the Ba'th regime from an evolving Iraqi society. Chapter 4 concludes the discussion of the outbreak of war by addressing the interstate struggles immediately associated with Iraq's attack. This discussion is assisted by recent contributions to the study of security—contributions that offer four specific cautions to researchers: (1) avoid extending the security discourses beyond the regimes that controlled the state apparatuses in 1980. Hence the developing security problems are analyzed as a thoroughly political manifestation between two regimes struggling to maintain control of the state apparatus within their respective social formations; (2) avoid reifying the analysis by grounding it firmly in the sociopolitical struggles of the two countries; (3) avoid approaching the discussion of the security problems between Iran and Iraq in correlative terms; that is, as a natural or insuperable problem rooted in the objective conditions of the Iraqi state or the Iranian state; and (4) fully acknowledge the political project that necessarily inheres in any discussion of security.[70] With this guidance, the discussion of the mounting security problems between Iran and Iraq is linked directly to the broad socioeconomic transformations outlined in chapters 2 and 3.

The critical method alerts us to the reality that the sociopolitical struggles that undergird war do not bottom-out when the war begins. Although wars often appear as collective national efforts, and although the prosecution of a war might appeal to somewhat more universal features of any society, the conflict among countervailing social groups nevertheless continues. The Iran-Iraq War was no exception to this general observation. Chapter 5 addresses this aspect of the war, examining the turbulent process of revolutionary consolidation in Iran—a process that pitted the traditional middle class of Iran against a number of other social forces within Iranian society. The war helped to sustain the difficult process of clerical consolidation in Iran and contributed to the marginalization of numerous social constituencies that originally had figured prominently in the 1979 revolution. Chapter 6 similarly addresses the sociopolitical struggles associated with the war and Ba'thist political consolidation in Iraq, especially the populist wartime strategies of Saddam Hussein. Both chapters argue that the war brought profound political advantages to each of the regimes—a fact that contributed greatly to its disturbing prolongation. Chapter 7 concludes with a brief examination of the long shadow of the Iran-Iraq War, especially the continuity of regional instability and the outbreak of a more generalized war in 1991.

Notes

1. For example, see discussion in Samir al-Khalil, *Republic of Fear: The Politics of Modern Iraq,* (University of California Press, 1989), p. 261.
2. This claim is pressed by Dilip Hiro in *The Longest War: The Iran-Iraq Military Conflict,* (Paladin, 1990), p. xxii and p. 1.

3. Statistics on human and village losses extracted from Amir Taheri, *The Cauldron: The Middle East Behind the Headlines,* (Hutchinson, 1988), pp. 198–199. On refugees, see Martha Wenger and Dick Anderson, "The Gulf War," in *MERIP Middle East Report,* 17:5, (Sept.–Oct. 1987), p. 25. Estimates on the overall cost of the war appear in Hiro, *Longest War,* op. cit., p. 1.

4. For example, see Bijan Mossavar-Rahmani, "Economic Implications for Iran and Iraq," in *The Iran-Iraq War: Old Conflicts, New Weapons,* eds. Shirin Tahir-Kheli and Shaheen Ayubi, (Greenwood Press, 1983).

5. Michael Walzer, *Just and Unjust Wars,* (Basic Books, 1977), p. 3.

6. F. H. Hinsley, *Power and the Pursuit of Peace: Theory and Practice in the History of Relations Between States,* (Cambridge University Press, 1963), p. 1.

7. Michael Howard, "The Causes of Wars," in *The Causes of Wars,* (Harvard University Press, 1984), pp. 9–12.

8. Luther Lee Bernard, *War and Its Causes,* (Garland Publishing, 1972), p. 6.

9. Note the title of Ronald J. Glossop's *Confronting War: An Examination of Humanity's Most Pressing Problem,* (McFarland, 1983).

10. Betty Crump Hanson and Bruce M. Russett, "Introduction," in *Peace, War, and Numbers,* ed. Bruce M. Russett, (Sage Publications, 1972), p. 9.

11. Louis Kriesberg, "Peace Promotion," in *Handbook of Applied Sociology: Frontiers of Contemporary Research,* (Praeger, 1971), p. 539.

12. Richard J. Bernstein, *The Restructuring of Social and Political Theory,* (Harcourt Brace Jovanovich, 1976), p. 227.

13. Luther Lee Bernard, *War and Its Causes,* op. cit., p. 213.

14. For example, see *The Correlates of War,* vols. 1 and 2, ed. J. David Singer, (Free Press, 1980).

15. See the discussion in David Wilkinson, *Deadly Quarrels: Lewis F. Richardson and the Statistical Study of War,* (University of California Press, 1980), especially Chapter 11 and quote p. 106.

16. See, for example: Evan Luard, *War in International Society: A Study in International Sociology,* (I. B. Tauris & Co, 1986), pp. 7–12.

17. See discussion on the nature of the scientific enterprise and the study of war in Dean G. Pruitt and Richard C. Snyder, *Theory and Research on the Causes of War,* (Prentice-Hall, 1969), p. 3.

18. Hanson and Russett, *Peace, War, and Numbers,* op. cit., p. 9.

19. Commentary by M. Nettleship, in *War, Its Causes and Correlates,* eds. Martin Nettleship, R. Dalegivens, and A. Nettleship, (Mouton Publishers, 1975), p. 52.

20. See "Introduction," *War, Its Causes and Correlates,* op. cit., p. 5.

21. Anatol Rapoport, "Approaches to Peace Research," in *War, Its Causes and Correlates,* op. cit., p. 50.

22. Ibid.

23. Leon Bramson and George W. Goethals, eds., *War: Studies from Psychology, Sociology, Anthropology,* (Basic Books, 1968), p. 5.

24. Melvin Small and J. David Singer, *Resort to Arms: International and Civil Wars, 1816–1980,* (Sage Publications, 1982), p. 14.

25. Brian Fay, *Critical Social Science,* (Cornell University Press, 1987), p. 88.

26. Michael Nicholson, *Conflict Analysis,* (English Universities Press, 1970), p. 1.

27. For example, see Norman Alcock, *The War Disease,* (Canadian Peace Research Institute, 1972).

28. Francis A. Beer, *Peace Against War: The Ecology of International Violence,* (W. H. Freeman and Co., 1982), p. 1.

29. Robin Clarke, *The Science of War and Peace*, (Jonathan Cape, 1971), p. 225.

30. Kenneth Waltz, *Man, the State and War*, (Columbia University Press, 1959), p. 14.

31. Anatol Rapoport, *The Origins of Violence: Approaches to the Study of Conflict*, (Paragon House, 1989), p. xvii.

32. For two reviews of the critical theory of the Frankfurt School, see David Held, *Introduction to Critical Theory*, (University of California Press, 1980), and Martin Jay, *The Dialectical Imagination*, (Boston: Little, Brown, 1973). Recent inquiries into the nature of critical social science may be found in Richard J. Bernstein, *The Restructuring of Social and Political Theory*, (University of Pennsylvania Press, 1976); Brian Fay, *Critical Social Science*, (Cornell University Press, 1987); and Douglas Kellner, *Critical Theory, Marxism and Modernity*, (Johns Hopkins University Press, 1989).

33. See discussion in Charles Taylor, "Foucault on freedom and truth," *Political Theory*, 12:2, (May, 1984), reprinted in *Philosophy and the Human Sciences: Philosophical Papers 2*, (Cambridge University Press, 1985), p. 152.

34. One of the most exemplary efforts to conceive of social power in these terms can be found in the writings of Antonio Gramsci. Gramsci's notion of a *war of position* (as opposed to a war of maneuver) is entirely contingent upon his theoretical conceptualization of the nature and distribution of power within civil society. See the discussion in Ellen Meiksins Wood, "The Uses and Abuses of Civil Society," in *The Socialist Register: 1990*, (Merlin Press, 1990), pp. 62–63.

35. Within the field of conflict studies the idea of oppression has been labeled as *structural violence*. As Johan Galtung writes: "Let us say that violence is present when human beings are being influenced so that their actual somatic and mental realizations are below their potential realizations." Later Galtung adds: "The violence is built into the structure and shows up as unequal power and consequently as unequal life chances." See "Violence, Peace, and Peace Research," *Journal of Peace Research*, 6, (1969), p. 168 and p. 171.

36. Enloe continues in *Bananas, Beaches and Bases*, (Pandora Press, 1989), p. 3.

> As one learns to look at this world through feminist eyes, one learns to ask whether any thing that passes for inevitable, inherent, "traditional" or biological has in fact been made. One begins to ask how all sorts of things have been made—a treeless landscape, a rifle-wielding police force, the "Irishman joke," an all-women typing pool. Asking how something has been made implies that it has been made by someone. Suddenly there are clues to trace; there is also blame, credit and responsibility to apportion, not just at the start but at each point along the way.

37. On the normative foundations of critical theory see Seyla Benhabib, *Critique, Norm, and Utopia: A Study of the Foundations of Critical Theory*, (Columbia University Press, 1986).

38. An excellent example of this effort is Douglas Kellner's *Television and the Crisis of Democracy*, (Westview Press, 1990).

39. For the most involved efforts to date see Herbert G. Reid and Ernest J. Yanarella, "Toward a Critical Theory of Peace Research in the United States: the Search for an Intelligible Core," *Journal of Peace Research*, 13:4, (1976); Ole Jess Olsen and Ib Martin Jarvad, "The Vietnam Conference Papers: a case study of a failure of Peace Research," *Peace Research Society: Papers*, 14, (1970); Lars

Dencik, "Peace Research: Pacification or Revolution?" *Contemporary Peace Research,* ed. Ghanshyam Pardesi, (Harvester, 1982). For a response to this literature see William Eckhardt, "The Radical Critique of Peace Research: A Brief Review," *Peace Research,* 18:3, (1986).

40. It is appropriate here briefly to speak of the term *critical.* It is important to recognize that the suggestion is not being made that the critical study of war is imbued with greater incisiveness than is traditional science. This would be an arrogating claim to say the least. There is a considerable terminological lineage of the word, including the way the term was employed in Marx's *Contribution to the Critique of Political Economy.* It is beneficial to quote from a footnote in Horkheimer's programmatic essay entitled "Traditional and Critical Theory": "The term is used here less in the sense it has in the idealist critique of pure reason than in the sense it has in the dialectial critique of political economy. It points to an essential aspect of the dialectial theory of society." From Max Horkheimer, "Traditional and Critical Theory," *Critical Theory: Selected Essays,* (Continuum Publishing Corporation, 1989), p. 206.

41. This last observation reflects the etymological link between critique and crisis, with the former word signifying the body of commentary upon the latter. This meaning is still in use, as in the idea of a critical care unit in a hospital, an expression linking the word critical to bodily crises.

42. Kenneth Waltz, *Man,* op. cit, p. 232.

43. Raymond Aron, *War and Industrial Society,* (Oxford University Press, 1958).

44. Nazli Choucri and Robert C. North, *Nations in Conflict: National Growth and International Violence,* (W. H. Freeman and Company, 1975).

45. Manus I. Midlarsky and Stafford T. Thomas, "Domestic Social Structure and International Warfare," in *War, Its Causes and Correlates,* op. cit., p. 531.

46. For an example of transnational class dynamics infused with a Gramscian understanding of hegemony and its effects upon international relations see Robert W. Cox, *Production, Power, and World Order: Social Forces in the Making of History,* (Columbia University Press, 1987).

47. E. P. Thompson has written "Class itself is not a thing, it is a happening," *The Making of the English Working Class,* (Penguin, 1968), p. 939.

48. Thomas Paine, *Rights of Man,* (Pelican Books, 1969), p. 99.

49. Herbert Marcuse, *One-Dimensional Man,* (Beacon Press, 1964), p. ix.

50. Michael Walzer's *Just and Unjust Wars* (Basic Books, 1977) does not adequately deal with this particular conception of a just war.

51. See Alberto Ascherio et al., "The Gulf War and Paediatric Mortality in Iraq," *The New England Journal of Medicine,* 327:13, (September 1992).

52. Herman Schmidt, "Peace Research and Politics," *Journal of Conflict Resolution,* 13, (1968).

53. Even if an objective social science were possible, it is not clear that it should enjoy exclusivity; that is, critical social science enlists the more general observation that positivist social science unfortunately reflects the Enlightenment bias that subordinates imagination to truth, metaphysical play to rationalistic dogma, and religio-mythic structures to scientistic-mythic structures. George Steiner wrote: "Reason itself has become repressive. The worship of truth and of autonomous facts is a cruel fetishism. . . . The disease of enlightened man is his acceptance, itself wholly superstitious, of the superiority of facts to ideas." George Steiner, *In Bluebeard's Castle: Some Notes Towards the Redefinition of Culture,* (Yale University Press, 1971), p. 138. Behind the slavish insistence that theories of war be objective lurks the relegation of normative speculation about war to secondary standing.

54. One of the clearest statements of this antipositivist position may be found in Charles Taylor's "Interpretation and the Sciences of Man," *The Review of Metaphysics,* 25, (September 1971), 3–51.

55. Brian Fay, *Critical Social Science,* op. cit., p. 89.

56. Ibid., p. 95.

57. For a brief sampling of this vast literature, see Zahair Kashmari, *The Gulf Within: Canadian Arabs, Racism and the Gulf War,* (Toronto: Lorimer, 1991); Albert Russel Buchanan, *Black Americans in World War II,* (Clio Books, 1977); Alison R. Bernstein, *American Indians and WWII: Towards a new era in Indian Affairs,* (University of Oklahoma Press, 1991).

58. Some examples of this literature would include William H. Durham, *Scarcity and Survival in Central America: the Ecological Origins of the Soccer War,* (Stanford University Press, 1979); Richard Price, *An Imperial War and the British Working Class: Working Class Attitudes and Reaction to the Boer War 1899–1902,* (Routledge, Kegan Paul, 1972).

59. For a sampling of the literature addressing some of these questions, see Karen Anderson, *Wartime Women: Sex Roles, Family Relations, and the Status of Women during World War II,* (Greenwood Press, 1981).

60. See Allan Bérubé, *Coming Out Under Fire: the History of Gay Men and Women in World War II,* (Free Press, 1990).

61. For an illustration of this position, see Stephen R. Grummon, *The Iran-Iraq War: Islam Embattled,* The Washington Papers 92, (Praeger Publishers, 1982), pp. 1–2.

62. Samir al-Khalil, *Republic of Fear,* p. 272.

63. For an example of this position, see Shahram Chubin, "Iran and the War: From Stalemate to Ceasefire," in *The Gulf War: Regional and International Dimensions,* eds. Hanns W. Maull and Otto Pick, (Pinter Publishers, 1989), p. 6.

64. For example, see Albert Hourani, *A History of the Arab Peoples,* (Harvard University Press, 1991), p. 432.

65. Daniel Pipes, "A Border Adrift: Origins of the Conflict," in *The Iran-Iraq War,* op. cit., p. 21.

66. Their are some exceptions but they are rare. With respect to the outbreak of war see Ìsam al-Khafaji, "The Parasitic Base of the Ba'thist Regime," in *Saddam's Iraq: Revolution or Reaction,* ed. Committee Against Repression and for Democratic Rights in Iraq, (Zed Books, 1989), pp. 73–88.

67. Samih K. Farsoun and Lisa Hajjar, "The Contemporary Sociology of the Middle East: An Assessment," in *Theory, Politics and the Arab World: Critical Responses,* ed. Hisham Sharabi, (Routledge, Chapman and Hall, 1990), p. 161.

68. It would be misleading to suggest that any agreement on the *scope* of critical social enquiry translates into an agreement on *method.* The analysis of class, for example, proceeds in numerous, and often uncomplimentary, directions. Moreover, in the analysis of the Middle East, there is still an unfortunate superimposition of Western concepts and paradigms due in part to the lack of an organic—*oops, Gramsci again*—critical tradition. At a minimum, this requires acknowledgement and sensitivity on the part of the analyst, and a healthy receptivity to critical traditions emanating in direct response to the Middle East itself. See Hisham Sharabi, "The Scholarly Point of View: Politics, Perspective, Paradigm," in *Theory, Politics and the Arab World: Critical Responses,* op. cit., pp. 1–51.

69. An exemplary study in the case of Iran is Ervand Abrahamian, *Iran Between Two Revolutions,* (Princeton University Press, 1982). A comparable study on Iraq is still Hanna Batatu, *The Old Social Classes and the Revolutionary Movement in Iraq,* (Princeton University Press, 1978). For a provocative review of

Abrahamian's work see Eric Hooglund in *MERIP Reports,* 13:3, (March–April 1983); and on Batatu's work see articles by Tom Nieuwenhuis, Marion Farouk-Sluglett, Peter Sluglett, and Joe Stork in *MERIP Reports,* 97, (June 1981).

70. These alternative writings dramatically depart from and improve upon the revisionist analyses of security during the 1980s most notably associated with Barry Buzan, Edward Azar, and Mohommed Ayoob. For a sampling of this alternative literature see R. B. J. Walker, *The Concept of Security and International Relations,* Working Paper no. 3, Institute on Global Conflict and Cooperation, University of California; Brad Klein, "After Strategy: The Search for a Post-Modernist Analysis of Peace," in *Alternatives* (July 1988).

Part I
THE SOCIAL ORIGINS OF THE WAR

2

Social Transformation and Revolution in Iran

The Islamic Revolution triggered the slide to war between Iran and Iraq. The intense postrevolutionary struggles that followed the collapse of the Pahlavi monarchy enveloped the Gulf region and riveted the entire world. In the revolutionary aftermath, new political conflicts arose and older animosities were revived. The Iraqi regime in particular was alarmed seriously by Iran's aggressive postrevolutionary posture—a posture that abruptly halted the brief period of peaceful relations that had emerged during the second half of the 1970s. The political turmoil within the new Islamic Republic created a unique opportunity for Baghdad to redress some of its historical grievances with Iran. Alarmed by the contagions of revolution and buoyed by a sense of military opportunity, the Iraqi regime attacked Iran in September 1980. It was not a coincidence that the war followed so closely on the heels of the Islamic Revolution. The fall of the monarchy was the pivotal event in the outbreak of war in the Gulf.

A thorough account of the social origins of the Iran-Iraq War must address the sociohistorical foundations of Iran's revolutionary struggle. Accordingly, two broad themes are entertained in this chapter. First, the Islamic Revolution was rooted in Iran's twentieth-century socioeconomic trajectory. It was the last of a series of salient political upheavals that included the Constitutional Revolution, the overthrow of the Qajar dynasty, the ousting of Reza Shah in 1941, and the Mossadeq crisis of 1953. In the matter of a few decades, Iran was transformed from a largely disconnected collection of villages and nomadic tribes into a highly centralized, urbanized, and proletarianized society replete with the attendant social and political tribulations of modernity. The Pahlavi drives for modernization resulted in a significantly transformed class structure. This included the creation of a politically vibrant working class, dense pockets of urban poor, the expansion of a modern middle class, and a progressively alienated traditional middle class composed of *bazaaris* (merchants) and the Shi'i clerics.

Secondly, Iran's socioeconomic modernization was not accompanied by the democratization of its political system. The social forces unleashed by Iran's modernization drives thus were denied any meaningful opportunity to voice their grievances. The evolution of modern Iran can be characterized as a growing incommensurability between social modernization and political stagnation, between the proliferation of social forces under capitalist development and the progressive deterioration of meaningful channels of political expression. This development alienated the Iranian population and cleared the way for the emergence of strong revolutionary sentiments. Conjunctural conditions in the latter half of the 1970s cradled the growing opposition and ultimately led to the collapse of the Pahlavi dynasty.

Iran in the Nineteenth Century:
The Constitutional Revolution

For most of its history Iran was a loosely connected region.[1] Its sheer vastness, mountainous terrain, and massive central dessert, and its lack of a central waterway similar to the Nile or the Tigris-Euphrates river systems, effectively stalled the political centralization of the region. Iran's geography insured that its ruling cities were peripheral and constantly changing.[2] This political diffusion was reinforced by extensive ethnic and religious differences. These factors combined to nurse economic self-sufficiency in Iran's numerous towns and supported the nomadism and tribalism that historically characterized the majority of the Iranian population.

At the outset of the nineteenth century, there were four distinct levels in the class structure of Iran. The upper class of the Qajar dynasty included those directly associated with the monarchy—provincial aristocrats and tribal leaders. The intermediate strata was composed of merchants, shopkeepers, and small workshop owners. These groups were organically linked with the *ulama* (Islamic clerics). The third class was made up of wage earners—apprentices, hired artisans, construction workers, and so forth. The fourth, lower echelon of Iranian society was composed of tribal members and the peasantry.[3] But these classes did not behave as politically conscious entities: there was a strong presence of local, nonclass ties. In Abrahamian's words:

> Communal ties—especially those based on tribal lineages, religious sects, regional organization, and paternalistic sentiments—cut through the horizontal classes, strengthened the vertical communal bond, and thereby prevented latent economic interests from developing into manifest political forces. In so far as numerous individuals in early nineteenth-century Iran shared similar ways of life, similar positions in the mode of production, and similar relations to the means of administration, they constituted socioeconomic classes. But in so far as these individuals were bound by

communal ties, failed to overcome local barriers, and articulated no state-wide interests, they did not constitute socio-political classes.[4]

The vertical cleavages of Iranian society thus retarded the development of a class-based politics. In short, the political significance of the class structure of Iranian society during this period should not be accorded undue weight.

This feature of Iran began to change as the Iranian economy was penetrated increasingly by European merchants during the nineteenth century. Nursed by the Gulistan Treaty of 1813 and the Turkmanchai Treaty of 1828, both with Russia, and the Anglo-Persian Commercial Treaty of 1841, Iran's international trade rose dramatically. Between the turn of the century and the 1850s, Iranian trade increased threefold. By the outbreak of World War I, Iran's trade had quadrupled.[5] One salient effect of these changes included the development of a politically conscious intermediate strata, especially a disaffected traditional middle class adversely affected by Iran's new economic trajectory. The growing disaffection of Iran's merchants in the face of the new economic relations with Europe contributed to their heightened sense of unity and task. The gradual extension of European market relations throughout the Iranian economy had resulted in the erosion of local artisan production and merchant activity. The following observations, recorded by the son of an Isfahanian cashier, for example, demonstrate the reverberating effects of the influx of European textiles upon the weavers' guilds:

> It was for the sake of elegant appearance and easy handling that they employed European yarn in weaving *qadaks*. Their work became ugly and, as a result of mixing European and Iranian materials, it became progressively defective and tore and went to pieces while worn; it also lost its stiffness, fluff, and durability. Spinners lost their jobs and gradually perished. Russia stopped buying. Iranians turned away from their own products, and the weavers' guild suffered a tremendous loss. Consequently, other guilds began to face deficits and loss. At least one-tenth of the guilds in this city were weavers, of whom not even one-fifth has survived. About one-twentieth of the needy widows of Isfahan raised their children by spinning thread for the weavers; they all have perished. Likewise other large guilds, such as dyers, carders, and labourers in the bleaching house, which were related to this guild, have mostly disappeared.[6]

The developing political cohesiveness among the merchants was aided by a significant growth in communications throughout the region.

A second crucial trend in the development of a politically conscious intermediate strata centered around the influx of Western ideas and the formation of a modern middle-class intelligentsia. An embryonic nationalist discourse increasingly permeated the Iranian political atmosphere. The nationalist group specifically articulated a political critique of the Qajar dynasty, calling attention to the interference of European powers in Iranian affairs and to the tyrannical tendencies of some Muslim rulers.[7] The Qajar dynasty was increasingly viewed as weak and corrupt. Moreover, the agitated Shi'i clergy, an integral element of the traditional middle class, insured that this Western-influenced political discourse would have a distinctive Islamic hue. Through the *minbar* (pulpit) they kept the political public aware and aroused.[8] The combination of the traditional merchant/ clerical class and the Western-influenced middle-class intelligentsia resulted in a political force that firmly believed that the so-called religionational community was in danger.[9] The ensuing confrontation with the Qajars manifested itself in the sustained struggle to subordinate the dynasty to constitutional rule. The prolonged civil war lasted from 1905 to 1911. In the end the Qajar dynasty assented to constitutional restrictions including an elected assembly *(Majlis)*. These constitutional restrictions were gradually undone as the dynasty regained de facto political power over the ensuing decade. "In the final analysis," summarizes Fred Halliday, "no revolution occurred, and the state was not fundamentally altered by these events."[10] The alliance of the traditional middle class and the modern middle class, however, established a powerful historical precedent that would leave a far more enduring mark towards the end of the twentieth century.

Reza Shah and the Pahlavi Monarchy

While the Qajar dynasty managed to wrestle back most of its lost power in the aftermath of the Constitutional Revolution, its control over the country extended little beyond Tehran and a few other major cities. Travel between towns was hazardous. Iran was increasingly beset by centrifugal forces that threw its multicommunal character into full relief.

> In every corner of the land [wrote Elwell-Sutton] local chiefs and tribal khans were taking the law into their own hands—Turcomans in the northeast, Kurds in the northwest, Bakhtiaris and Qashqaís in the south, Baluchis in Kerman and Bulchistan, Lurs in the mountain ranges of the west. In Khuzistan, the Arab Shaykh Khazál reigned as an independent ruler, confident in the support of his British allies. In Gilan, Marza Kuchek Khan established an independent, republican regime from his Jangali "forest" headquarters, and collaborated with other rebels and Bolshevik troops along the whole coast of the Caspian Sea.[11]

As the country disintegrated, new fuel was added to the nationalist struggle with the signing of the Anglo-Persian Agreement of 1919. The accord essentially turned Iran into a British protectorate; it was loathed throughout the country. "Once again," wrote one commentator, "a comprehensive agreement had run foul of nascent Persian nationalism and after another half-century of development, a revolution and a war, that nationalism had a new cause."[12] The crescendo of opposition culminated on 20 February 1919 in a coup d'etat organized by Sayyid Zia and Reza Khan. In the ensuing year, Reza Khan (later Reza Shah) emerged as the unrivaled political authority in the country. In April 1926 the Majlis ended the Qajar dynasty and formally established the Pahlavi monarchy.

With the full accession of Reza Shah, the gradual ferment of Western ideas began to induce change. Reza Shah's embrace of Western ideas, however—especially those of nationalism and statehood—centered around the practical solution they offered for Iran's political ills. Western ideas embodied a coherent response to external interference and the internal forces of disintegration that plagued Iran. As Banani wrote: "Reza Shah was imbued with this spirit; it had come to him not from abstract contemplation of Western ideologies but from distress and anger at the helplessness of backward Iran in the face of foreign intervention."[13] Reza Shah's political orientation guaranteed strong support from the growing modern middle class—a class that widely accepted Western notions of nationalism, development, and progress.

The task of building a distinctly modern state had begun during Reza Shah's initial tenure as minister of war in the early 1920s. The state of the armed forces during the final years of the Qajar dynasty reflected the political fragmentation of the country. The Persian Cossack Brigade, the gendarmerie, and the South Persia Rifles each were tied to different power bases within the country. Reza Shah immediately dissolved all independent military units and created the first unified standing army in Iran. The tradition of foreign-officered armed forces was ended. On 6 June 1925, the Majlis passed a law of compulsory conscription for every male at age twenty-one. On 15 February 1936 the armed forces were further professionalized. New ranks with Persian names were established and there was now a regulated basis of promotion, retirement pay, and other pensions. By 1941, Reza Shah could mobilize an army of four hundred thousand men. The centralized army allowed Reza Shah to pacify the country, and by the end of 1923 his task was completed everywhere except in the southwestern Arab province of Khuzestan. By the 1930s, travel throughout the country was relatively safe.

Within a decade, Reza Shah had taken a fragmented army and turned it into a centralized, professional military force, and he employed it to conquer all autonomous forces in Iran. Amin Banani commented: "He instinctively understood the lesson of European history—the emergence of a unified national state coincides with the development of a standing national army."[14] Political and economic reforms complemented Reza Shah's reorganization of the armed forces. The nepotism of the poorly organized and corrupt Qajar bureaucracy was replaced by a Westernized, meritocratic, and vastly expanded civil administration. As testimony to the nature and extent of these administrative reforms, the *madakhel* system of official bribery was replaced by a strict system of penalties for corrupt practices. Public health laws were passed regarding the quality of food supplies, the licensing of physicians, and the prevention and combating of infectious diseases. A scientific research institute and a medical school were established in Tehran. The construction of hospitals was energetically pursued. Extensive education reforms included the creation of a high council of education in 1921; in 1934 the University of Tehran was established. An elementary and secondary school system with standardized, secular curricula was established, bypassing the cleric-controlled *maktab* (elementary schools) and *madrasah* (seminaries) in Qom and Isfahan.

The most extensive changes during the reign of Reza Shah were in the economy.[15] Under the Qajar dynasty, Iranian economic development was hindered by a number of factors, especially the weakness of the central government. This changed with the political consolidation of Reza Shah. Enhanced internal security meant better communication and safer travel. Educational, administrative, and health reforms were largely designed to complement economic growth and development. Iran's infrastructure was continually developed and expanded. Between 1927 and 1938, for example, approximately fourteen thousand miles of roads were constructed. The number of vehicles in the country jumped from one lone car in 1910 to eight thousand cars and six thousand trucks by 1929.[16] By 1938, the trans-Iranian railway connecting Tehran in the north and Ahwas in the south was completed. By 1941, half of the east-west link between Mashhad, Tehran, and Tabriz was completed. The Iranian state also became involved directly in the economy, establishing a number of state monopolies to import and export commodities such as sugar, tobacco, tea, cotton, jute, rice, and carpets. By 1931, the state had established twenty-seven monopolies in essential commodities.

The state also encouraged private industrialization. This was done through tax exemptions, by supplying credit through the Agricultural and Industrial Bank, established in 1933, and through other protective measures such as tariffs, quotas, and exchange controls. The cumulative effect of the state's direct and indirect encouragement to industrial development was substantial. Between 1929 and 1941, ninety large manufacturing plants were established. Between 1934 and 1938 alone, at least fifty-eight industries began operation. These figures compare with the establishment of two new operations in 1926, none in 1927, and none in 1928. Iran also continually increased its oil exports, which rose from 3.8 million metric tons in 1925 to approximately 9.6 million metric tons in 1938.[17]

During Reza Shah's rule, there was continuing expansion of the number of professionals—lawyers, judges, doctors, and teachers. Industrialization also had led to the rise of a working class. At the same time, the social standing and political influence of the traditional middle class (ulama and bazaar merchants) continued to decline. In the countryside, the growth of a

landed class and a massive Iranian peasant class characterized rural relations of production.[18] Tribal identities were progressively eroded: the
monarchy had managed to engineer almost absolute control over the political system. The social forces taking shape under Reza Shah's autocratic
rule were denied the opportunity freely to voice their concerns. The state,
paradoxically, was on the one hand stable and resilient, and vulnerable on
the other. With respect to the former, the political structure under two
decades of Reza Shah's rule was stronger and more politically centralized
than at any other time in Iranian history. In the latter sense, however, the
regime lacked strong social foundations. "Reza Shah's state hovered somewhat precariously," Abrahamian commented, "without class foundations,
over Iran's society."[19] Reza Shah alienated the traditional middle class and
maintained a tight reign over the burgeoning working class. Trade unions
were banned in 1926; in 1931, a law prohibiting the propagation of all "col-
lectivist ideologies" was promulgated. Class and ethnic conflict was
increasingly controlled through direct state repression.

In 1941, Iran was occupied by the Soviet Union, Turkey, and Britain.
Reza Shah, lacking a strong social base and suspected by the Allied forces
of being sympathetic to Germany, was easily deposed and replaced by his
son. Mohammed Reza was just twenty-two years of age. In the aftermath of
the occupation, Iran embarked on a process of political liberalization. The
social forces that had developed during the reign of Reza Shah were
allowed to organize and operate with relative freedom. The result was a
lively and fluid political struggle among organizations representing the traditional middle class, the modern middle class, the working class, and various factions of the ruling elite.[20] The most salient struggle of the period
was between the young shah and the politically vibrant Majlis. The struggle
could be characterized as the call for an open, liberal democracy (the forces
represented in the Majlis) against efforts to reestablish an authoritarian
monarchy. Turning points in this conflict included the banning of the
Tudeh Party in 1949 and the oil nationalization crisis of 1951–1953.
Toward the end of the 1940s, the drift back toward a closed political system
was patently clear. The turbulence of the twelve-year interregnum was
brought to an abrupt close with the ousting of the Mossadeq government
through a CIA-sponsored coup in 1953. Although the power of the court
had been steadily accumulating, the coup unequivocally signalled the
return of autocratic rule in Iran. In effect, "the potentially viable alternative
to royal authoritarianism" was closed off for decades.[21]

Developments Under the Shah

The undisputed accession of the shah to power in 1953 ushered in the second period of concentrated economic growth and social transformation in

Iran. The centerpiece of the shah's development program was a package of economic and social reforms known as the White Revolution of 1963. The six-point program included (1) land reform provisions, (2) the sale of government-owned factories, (3) a revised election law granting women's suffrage, (4) the nationalization of Iran's forests, (5) a literacy corps, and (6) a plan to give workers a share of industrial profits. Iranian economic growth under the shah was spectacular. Between 1959/1960 and 1970/1971 the gross national product (GNP) in Iran rose by 143 percent, or at an average rate of approximately 8.5 percent each year. Annual growth rates in the first half of the 1970s were approximately 30 percent per year, a jump largely due to the sharp rise in world oil prices after 1973.[22] The rapid growth throughout the 1960s and 1970s reinforced shifting trends in the relative size of the various sectors of the Iranian economy. The agricultural sector continued to decline. Although it had accounted for more than 80 percent of the Iranian gross domestic product (GDP) at the turn of the century, by 1959 it had fallen to 33 percent and by the close of the 1960s it had fallen to 23 percent. In contrast, the manufacturing and mining sectors of the Iranian economy, which made negligible contributions at the turn of the century, accounted for one-third of GNP by 1969. The service sector, including banking, communications, and power supplies, grew to over forty percent of the Iranian economy by the end of the 1960s.[23]

Iranian economic development under the shah is subject to important qualifications. Successful growth in manufacturing and mining was accompanied by the growing inefficiency of the agricultural sector. Iranian agricultural production was incapable of meeting domestic needs and the monarchy had to import foodstuffs.[24] The industrial sector, moreover, had few backward or forward linkages, which limited the opportunity for economic development. The growth of the economy became increasingly dependent upon the steady supply of oil revenues. Those that remained in the countryside often endured extreme privation and hardship. Large-scale urban migration put great strain upon Iran's cities. Shantytowns with deplorable living conditions arose in the major urban centers, especially Tehran. The economic boom after 1973 was accompanied by rampant inflation that significantly worsened the lives of many Iranians. In short, although some social constituencies prospered, particularly those groups directly linked to the court—the businessmen, many large landowners, and the upper segments of the modern middle classes—the majority of Iranians became worse off.

The shah's economic successes were overshadowed by political stagnation. Although the Majlis continued to sit, it provided little more than official approbation of royal decrees. The shah's autocratic approach manifested itself most visibly in his control over the two parliamentary parties, the National Party and the People's Party, which were known colloquially as the "yes" and "yes sir" parties. The shah maintained his political control through a well-developed internal policing apparatus, known by its acronym SAVAK. In 1975 the shah dissolved the two-party system and replaced it with the Resurgence Party. Iran's latent opposition viewed the formation of the one-party system as a brazen move toward absolute political closure.

Social discontent with the shah's monarchy had registered as early as 1963. During the mourning month of *Muharram,* thousands of Iranians poured into the streets to protest against the regime. The protests lasted three days and left hundreds dead. A state-enforced calm held for little more than a decade. The economic downturns of the mid-1970s inspired the dormant opposition and rallied the population. The monarchy began to unravel in 1977 when a series of letters criticizing government policies and demanding greater political freedom were widely circulated. These protests were accompanied by student rallies and events. The sporadic nature of the protests was soon transformed into sustained opposition against the regime. Clashes between police and students early in 1978 resulted in several student deaths. The Tehran bazaar, which had not closed since 1963, suspended operation to protest the killings. By the summer of 1978, confrontations between the revolutionary opposition and the monarchy were unbroken. Any religious date or anniversary occasioned large-scale demonstrations and protests. The second half of 1978 saw a series of crippling strikes and marches involving hundreds of thousands of Iranians. By the end of 1978, the Pahlavi monarchy teetered on the verge of collapse. Political patronage and brute force could no longer stem the oppositional tide.

Two factors worthy of detailed attention stand out with respect to the Iranian revolution. The first concerns the wide coalition of social forces—including the traditional middle class, the modern middle class, and the working class—that ultimately brought the shah's regime down. The political character of each social force was essentially the product of the Pahlavi modernization drives. Only by banding together could the political momentum capable of toppling the monarchy be achieved. Second, a combination of unique historical and conjunctural circumstances combined to give the revolution its unmistakable Islamic hue. Both of these factors must be examined separately in order to adequately comprehend the 1979 revolution. The discussion appropriately begins where the revolution began; that is, with Iran's modern middle class.

Modern Middle-Class Opposition

The Iranian revolution received its initial impetus from the modern middle classes. In his pathbreaking study, James Bill defined this class as one composed of individuals who rest their power position upon employment utilizing those skills and talents which they possess thanks to modern education. This is a nonbourgeois middle class many of whose members relate themselves to the other classes and the system through function, performance, and service rather than through material wealth, family ties, or property. The members of this class are engaged in professional, technical, cultural, intellectual, and administrative occupations and are by and large a salaried middle class.[25]

The modern middle class was a direct creation of the socioeconomic trajectory of contemporary Iran, especially under the Pahlavi monarchy. The modern middle class displayed a refusal to accept the power relationships that characterized traditional Iranian society. They had considerable exposure to Western ideas and they tended to be less inclined to religious dogmatism (as manifested in their embrace of the Baha'i religion).[26] This class grew approximately 60 percent between 1956 and 1966. By the middle of the 1960s, one in every twelve Iranians belonged to the burgeoning middle class.[27] The growth of the "new technocrats" of Iranian society was partly bound up with the expansion of the state apparatus. Between 1956 and 1963, for example, Iran's Ministry of Economy tripled in size and the Ministry of Education doubled in size.[28]

Under the shah, the modern middle class was denied the opportunity to organize politically. This condition began to change in the late 1970s. The shah's promises of political liberalization and the human rights pronouncements by the U.S. president, Jimmy Carter, in January of 1977 sparked a sharp increase in the political activity of the modern middle class. These openings invited the rebirth of dormant organizations and the formation of entirely new ones. The Writers' Association, for example, was reactivated in the spring of 1977. The Iranian Committee for the Defense of Freedom and Human Rights, the Association of Iranian Lawyers, and the National Organization of University Teachers were formed in the autumn of 1977. During 1977, the National Front was revived by Karim Sanjabi, and Mehdi Bazargan revitalized the Freedom Movement of Iran.[29] In June of 1977, the National Front sent a letter directly to the shah asking for observance of the national constitution by the regime. Its authors wrote:

> The only way . . . to restore individual freedoms, reestablish national cooperation and solve the problems that threaten Iran's future is to desist from authoritarian rule, to submit absolutely to the principle of constitutionality, revive the people's rights, respect the Constitution and the Universal Declaration of Human Rights, abandon the single-party system, permit freedom of the press and freedom of association, free all political prisoners, allow exiles to return and establish a government based on a majority that has been popularly elected and which considers itself answerable to the Constitution.

The letter began with the following extremely candid assessment of where the blame for Iran's malaise lay: "No one in parliament, the Judiciary or the Administration is capable of listening to this statement since they possess no authority or responsibility, but merely observe the Royal Will. All the Nation's affairs are discharged through Imperial Writs."[30]

The Writers' Association was a leader in activity against the regime. The association was originally formed in 1967 but at that time was immediately dissolved by the government. Revived in 1977, at its peak the Writers' Association had some two hundred members, who adhered to a wide spectrum of political ideologies. The main venue for the Writers' Association during the initial stages of unrest was its poetry nights. The readings were instrumental in the initial stages of the 1977 mobilization against the regime. The following account of one poetry night, when the well-known Iranian Marxist poet and playwright Saeed Soltanpour was scheduled to speak, reveals the political character of this forum:

> The organizers had sent out two thousand invitations, but ten thousand people showed up to hear the talk. The police prevented the rest from entering the university. There was a confrontation between thousands of these people and the police outside the doors. Fifty students who had been denied permission to enter the amphitheatre were arrested. To protest this act of government repression, Soltanpour refused to give his scheduled speech on art and its influence on society and instead read one of his most revolutionary poems, written while he was incarcerated in a Savak jail. His reading generated great excitement. A massive overnight sit-in was spontaneously organized inside the amphitheatre and just outside the door to protest the students' arrests. The building that held the amphitheatre was surrounded all night and into the morning by police, who threatened more arrests if the demonstrators refused to disperse. Throughout the night, those inside sang revolutionary songs. . . . In the morning a message of solidarity was sent by workers from south Tehran and read to the audience. The protesters then left the amphitheatre for a street demonstration during which several students were slain or injured in clashes with the police. Three days later students called for a national day of mourning. Tehran merchants quickly responded by closing down the entire bazaar. That day more demonstrations took place and additional people were killed and injured.[31]

The activities of the Writers' Association epitomized the gathering opposition against the regime.

Collectively, organizations of the modern middle class can be credited with triggering the revolutionary movement. Elements of the modern middle class also provided considerable revolutionary momentum during 1978. Strikes by bank clerks, civil servants, and customs officials crippled the economy. "The wheels of government," commented one writer, "ground to a halt."[32] The revolution's final blow to the regime was also dealt by insurgent groups that drew almost exclusively upon members of the modern middle class.[33] By the late 1970s, a number of insurgent organizations were operating in the country. These included the Marxist Fedayi *(Sazman-i Cherik-ha-yi Feda'-i Khalq-i)*, the Islamic Mujahadin *(Sasman-i Mujahidin-i Khalq-i Iran)*, Paykar or Marxist Mujahidin *(Sazman-i Paykar dar Rah-i Azad-i Tabaqeh-i Kargar)*, smaller Islamic organizations frequently limited to one town, and smaller Marxist organizations. Almost all the members of these organizations came from the ranks of the young intelligentsia and took up arms out of moral and political indignation rather than material privation. During the last days of the shah's regime, the major insurgent organizations mounted assaults on the shah's army. During the insurrection of 1979, the guerrillas successfully opposed the elite imperial guards and gained control of the prisons, police stations, armories, and five military bases in Tehran. Similar seizures took place in Tabriz, Abadan, Hamadan, Mermanshah, Yazd, Isfahan, Mashad, Mahabad, and Babol.

The Traditional Middle Class

Although the modern middle class provided the revolution with its initial push, it was the traditional middle class that mobilized the Iranian population on a massive scale. The main components of the traditional middle class, the ulama and the bazaaris, were thoroughly alienated by the socioeconomic path of the Pahlavi monarchy. The standing of both groups waned as a direct result of the monarchy's modernization and secularization policies. Predictably, the traditional middle class was active in the uprisings of 1963. As small windows of opportunity appeared in the late 1970s, the disaffected traditional middle class moved quickly. Each component of the traditional middle class warrants separate consideration.

The undisputed accession of Reza Shah dramatically increased the strain upon the bazaaris. Social and economic policies during the 1930s prompted one contemporary observer to remark that "the merchant class in Persia is practically ruined, and the activity of former great trading centres like Tabriz, Isfahan, and Sultanabad paralysed."[34] Bazaari fathers no longer wanted their sons to be merchants.[35] The erosion of the traditional socioeconomic character of Iran under the rubric of modernization threw the bazaaris on the defensive. Specific economic trends—such as the rise of government-owned industrial enterprises, the increasing involvement of the state in the export-import businesses, and the expansion of the banking system that supplanted the credit capacities of the bazaaris—contributed to the general decline of the merchants' social and economic standing.[36] One writer noted: "Modernization in Iran was geared to bypassing the bazaar while rendering it politically and economically obsolete."[37]

The bazaaris were also subjected to direct attacks by the shah, especially after 1975. The shah's contempt for the traditional merchant class is evident in this excerpt from his personal reflections:

> Bazaars are a major social and commercial institution throughout the Mideast. But it remains my conviction that their time is past. The bazaar consists of a cluster of small shops. There is usually little sunshine or ventilation so they are basically unhealthy environs. The bazaaris are a frantic lot, highly resistant to change because their locations afford a lucrative monopoly. I could not stop building supermarkets. I wanted a modern country. Moving against the bazaars was typical of the political and social risks I had to take in my drive for modernization.[38]

One of the most visible assaults on the bazaaris was an antiprofiteering campaign. In August of 1975, this price-control and antiprofiteering policy directed at the "parasitic middlemen" of Iranian society was launched.[39] The state recruited some ten thousand people from all walks of life—students, teachers and housewives—in order to enforce the antiprofiteering legislation. These enforcers reserved the right to "hand out fines and recommend stiff penalties which ranged from prison to deportation and closure of the place of business."[40] In the first few days of the policy, more than seven thousand shopkeepers had been arrested. In a little more than two years, at least half the shopkeepers in Tehran had been investigated for price-control violations. By the end of 1977, some twenty thousand shopkeepers had been jailed for violating the new law. Convicted shopkeepers were humiliated through the closure of their shops and the hanging across their doorways of a banner proclaiming that the owner had been convicted of profiteering.[41] Throughout 1978, the bazaaris were increasingly subjected to violent attacks by SAVAK-hired hooligans.[42]

The clerical component of the traditional middle class fared worse than the bazaaris. Socioeconomic reforms relentlessly cut into their traditional roles and functions. Their social prestige and power within the Iranian social tapestry greatly declined. Attempts to regain their lost social stature seemed forever futile in view of the overwhelming forces of modernization and secularization at work under the Pahlavi monarchy.

Although the decline of the clergy could be detected prior to the rise of Reza Shah, the period between 1926 and 1941 marked the first rapid and sustained eclipse in their social standing. The growing body of intellectuals that nursed the socioeconomic program of Reza Shah "recognized in the power of the clergy the strongest obstacle to progress."[43] The revisions to the universal military training law of 1938 made all clergy subject to two years of compulsory military duty. Educational reforms under Reza Shah, especially the development of new institutions and curricula, undercut the traditional role of the clergy in Iranian education. Legal functions such as the registration of private property, traditionally monopolized by the *shari'ah* courts, and an important source of prestige and income for the clergy, became the prerogative of secular courts. Further legal reforms, especially the civil and penal codes of 1939 and 1940, continually abandoned the shariah to the point where traditional Islamic jurisprudence was left little room at all. Clerical resistance, especially against such reforms as the unveiling of women, was sustained throughout Reza Shah's reign.

The decline of the clergy was aggravated in the post-1953 era. Initially, the shah appeared extremely sensitive to the potential power of the ulama. Prominent religious leaders, for example, enjoyed easy access to the court. Nonetheless, the shah did nothing to reverse the setbacks suffered by the ulama. Moreover, by following development policies similar to his father's, the shah contributed to a further deterioration in the ulama's condition.[44] The growth of the modern middle class under the shah constituted a direct challenge to the clergy. As James Bill summarized in 1972:

> That which was sacred to the traditional middle classes is either ignored or attacked by the new class which is little impressed by either history or prophets. It is perhaps natural that the secularization of the education process would result in a different view of Shi'i Islam. The result has been a sharp move away from this most basic of value systems which organized all phases of a Muslim's life. Thus, a mujtahid stated in 1967 that whenever he spoke and worked with university students, he left his *'ammamah* (turban) at home and wore only a plain suit. The students of today, he pointed out, had little respect for the cleric. Within the intelligentsia in general, there is a deep sense that Islam represents an alien incursion forced upon Iranians by foreign invaders. It is often stated that the social problems of Iran stem from the Islamic intrusion.[45]

Events in the 1960s and 1970s aroused further opposition from the clergy. The ulama were opposed to elements of the shah's White Revolution—especially the proposed land reform and the enfranchisement of women. The shah also directly acted to weaken the clergy. The stipends given to clerical students *(tullab)* were abolished, and the new program resulted in considerably less money for aspiring students of Islam. Religious leaders, such as Ayatollah Taleqani, were persecuted by the regime. The shah directly affronted the clergy by destroying most of the theological seminaries in the holy city of Mashhad in 1975 under the pretext of creating green areas around the eighth imam's shrine.[46] The regime flouted established Islamic symbols, including the Islamic calendar. The shah also created a religious corps (in 1971) that was widely viewed as a direct attempt to undermine the clergy. As Parsa noted: "The Shah's opponents charged that he was creating his own brand of Islam and clergy, and that the corps was designed to 'nationalize religion' and undermine the traditional spiritual leaders."[47] Under the shah's land reform program, many religious lands *(awqaf)* were redistributed. The shah, in short, tended to view the clergy as a drag on his development policies. He himself wrote:

It must be acknowledged that, had my father not curtailed political efforts of certain clerics, the task which he had undertaken would have been far more difficult. It would have been a long time before Iran became a modern state. . . . The moral primacy of the spiritual over the temporal being indisputable and undisputed, it was a matter of bringing Iran into the twentieth century, whereas today's efforts are towards turning the clock back. Reza Shah asserted that in the twentieth century it was impossible for a nation to survive in obscurantism. True spirituality should exist *over and above* politics and economics.[48]

The ulama became déclassé: disengaged from the political power structure of Pahlavi Iran and disembedded from the Iranian social canvas.[49]

The mounting frustration of the ulama was cemented by their cohesiveness as a social group. Their collective animosity toward the regime articulated well with the alienation of the bazaaris, the other faction of the traditional middle class. An organic link between these two elements created a powerful social force. The *bazaaris* formed the traditional financial base for the ulama, providing up to 80 percent of the clergy's operating expenses.[50] The bazaaris also ran religious centers including the Hosseinieyeh, used for incidental religious gatherings to mourn the dead, the Mahdiyeh, used for religious instruction or the recital of the Quran, and the Takyeh, used for forty days beginning with the first of Moharram, the holy month of martyrdom of Imam Hussein.[51] The bazaaris and the clergy also shared physical linkages. Nikki Keddie's discussion of the shah's attacks upon the traditional middle class in Mashhad sheds light on the extent of these links. Keddie writes:

The Shah's scheme to redevelop the area around the holy shrine of the Imam Reza at Mashhad, which, like many shrines, was surrounded by a dense bazaar area, helped unify the bazaaris and the ulama. The plan was carried through and razed all buildings around the shrine, creating instead a green space and a broad traffic circle. It was so unpopular that bulldozers and construction equipment were often bombed or sabotaged, but it created something more attractive to "modern" taste. It dispersed Mashhad's bazaaris and further kindled their resentments. A related scheme for the Tehran bazaar, to cut through it with broad boulevards, which would, as in Mashhad, have dispersed potentially dangerous bazaaris, aroused so much opposition that it was not carried through.[52]

These linkages were complemented by strong ideological bonds between the ulama and the bazaaris. The ulama provided the bazaaris with moral, intellectual, and political guidance. This guidance was undoubtedly nurtured by the fact that Shi'i Islam has never called the sanctity of private property into question.[53] The bazaaris, in turn, tended to exert a moderating economic influence on the clergy.[54] The organic link between the two groups helped to insure that they would unify as an active social force against the monarchy as soon as circumstances permitted.

Although elements of the modern middle class began the revolutionary process, it was the traditional middle class that seized the openings and carried the revolution to fruition. Throughout 1978 and into 1979 the ulama mobilized the Iranian population on a scale unmatched in modern history. In the end, however, they were joined by the third integral element of the revolutionary opposition; namely, the working class.

Working-Class Opposition

The Iranian working class was largely the product of Pahlavi industrialization policies. There is some dispute concerning the overall significance of the working class in the revolutionary struggle, but most assessments contend that its participation was integral and substantial.[55] As Ervand Abrahamian concluded: "If the two middle classes were the main bulwarks of the revolution, the urban working class was its chief battering ram."[56] The Iranian working class oscillated between periods of growing organization and development and periods of repression under the autocratic rule of Reza Shah and his son.[57] The development of a nascent working class arose during the gradual changes at the turn of the century.[58] The labor movement developed strongly during the period between the Constitutional Revolution and the rise of Reza Shah. Any advances, however, were forfeited in the face of Reza Shah's direct repression. In particular, the Regulations for Factories and Industrial Organizations of 1936 prohibited employees from "faction formation, connivance, and other activities leading to disturbance of the smooth running of factory affairs and progress in production."[59] Reza Shah tried to supplant the need for independent trade unions by issuing labor regulations, but these palliative gestures tended to leave the condition of the working class unchanged during his rule.

The working class went through a period of renewal in the aftermath of the Allied occupation of 1941. In the more relaxed political atmosphere of the early 1940s, worker militancy increased substantially. The Tudeh Party was founded in 1941. The intensification of trade union organization culminated in the formation of the Central United Council of the Trade Union of Workers and Toilers of Iran. The growth of the labor movement after 1941 contributed to the development of new labor legislation enacted in 1946 by the Qavam government. This law contained a number of provisions, including limitations on the permitted number of hours of factory work, restrictions on child labor, maternity provisions for women, and minimum wage laws. The gathering strength of the working class during the interregnum was accompanied by several important strikes; e.g., the oil workers strike in the Anglo-Iranian fields in 1951.[60]

Despite these modest gains, repression against the labor movement began in earnest with the gradual accession of the shah.[61] In the aftermath of the coup d'etat that overthrew the government of Mohammed Mossadeq, the relationship between labor and the state reacquired the characteristics of Reza Shah's reign. Fred Halliday, describing 1953, wrote: "In that year a long night fell over the Iranian working class—a darkness from which it only began to emerge after the passage of twenty years."[62] Labor was directly attacked through a process that was colloquially summarized as "putting them [workers] in their place."[63] The labor law of 1959 established that unions could be established only if recognized by the Ministry of Labor. Labor organizations were increasingly penetrated and organized by SAVAK. As a result of the shah's policies, the number of major industrial strikes fell from seventy-nine in 1953 to seven in 1954, and between 1955 and 1957 to three in total.[64]

The repression of the working class sat awkwardly against the significant growth of labor during the shah's rule. The working class—defined as employees working in construction, mining, and manufacturing—grew far more rapidly than any other segment of the Iranian workforce. Total growth between 1956 and 1977 approached 2.5 million workers. By 1977, only the agricultural sector employed more people.[65]

A realm of unobserved oppression plagued Iranian workers. This included industrial accidents such as amputations and the loss of sight. Other problems included chemical hazards, noise pollution, foul odors, and poor lighting.[66] Attempts to raise worker productivity in key economic sectors resulted in the implementation of the profit-sharing scheme of 1963 (part of the White Revolution) and the workers' share scheme of 1975. Neither program proved successful in placating labor or in raising worker productivity.[67] Many wage gains were eroded by the high inflation that accompanied the economic boom of the mid-1970s.

In the repressive atmosphere of the shah, workers could only periodically resort to wildcat strikes. However, mounting inflation, labor shortages (with the ensuing enhanced job prospects in the event that a worker is fired for agitation), and oil revenue increases (which allow the state occasionally to grant concessions) contributed to a growth in strike activity during the mid-1970s. Strikes rose from a handful in the early 1970s to at least twenty in 1974–1975 and twenty in 1977 alone. In the first three months of 1978, more than ten strikes were called.[68] Despite this growth in strike activity during the 1970s, workers were slow to join the revolutionary movement.[69] In September 1978, oil workers went on strike at the Tehran oil refinery. This was followed by strikes at the Abadan, Shiraz, Isfahan, and Tabriz refineries.[70] The strike by oil workers was heavily permeated with political demands, as evident in the following list submitted by Ahwaz staff workers on 29 October 1978. The strikers demanded:

1. An end to martial law
2. Full solidarity and cooperation with teachers who were also on strike
3. Unconditional release of all political prisoners

4. Iranianization of the oil industry
5. That all communications be in the Persian language
6. That all foreign employees leave the country
7. An end to discrimination against women—both staff employees and workers
8. The implementation of a law recently passed by both houses of Parliament dealing with the housing of oil workers and staff employees
9. Support for demands being made by production workers, including the dissolution of SAVAK
10. Punishment of corrupt high government officials and ministers
11. Reduced schedules for offshore drilling crews[71]

The oil workers' strike reverberated throughout the Iranian economy. Without access to oil revenues, the regime was severely weakened.[72] With the growing domestic oil shortage, buses and cars ceased to run. This led to the closing of many government ministries. Numerous factories were forced to close because of a lack of fuel. The strike by the oil workers also inspired other economic sectors to act against the regime. Eventually, the combined effect of the strikes by industrial and oil workers succeeded in bringing the Iranian economy to a virtual halt.

The Revolution: A Distinct Islamic Hue

Fifteen years after the Muharram uprisings of 1963, the Pahlavi monarchy was seriously faltering. Once again, during the mourning month of Muharram, and particularly on Ashurah, its most solemn day, hundreds of thousands of Iranians took to the streets, calling for the overthrow of the monarchy. Strikes had crippled the economy. The shah's army appeared incapable of restoring any semblance of calm or order. From his exile in France, Ayatollah Khomeini urged all Iranians steadfastly to oppose the monarchy. Repeatedly, he called for the shah's removal. By the end of 1978, major Iranian cities (e.g., Mashhad and Isfahan) were under the control of the revolutionary opposition.

In response to the growing crisis, the shah appointed his third government in six months. Shahpur Bakhtyar agreed to accept the task of seeking a political solution to the deepening crisis. His two immediate predecessors, Sherif-Amami and Gholam Reza Azhari, had failed in their bids to restore calm. Bakhtyar committed his government to a number of liberalization policies, including the disbanding of SAVAK and the lifting of press censorship. Despite these moves, his government was met with sustained opposition, especially from the National Front. Bakhtyar's efforts were radically undermined by the departure of the shah on 16 January

1979. This was followed by the return of Khomeini to Iran on 1 February. On 5 February, Khomeini appointed Mehdi Bazargan to head a provisional revolutionary government. Over the next two weeks, the decay of the old regime accelerated. On 11 February the army declared its neutrality and Bakhtyar resigned.[73] The Pahlavi monarchy had collapsed.

The monarchy fell victim to a broad coalition of revolutionary forces that included the urban middle class, the traditional middle class, and the working class. The monarchy authored its own fate in two senses. Its development strategy had profoundly conditioned the social forces that rose up to challenge it. The regime, moreover, deprived Iranians of the opportunity to air their social and political grievances. Iran's political development was incommensurate with its rich social permutations. By effectively shutting down the political system, the opposition gravitated toward an uncompromising revolutionary posture.[74]

Despite its diverse oppositional cast, the Iranian revolution acquired a distinct Islamic hue. A number of factors account for this outcome. First, the absence of alternative avenues for political expression provided an incentive for the structuring of political opposition in religious terms. Religion essentially became a political front. The following passage from Homa Katouzian's study reveals the extent to which religion masked political criticism:

> In the month of *Muharram*—in which Imam Husain, his family and his followers had been heroically martyred by an army of Yazid, the second Ummayid caliph—even the lampposts in the more traditional city districts were wrapped in black material. When in a mosque, or a private house, the audience roared approval of the ceremonial damnation of Yazid and his men by the officiating preacher, few people, including SAVAK agents, missed the allusions to the Shah and his henchmen, which were on everybody's mind. On the birthday of the twelfth Shi-ite Imam—Hujjat ibn al-Hasan al-'Askari; the Redeemer who is always present, but remains invisible until the moment of his advent—the huge banners put out in the streets carried thinly disguised political slogans: "Oh Redeemer of all humanity, hasten in your advent, for the world is now full of injustice"; "With the advent of the lord of the Time; may god Almighty hasten his deliverance; injustice will be completely uprooted in this world" and so on.[75]

This incentive was enhanced by the popular appeal of some widely read works by Ali Shari'ati that presented Islam as an ideology for social revolution—a revolution aspiring to establish a free and classless society.[76]

In the repressive regime of the shah, moreover, the mosque became a strategically important communication network. This network was well placed and relatively well insulated. It complemented the use of religious services, festivals, and mourning periods as political venues. The ulama thus became integral to the revolutionary process, and they developed close links to the revolutionary organizations that sprang up during the latter stages of the struggle. Finally, and perhaps most importantly, Ayatollah Khomeini stood at the head of the gathering storm. The influence exercised by Khomeini, especially during the autumn of 1978, was unequalled by any other opposition figure. Other elements of the opposition did not dare to contradict Khomeini's instructions from Paris. Khomeini's charisma and uncompromising stand against the monarchy, in effect, provided the benchmark for the revolutionary opposition.

Revolutionary Consolidation

The unity of the revolutionary opposition was achieved in the face of a common adversary. With the fall of the shah this unity began to unravel immediately. Clerical ascendency through 1978 and 1979 was not about to go unchallenged by other elements of the revolutionary coalition. As this became increasingly clear to the clerics, an intense and frequently violent process of revolutionary consolidation immediately set in. It is in the process of revolutionary consolidation that the seeds of the aggressive campaign against Iraq may be detected, a campaign that included direct calls for the overthrow of the Iraqi regime. Iran's aggressive posture evoked extreme concern among the Ba'th leadership in Iraq. At the same time, the postrevolutionary turmoil of Iran presented Iraq's leadership with a cherished opportunity to even recent diplomatic scores. In order to understand Baghdad's response, this analysis now turns to Iraq's contemporary history.

Notes

1. Except where specifically indicated for clarity and due recognition, this analysis is extracted from the following general histories of twentieth-century Iran: Ervand Abrahamian, *Iran Between Two Revolutions,* (Princeton University Press, 1982); H. Bashiriyeh, *The State and Revolution in Iran: 1962–1982,* (St. Martin's Press, 1984); Fred Halliday, *Iran: Dictatorship and Development,* (Penguin, 1989); Mehran Kamrava, *Revolution in Iran: The Roots of Turmoil,* (Routledge, 1990); H. Katouzian, *The Political Economy of Modern Iran: Despotism and Pseudo-Modernism: 1926–1979,* (New York University Press, 1981); N. Misagh Parsa, *Social Origins of the Iranian Revolution,* (Rutgers University Press, 1989).

2. For a full account of the political effects of Iranian geography, see Charles Issawi, "Geographical and Historical Background," in *The Economic History of Iran: 1800–1914,* ed. Charles Issawi, (University of Chicago Press, 1971), pp. 1–13.

3. Abrahamian, *Iran: Between Two Revolutions,* op. cit., pp. 33–34.

4. Ibid., p. 36.

5. Issawi, *Economic History,* op. cit., editor's summary, Chapter 3, p. 132.

6. Mirza Husain, "Crafts in Isfahan," selection 3, Chapter 6, in *Economic History,* ed. Charles Issawi, op. cit., p. 281.

7. See discussion in Malcolm E. Yapp, "1900–1921: The Last Years of the Qajar Dynasty," in *Twentieth Century Iran,* ed. Hossein Amirsadeghi, (Heinemann, 1977), p.7.

8. An interesting assessment of this role may be found in Asghar Fathi, "Preachers as Substitutes for Mass Media: The Case of Iran 1905–1909," in *Towards a Modern Iran: Studies in Thought, Politics and Society,* eds. Elie Kedourie and Sylvia G. Haim, (Frank Cass, 1980).

9. See discussion in Hamid Algar, *Religion and State in Iran 1785–1906: The Role of the Ulama in the Qajar Period,* (University of California Press, 1969), Chapter 14.

10. Halliday, *Iran,* op. cit., p. 22.

11. L. P. Elwell-Sutton, "Reza Shah the Great: Founder of the Pahlavi Dynasty," in *Iran Under the Pahlavis,* ed. George Lenczowski, (Hoover Institution Press, 1978), p. 9.

12. William J. Olson, "The Genesis of the Anglo-Persian Agreement of 1919," in *Towards a Modern Iran,* eds. Kedourie and Haim, op. cit., p. 211.

13. Amin Banani, *The Modernization of Iran: 1921–1941,* (Stanford University Press, 1961), p. 46.

14. Ibid., p. 54.

15. The following discussion on economic changes primarily draws upon Julian Bharier, *Economic Development in Iran: 1900–1970,* (Oxford University Press, 1971).

16. Ibid., pp. 194–197.

17. See discussion in Charles Issawi, "The Iranian Economy 1925–1975: Fifty Years of Economic Development," in Iran *Under the Pahlavis,* ed. George Lenczowski, (Hoover Institution Press, 1978), p. 131. Also see Bharier, *Economic Development,* op. cit., Chapter 5, pp. 84–88.

18. An excellent account of these social changes may be found in Farideh Farhi, "Class Struggles, the State, and Revolution in Iran," in *Power and Stability in the Middle East,* ed. Berch Berberoglu, (Zed Books, 1989), p. 92.

19. Abrahamian, *Iran Between Two Revolutions,* op. cit., p. 149.

20. The most comprehensive account of the political struggles of this period may be found in Fakhreddin Azimi, *Iran: The Crisis of Democracy, 1941–1953,* (I. B. Tauris and Company, 1989).

21. Ibid., p. 339.

22. Charles Issawi, "The Iranian Economy 1925–1975: Fifty Years of Economic Development," in *Iran Under the Pahlavis,* op. cit., p. 141.

23. Bharier, *Economic Development,* op. cit., pp. 59–61.

24. See Keith McLachlan, "The Iranian Economy: 1960–1976," in *Twentieth Century Iran,* ed. Hossein Amirsadeghi, (Heinemann, 1977).

25. James Alban Bill, *The Politics of Iran: Groups, Classes and Modernization,* (C. E. Merrill, 1972), p. 54.

26. See discussion in Bill, *Politics,* op. cit., pp. 57–62.

27. Ibid. (Figures extracted from pp. 66–67).

28. See discussion in Roger M. Savory, "Social Development in Iran during the Pahlavi Era," in *Iran Under the Pahlavis,* ed. George Lanczowski, (Hoover Institution, 1978), pp. 124–125.

29. For a discussion of the politics of this class under the shah and in the revolutionary aftermath, see Said Amir Arjomand, *The Turban for the Crown: The Islamic Revolution in Iran,* (Oxford University Press, 1988), pp. 198–114.

30. See discussion in Jerrold D. Green, *Revolution in Iran: The Politics of Countermobilization,* (Praeger Special Studies, 1982), pp. 64–67. (The letter is quoted on p. 65.)

31. Misagh Parsa, *Social Origins,* op. cit., pp. 178–179.

32. M. Reza Ghods, *Iran in the Twentieth Century: A Political History,* (Lynne Rienner Publishers, 1989), p. 218.

33. Discussion extracted from Ervand Abrahamian, "The Guerrilla Movement in Iran, 1963–1977," in *MERIP Reports* no. 86 (March/April 1980).

34. Violet Conolly, "The Industrialization of Persia," in *Journal of the Royal Central Asian Society,* (July 1935), p. 462, cited in M. Reza Ghods, *Iran in the Twentieth Century,* op. cit., p. 112.

35. See discussion in Michael Fischer, "Persian Society: Transformation and Strain," in *Twentieth-Century Iran,* op. cit., pp. 180–183.

36. See the discussion in Sepehr Zabih, *Iran's Revolutionary Upheaval,* (Alchemy Books, 1979), p. 27.

37. Jerrold D. Green, *Revolution in Iran: The Politics of Countermobilization,* (Praeger Publishers, 1982), p. 41.

38. Mohammed Reza Shah Pahlavi, *Answer to History,* (Stein and Day, 1980), p. 156.

39. Michael Fischer, "Persian Society: Transformation and Strain," in *Twentieth-Century Iran,* op. cit., pp. 180–183.

40. Sepehr Zabih, *Iran's Revolutionary Upheaval,* op. cit., p. 31

41. Figures and account extracted from Misagh Parsa, *Social Origins,* op. cit., pp. 102–104.

42. Ibid., pp. 115–119.

43. This analysis is indebted to Banani, *Modernization,* op. cit. (The quote is from p. 50.)

44. Discussion extracted from Parsa, *Social Origins,* op. cit., pp. 195–196.

45. James Alban Bill, *The Politics of Iran,* op. cit., (C. E. Merrill, 1972), p. 61.

46. Arjomand, *Turban,* op. cit., p. 86.

47. Parsa, *Social Origins,* op. cit., p. 196.

48. Mohammad Reza Pahlavi, *Answer,* op. cit., p. 55.

49. See discussion in Said Amir Arjomand, *Turban,* op. cit., pp. 83–84.

50. This figure is taken from John D. Stempel, *Inside the Iranian Revolution,* (Indiana University Press, 1981), p. 45.

51. Sepehr Zabih, *Iran's Revolutionary Upheaval,* op. cit., p. 29.

52. Nikki R. Keddie, *Roots of Revolution: An Interpretive History of Modern Iran,* (Yale University Press, 1981), p. 241.

53. For a detailed account of the relationship between the bazaaris and the clerics see Ahmad Ashraf, "Bazaar and Mosque in Iran's Revolution," in *MERIP Reports,* 13:3, (March–April 1983).

54. See discussion in Farideh Farhi, in *Power and Stability,* op. cit., p. 103.

55. For a dissenting view see Arjomand, *Turban,* op. cit., note 14, p. 236.

56. Abrahamian, *Iran Between Two Revolutions,* op. cit., p. 535.

57. The following summary primarily relies upon Habib Ladjevardi, *Labour Unions and Autocracy in Iran,* (Syracuse University Press, 1985).

58. See the discussion of Z. Z. Abdullaev, "Bourgeoisie and Working Class, 1900s," in Issawi, *Economic History,* op. cit., especially pp. 48–52.

59. Ladjevardi, *Labour Unions,* op. cit., p. 61.

60. See discussion in Keddie, *Roots of Revolution,* op. cit., pp. 121–129.

61. See especially Ladjevardi, *Labour Unions,* op. cit., Chapter 4.

62. Fred Halliday, *Iran: Dictatorship and Development,* op. cit., p. 202.

63. Ladjevardi, *Labour Unions,* op. cit., p. 198.

64. Abrahamian, *Iran Between Two Revolutions,* op. cit., p. 420.

65. Statistics from Halliday, *Iran: Dictatorship or Democracy,* op. cit., p. 176.

66. Assef Bayat, *Workers and Revolution in Iran,* (Zed Books, 1987), pp. 65–74.

67. See discussion in Halliday, *Iran: Dictatorship or Democarcy,* op. cit., pp. 193–197.

68. Figures and analysis extracted from Parsa, *Social Origins,* op. cit., pp. 140–144.

69. See discussion in Abrahamian, *Iran Between Two Revolutions,* op. cit., p. 537.

70. A detailed firsthand account of the oil workers' strike may be found in "How We Organized the Strike that Paralysed the Shah's Regime," in *Oil and Class Struggle,* eds. Petter Nore and Terisa Turner, (Zed Press, 1980).

71. Terisa Turner, "Iranian Oilworkers in the 1978–1979 Revolution," in *Oil and Class Struggle,* op. cit., p. 282.

72. Discussion extracted from Misagh Parsa, *Social Origins,* op. cit., pp. 157–167.

73. For a more detailed account of the military during this period, see Sepehr Zabih, *The Iranian Military in Revolution and War,* (Routledge, 1988).

74. See discussion in Abrahamian, "Structural Causes of the Iranian Revolution," in *MERIP Reports* no. 87 (May 1980).

75. Homa Katouzian, *The Political Economy of Modern Iran: Despotism and Pseudo-Modernism, 1926–1979,* (Macmillan Press, 1981), p. 339.

76. For a discussion of Shari'ati's works see Mangol Bayat-Philipp, "Shi'ism in Contemporary Iranian Politics: The Case of Ali Shari'ati," in *Towards a Modern Iran: Studies in Thought, Politics and Society,* eds. Elie Kedourie and Sylvia G. Haim, (Frank Cass, 1980).

3

The Tenuous Social Base of the Ba'th Regime in Iraq

The Iranian revolution had a far-reaching impact on Iraq. Ultimately, political fallout from the revolution undergirded the catastrophic drift to war in 1980. In order to properly understand these revolutionary reverberations, it is necessary to concisely outline the development path of contemporary Iraqi society. As Iraq was inserted into the global economy over the century prior to the war, its social tapestry was rewoven thoroughly. The country was transformed from a mainly rural, nomadic, tribal-based populace into a largely urbanized, sedentary, and extensively proletarianized society. Iraq's new social forces, often succoured by Western ideas, irrevocably altered the contemporary political terrain of the country. The extensive changes in the social and political canvas of Iraq nourished a string of historical upheavals. These included the British occupation in 1914, the founding of the Iraqi monarchy in 1921, the al-Wathbah popular uprising against the Portsmouth Treaty in 1948, and the subsequent fall of the monarchy in 1958.

Iraq's development can also be reviewed in terms of the repetitive alienation of its political elite from the wider population. The Iraqi monarchy, for example, was wholly estranged from the Iraqi people—a fact that figured prominently in its collapse. Most of Iraq's republican era, post-1958, can also be characterized in terms of an untraversable distance between the country's political leadership and the general population. This trend was magnified after the second accession of the Ba'th party, in 1968. Iraq's vibrant social floor was systematically choked off from the corridors of Ba'th power. Kurdish nationalist groups, the working class, women, and the Shi'i poor were forced to play by the politically restrictive rules of the Ba'th regime. Genuine calls for social and political reform were routinely greeted harshly by Baghdad. The social foundations of the Ba'th regime became increasingly slender, and its policing apparatus accordingly expanded exponentially. By the end of the 1970s, the Ba'th regime was tenuously poised above a severely fractured and politically volatile society.

It is within this context of a society wrestling beneath an obtrusive and repressive state that the reaction to events in nearby Iran must be placed. Iraq's contemporary social and political trajectory rendered the country susceptible to the revolutionary upheaval of its neighbor. The Iranian revolution charged Iraq's political atmosphere and seriously alarmed the Ba'th regime. Iran's postrevolutionary turmoil and its determination to export the Islamic Revolution sharpened Iraq's explosive political climate. The Ba'th regime, facing sustained opposition from a number of political quarters, became sufficiently motivated to move against its extraterritorial agitant. In complementary terms, the Islamic Revolution echoed within a society that had been extensively transformed over the previous century, intensified its social fissures, and nourished its political struggles. Ultimately, the events in Iran triggered an aggressive military response from Baghdad.

The Decline of Ottoman Rule

As Iraq was drawn into the European economic fold during the latter half of the nineteenth century, the country's tribal-centered way of life was abruptly interrupted.[1] The tribes had traditionally practiced subsistence agriculture along with camel, sheep, and goat herding. Tribal life tended to oscillate between periods of relative calm and periods of turmoil among feuding clans. Three particular developments stimulated Iraq's links with the European economy: the growth of commercialized river transport along the Tigris between Basra and Baghdad during the 1850s, the Ottoman land code of 1858, and the opening of the Suez Canal in 1869. It is helpful to address each of these stimuli separately.

Growth of River Trade

Prior to the mid-1800s, Iraqi exports were destined primarily for the Arabian peninsula and India. Exports from Basra (one of the three Ottoman provinces—Basra, Baghdad, and Mosul—that came to form Iraq) at midcentury were primarily horses and dates. To a lesser extent, wool, rice, and grain were exported. Imports included coffee from Yemen and indigo, sugar, and textiles from India. As Roger Owen writes, the internal obstacles to increased trade were considerable:

> The major obstacles to any increase in trade remained more or less the same. Goods traffic along both the Tigris and the Euphrates remained difficult, slow and subject to heavy duties imposed by both the government and the tribes which controlled strategic points along the river banks. The cargoes of the small boats engaged in this traffic were still held to ransom or plundered at regular intervals. Sea-going ships face other problems, notably the monsoons which made it hard for a sailing vessel to make

more than one trip to India a year. With access to external markets so difficult there was little incentive to increase production and the captains of the few British ships which reached Basra with goods from England generally complained of being unable to find a return cargo.[2]

The development of commercialized river transport along the Tigris and the Euphrates during the nineteenth century provided the first incentive to expand Iraq's trading relations. Although initial surveys of the Mesopotamian rivers undertaken in the early 1830s met with limited success, a major impetus came from a decision of the British House of Commons favoring the Mesopotamian rivers as an alternative route to India. This decision spawned more intensive surveying of the Tigris and the Euphrates and led to the foundation of the Lynch Firm's operation of two steamers in 1841. By the 1860s, travel time and transportation costs had been reduced significantly. Upstream travel time between Baghdad and Basra was reduced to a maximum of eight days. Initially it was a journey of forty to sixty days.[3]

The Land Code

The second factor that changed Iraq's socioeconomic canvas came during Midhat Pasha's tenure as governor of Baghdad. Previous reforms inaugurated under Da'ud during the Mamluk era, including the establishment of a printing press, the clearing of canals, and the setting up of small-scale industries, had planted the first seeds of economic change. But it was Midhat Pasha's administrative, educational, and rural reforms that really ushered in the era of modernization in Iraq. Administrative reforms strengthened the position of the towns, particularly Baghdad, and educational reforms laid the foundations for the secularization of Iraqi education by establishing schools outside the ambit of the *maktab* (elementary educational facilities run by the clergy) and the *madrasah* (advanced educational institutions, also run by the clergy).[4] Midhat Pasha's implementation of the Ottoman land code of 1858 had an enduring effect upon Iraq's economic development and, ultimately, its social structure. Prior to the 1858 land code, most of the cultivated areas of Iraq were held communally among all members of the tribe. Although much of the product of the cultivated land of the *dira* (area claimed by the tribe) eventually found its way to the tribal *shaikh* (chief), the revenues, in theory, went to support the tribe writ large—maintaining, for example, the tribal militia. The remainder of the tribal lands was held by tribal subchiefs *(sirkal)* on conditions similar to the tribal shaikh. The unit of cultivated land (known as the *quit'a*) was subdivided into plots *(faddan)* that were worked by groups of cultivators *(juaq)*.[5] Midhat Pasha's rural reforms, aimed at strengthening the influence and financial position of the Ottoman state, established a legal land-tenure system by granting title deeds *(tapu sands)* in place of *miri* (state or unalienated) land. The simple goal was to have the security of state-authorized land tenure give prospective taxpayers a much greater incentive to pay their taxes.[6] The absence of any effective machinery to enforce tax laws, however, resulted, from the Ottoman standpoint, in the failure of the policy. *Tapu* grants were banned after 1881. Nonetheless, Midhat Pasha's reforms established a strong precedent with respect to the private ownership of land in Iraq.

Opening of the Suez Canal

The process of detribalization and pacification of the countryside received its third, and perhaps most significant, boost with the opening of the Suez Canal in 1869. The canal effectively plugged the region into the European economy. The arrival of the first British steamer via the Suez Canal in June 1870 symbolically underscored the removal of traditional barriers to trade in Iraq. The combined effect of the growth of tapu lands, the development of commercialized river transport along the Mesopotamian rivers, and the opening of the canal insured Iraq's movement away from a subsistence economy to a seaborne, export-oriented economy primarily based on agricultural and pastoral exports. In the first decade after the opening of the Suez Canal, Iraqi trade jumped dramatically. Between 1870 and 1880, total exports rose from £206,000 to £1,275,000. In the same period, imports jumped from £314,000 to £722,000. Between 1880 and 1913, the total value of Iraq's exports of dates, wool, wheat, and barley rose from £940,000 to £2.7 million.[7]

The net effect of these changes during the nineteenth and early twentieth centuries was the unmistakable process of detribalization and pacification of the Iraq countryside. The evolution of the latter part of the nineteenth century broke a pattern of undulating power balances between the towns and the tribes that had characterized Iraq for centuries. The strengthening of the towns in the context of the region's new trading relations now meant the permanent satellitization of rural life.[8] The tribal member, moreover, was transformed from a warrior into a peasant in a few short decades. As economic historian Mohammad Salman Hasan described it, "Nomads who were no longer in a position to rely on the camel or plunder for their livelihood, but were still subject to the discipline of tribal organization regarding the relations between the followers and their leaders, had no alternative but the follow their shaykhs into settlement on the land."[9] The transformation of the countryside and the erosion of tribal life is also reflected in the shifting demographic patterns of the period. The growth of the agricultural export economy contributed to the settlement of the population. In 1867 the nomadic population of Iraq stood at 35 percent of the total population. By 1890, this figure had declined to 25 percent; by 1905, to 17 percent; and by 1930, to a mere 7 percent. The spectacular growth of the agricultural economy also resulted in considerable growth in the rural population. In 1867, the rural population as a percentage of the total Iraqi population stood at 41 percent. By 1930, this figure had climbed to 68 percent.[10]

British Influence and the Iraqi Monarchy

World War I saw a rapid decline in Ottoman influence and a corresponding rise in British control in Iraq. British interest centered around securing access to the region's oil, especially after Britain's navy converted to diesel power. In November 1914, British troops landed at the head of the Gulf in order to protect its oil interests at Abadan. By the end of the war, Britain had acquired relative control of Iraq. In 1920, the League of Nations awarded Britain mandatory power over Iraq under the terms of the San Remo Agreement. Britain proceeded to establish a monarchy, discharging some of its regional political debts by installing Faisal on the Iraqi throne in the summer of 1921.

Iraq's evolving social character began to congeal under the monarchy. At the apex of Iraqi society stood the landed shaikhs, a group that had benefited directly from the transformation in rural productive relations throughout the late nineteenth and early twentieth centuries. This landowning class was bolstered by favorable agricultural policies under the monarchy.[11] The early years of the monarchy also saw the accelerated rise of the urban—primarily mercantile—bourgeoisie. In part, the bourgeoisie expanded due to the opportunities afforded by the two world wars—such as the presence of troops (which increased the size of the market) and rapidly fluctuating prices (which promoted profiteering). The bourgeoisie also benefited by the considerable growth in cultivated lands, improved infrastructural facilities (especially in transport and travel), and weak tax structures. Some elements of the mercantile bourgeoisie branched out into manufacturing (textiles, beverages, soap, vegetable oil, cigarettes, and building materials), and in the latter stage of the monarchy, the rising demand for consumer goods contributed to their growth. There was also, after 1951, the influx in oil revenues.[12]

The constellation of the middle classes was likewise falling into place. The *sadah,* or traditional clerical class, maintained some influence in the government, but their political influence and social position, especially during the latter years of the monarchy, appreciably declined. As noted by Batatu:

> The building up of the state apparatus, the growth of the army . . . the spread of modern learning, the rise of the oil industry, the rapid increase

in the country's revenue, the widening links of Iraq with the outside world, had created new forces, new opinions, a new psychological climate. The old activities of many of the *sadah* families, their function as 'ulama, or keepers of shrines, or leaders of mystic orders, had declined in social value.[13]

At the same time, the gradual expansion of the modern middle class could be detected. The expansion of the state apparatus in particular encouraged the rise of this class. The concomitant growth of modern education facilities and new occupational opportunities helped to give this class a relatively cohesive view of the world. The new middle class included civil servants, professionals (among them teachers, doctors, lawyers, and army officers), retailers, and the operators of small businesses and industrial establishments. By the time of the collapse of the monarchy in 1958, this class constituted slightly more than 10 percent of the Iraqi workforce.[14]

The majority of Iraqis, of course, stood at the bottom of the social hierarchy. The evolving agricultural system bore down heavily upon the Iraqi peasantry. Agricultural production had come to revolve around a system of sharecropping. The peasant, or *fallah,* was paid in kind. If the fallah was unable to supply seed or tools for cultivation, he would be forced to borrow money, frequently at exorbitant interest rates, which would result in the perennial indebtedness of the peasant. The condition of the peasants (*fallahin*) was aggravated by the Rights and Duties of Cultivator Act of 1933. Elie Kedourie's masterful essay on the Iraqi monarchy testifies to the social effects of this law:

> The notorious Rights and Duties of Cultivator Act . . . deprived the *fellah* of all rights, and made him into a serf. Under this law, the landowner could evict the *fellah* for any activities deemed "harmful to agriculture". On the other hand, the agricultural worker was virtually tied to the land; so long as he was in debt to the landowner, it was laid down in the law, he could not be employed by another landowner; and should he be dismissed or evicted, his debts were recoverable from his personal property. This law thus transformed a large—perhaps the largest—number of Iraqis from free persons into mere *adscripti glebae.*[15]

The wretched condition of the Iraqi peasantry was unenviable in the extreme.[16] One historical reference to the typical Iraqi cultivator revealed the extent of their misery: "The health condition of the fallah was so appalling that Professor Critchley described him as a 'living pathological specimen.' His life expectancy did not improve much throughout the regime of the monarchy . . . it stood at 35–39 years."[17]

The prevailing relations of agricultural production and the perilous condition of the fallahin contributed to a growing tendency to leave the land. Between 1930 and 1947, the rural population dropped from 68 percent to 57 percent of the total. During the same period, the urban population, after hovering around 25 percent between 1867 and 1930, had risen to 38 percent by 1947.[18] The growing migration to the urban areas put pressure upon the cities. New residents were usually absorbed into the workforce in menial capacities such as porters and servants.[19] The migrants in Baghdad crowded into open spaces in the city and lived in *sarifah* (mud huts with reed mats on the roof). It is estimated that in 1956 there were 16,400 sarifas in the Baghdad area.[20] Privation, unsanitary conditions, and disease were common in the new urban slums.

The Iraqi working class was expanding throughout the monarchy, although the tempo of this growth was retarded by the slow pace of industrial development.[21] The working class was concentrated almost exclusively in the urban areas. In 1954, fewer than one hundred thousand workers were employed in non-oil industry; approximately fifteen thousand workers were in the oil industry. Large-scale manufacturing enterprises were relatively uncommon: only approximately thirty thousand people worked in manufacturing units employing more than ten workers.[22]

Although the social structure of contemporary Iraq was falling into place during the monarchy, the country's political apparatus was captive of a relatively narrow power axis. This was comprised of Britain, the court, and the large landowners. The latter group was the truly privileged class of the monarchy. The consumption tax of 1931 (which established favorable tax schemes for the landlords), the settlements law of 1932 (which turned landholdings into private property), and the above-mentioned Rights and Duties of Cultivator Law of 1933 attest to the degree to which monarchic policies accommodated the landowning class.[23] The political base of the monarchy, in corollative terms, did not reside in the social forces forming beneath it. The subordinate classes were denied access to Iraq's authority structures. As a result, these classes became increasingly disaffected with the prevailing political arrangements. One manifestation of this discontent—noticeable as early as the 1920s—was the growth of the nationalist political discourse. The alienation of the middle classes from the monarchic power structure is also evident between 1936 and 1941 in the series of coups by military officers. As Batatu summarizes:

> The coups represented a successful, even if shortlived, break by the armed segment of the middle class into the narrow circle of the ruling order . . . [and] the coups succeeded, if briefly, because they appealed to sentiments or manifested tendencies—reformism, or pan-Arabism, or neutralism, or intense opposition to English influence, or sheer discontent at the exclusion of all but a few from any effective role in the political life of the country—sentiments and tendencies that were shared by substantial portions of the officer corps and of the middle class from which the corps largely stemmed.[24]

In other instances, the intermediate classes increasingly articulated demands aimed at thoroughly transforming the existing social and political order. This tendency toward a more radical social posture was evident in the growing strength of the Iraqi Communist Party (ICP), particularly in the 1940s and 1950s. A number of separate elements blended together to increase the attractiveness of the ICP during the latter years of the monarchy. British interference was widely recognized and even more widely held in contempt, thus decreasing the legitimacy of the monarchy in the eyes of many Iraqis. The critique levelled by the ICP could be easily absorbed by many Iraqis. The Communists also articulated a world view that meshed with Iraqis' experiences. In addition, the spectrum of Iraqi society that formed the nucleus of Communist Party support—students, unskilled laborers, shantytown dwellers, and civil servants—was concentrated, both geographically and occupationally.[25]

The ICP organized numerous protests against the monarchy. In January 1948 it coordinated a massive urban-centered uprising known as the al-Wathbah (the Leap). The al-Wathbah was precipitated by the signing of the Portsmouth Treaty on 15 January 1948—a treaty popularly viewed as an unmitigated capitulation to British interests. Between 5 and 8 January, students staged protests and strikes against the regime. These initial stirrings did not infect the remainder of the population. The day after the treaty was formally signed, students again demonstrated against the regime. This time their protests fired up other segments of the population, and by 20 January the urban poor and workers had joined in the demonstrations. Over the next few days, Baghdad's streets regularly filled with enormous crowds. On 27 January, however, the al-Wathbah came to an abrupt end as the regime clamped down on the protestors, killing hundreds of people in the process.

The al-Wathbah was unique only by dint of its size. Social protests were common throughout the monarchy. In 1931, for example, a fourteen-day general strike that began in Baghdad quickly spread to other parts of the country. Tribal uprisings in the Iraqi south and Kurdish rebellions in the north were common. Additional *intifadahs* (uprisings) took place in 1952 and 1956. The regime typically responded to political opposition and social unrest harshly. Article 79 of its Criminal Procedure Act Appendix, for example, permitted the arrest of any person "who for some reason, it is believed, may disturb the peace." Political parties were rarely allowed to operate openly, the press was heavily censored, and political incarcerations and abuse were routinely practiced.[26]

The monarchy lacked any strong links to Iraqi society. Growing social opposition during the 1950s was accompanied by the formation of the National Unity Front, composed of the National Democratic Party, the ICP, and the pan-Arab Ba'th Socialist Party. On 14 July 1958 a coup by the Free Officers, led by 'abd al-Karim Qasem, ushered in Iraq's republican period. The overthrow of the monarchy was greeted with widespread demonstrations of support by the Iraqi people and political support from the diversified opposition that had coalesced against the regime. The coup's success reflected the underlying alienation of the country's subordinate classes from the monarchy. The toppling of the monarchy essentially brought the urban-centered modern middle classes to Iraq's political fore. Intense struggles among different fractions of the heterogenous middle classes would destabilize Iraqi political life for the next decade until the second accession of the Arab Ba'th Socialist Party in 1968.

Republican Iraq and the Emergence of the Ba'th Regime

The early years of the nascent Iraqi Republic were marked by an evolving polarization around the issue of Iraq's participation in the political union *(wahda)* of Syria and Egypt.[27] In his struggle to rule, Qasem increasingly relied upon the tacit support of the left, especially the increasingly popular ICP. The other end of the political spectrum, including the Ba'th Party, grew suspicious of Qasem's relationship with the ICP. After an earlier, unsuccessful assassination attempt upon Qasem (the assassination team included Saddam Hussein), the Ba'th staged a successful coup in February 1963.[28] The maneuver was greeted with angry protests in favor of Qasem, who was still widely popular. In the months following the Ba'th coup, Iraq suffered from "the most terrible scenes of violence hitherto experienced in the postwar Middle East."[29] The ICP was the primary target in the initial wave of repression. On the evening of 8 February 1963, Baghdad Radio issued the following order specifically calling for the killing of Communists:

> As a consequence of the attempt of Communist agents, supporter of God's enemy 'Abd al-Karim Qasim, to disturb the ranks of the citizens and disobey order and instructions, we hereby confer authority on the commanders of military units, Police and National Guards to annihilate anyone who disturbs the peace. Faithful sons of the people are called upon to co-operate with the authorities by informing on these criminals and annihilate them.[30]

The *Sunday Times* reported that the Ba'th announcement sounded "like an open incitement to a massacre which would make St. Bartholomew's Day look like a Sunday School picnic."[31]

Growing tensions between the Ba'th and the military quickly led to a second coup in November 1963. This coup was headed by 'Abd al-Salam 'Arif, one of Qasem's peers in the toppling of the monarchy. The November 1963 coup was a bloodless affair. 'Arif successfully drew upon his political experience to bring calm to the country. The brief interlude of political stability was abruptly closed by 'Arif's untimely death in a helicopter crash in April 1966. The ensuing political struggle among contending nodes of power within the military, and to a lesser extent between the military and civilian political wings in Iraq, was resolved in favor of 'Arif's brother 'Abd al-Rahman 'Arif. Over the next two years, factions of the military expressed increasing disenchantment with the prevailing political arrangements. In the face of the growing restlessness of the 1960s, Ba'th Party members were able to gain the support of disaffected pockets within the military.[32] On 17 July 1968, the 'Arif regime was overthrown by the Ba'th, who quickly neutralized the military and secured full political control of the state. Ba'th command of the Iraqi state has since been unbroken.

In the first decade of the Iraqi Republic there were four leadership changes. Despite this political fluidity, there was continuity in the class composition of the regimes. The turmoil of the 1958–1968 period can be summarized broadly as the efforts of members of the modern middle class to forge a political hegemony within the country. A confluence of factors substantiates this characterization: (1) The middle classes supplied most of the post-1958 political leadership and stocked the upper echelons of the Iraqi bureaucracy. (2) The increasing autonomy of the state (created by its access to oil revenues) rendered control over private property a less important determinant of state policy. As commentators have written: "Under these circumstances [high oil revenues] control over the state, that is, the composition of the social and political forces in charge of the state apparatus, came to be of paramount importance for the development of the country and for the determination of the direction of future capitalist penetration."[33] Moreover, due in part to their common educational and social backgrounds, the groups coming to control the state in the post-1958 period tended "to look out into life from similar standpoints and tackle many problems in a similar manner."[34] This was reflected most clearly in the consistent economic and social programs introduced by the republican regimes. As noted by Marr:

> The old regime had been attacked by its opposition for the pace and direction of its development program and for the absence of social change. In particular, the regime's reliance on foreign oil companies for its revenue; its neglect of industry and emphasis on agriculture, which benefited mainly the landed classes; its disregard of the country's human resources, and the severe maldistribution of wealth that had resulted from the malfunctioning of the free enterprise system were all singled out for criticism. . . . The new regimes . . . set forth contrasting development aims. Regardless of the regime in power, all rebelled against foreign domination and control of the economy and the maldistribution of wealth, especially in land. They demanded an accelerated pace of development and a change of direction, particularly toward industrial development and social welfare.[35]

(3) The middle classes were also the primary beneficiaries of the development strategies under Qasem, the 'Arif brothers, and the Ba'th. The bene-

fits of expanded state activity in health and education, for example, accrued most visibly to members of the middle class.[36]

One of the salient policies in the post-1958 era was the land-reform program initiated under Qasem. The policy successfully broke the powerful landed classes. Earlier, in the mid-1950s, Doreen Warriner had provided a cogent analysis of the sociopolitical obstacles to land reform:

> The real obstacle to reform in Iraq is not a shortage of experts, or money, or administrative inefficiency. Nor is it, in reality, the "feudal" landowners. The town middle class represents the public opinion of the country in that it is conscious of the need for change; it provides the official class, criticizes development policy, and it is growing very fast. It cannot, however, link up with the *fellahin* and provide the political force which would recast the social structure of the country. There is no social or political force which can challenge the power of the sheiks. The educated townspeople do not, at present, constitute this force, though their number, their intelligence, and their importance in administration should qualify them to become it.[37]

The introduction of land reform clearly reflected the shifting balance of social forces in favor of the urban-centered middle classes. Writing in the late 1960s, Majid Khadduri noted: "Sympathy with the wretched conditions of peasants was not the only reason which prompted the new regime to promulgate an agrarian reform act; it wished also to eradicate the principal pillar on which the Old Regime had rested."[38]

The necessary political power quickly came with the overthrow of the monarchy. On 30 September 1958, just a few weeks after the revolution, the Agrarian Reform Law was promulgated. The main features of this program included upper limits on the size of landholdings and proposals for the extensive allocation of land to the fallahin. In 1970, the Ba'th enacted Law 117, further reducing land ceilings. By the mid-1970s, over half of Iraq's cultivable land had been affected by the land-reform measures.[39] The success of the measures, however, must be qualified. Although the policy clearly broke the power of the landed families, the predominance of private property in the countryside remained: a relatively new class of private landowners with smaller holdings arose. Many of the fallahin remained landless, and poor conditions in the countryside continually forced them into the cities.[40]

A second feature of the post-1958 regimes surrounds efforts to acquire greater domestic control over Iraq's oil resources. Between 1958 and 1972, the republican regimes wrestled for control of Iraq's oil resources with the foreign-owned Iraqi Petroleum Company (IPC).[41] After the collapse of the monarchy, it was widely believed that if economic growth and development were to be sustained, it was essential that greater oil revenues be in the hands of the state. To this end, the republican regimes entered into negotiations with the IPC. By October 1961, however, the talks had collapsed. The regime then enacted Law 80, greatly reducing the concession areas of the IPC to 0.5 percent of their original size. The next major move came early in 1964 when the government formed the Iraq National Oil Company (INOC). The INOC was put in charge of all phases of the oil industry, from exploration to the distribution of petrochemical products. In 1967, the INOC was granted exploitation rights in the areas earlier withdrawn from the IPC. On 1 June 1972 the continual conflict between the IPC and the republican regimes led to IPC being nationalized. In the wake of nationalization, the Ba'th regime quickly secured full control over all phases of the petrochemical industry.

Growing oil revenues throughout the post-1958 period allowed the republican regimes to play a greater role in the economic development of the country. During the 1960s, an average of 23 percent of the development budgets was allocated for industrial development.[42] Under the Ba'th regime, industrial allocations climbed as high as one-third of the total development budget.[43] Significant allocations were also made for infrastructural development, including transportation and communication grids. The development strategies of the republican regimes affected Iraq's class structure. New opportunities were created for capital accumulation and the growth of an indigenous capitalist class.[44] The greatest change, however, came in the expansion of the middle and lower segments of Iraq's class structure. By 1977, the middle class (professionals, civil servants, service and business workers, owners of small establishments, technicians) totalled 56.5 percent of the urban population (or more than one-third of the total Iraqi population). The urban working class also grew rapidly after 1958. By 1977, this group included more than one million workers, including more than a quarter of a million construction workers.[45]

In the early years of its rule, the Ba'th regime faced sustained opposition from numerous political quarters, including the Kurds and the Iraqi Communist Party. In 1973, the Ba'th attempted to enhance its legitimacy by forming the Progressive Patriotic National Front (PPNF) and managed to secure the participation of the ICP. The PPNF amounted to little more than an extensive cooptive strategy that contained political opposition and maximized societal compliance. By the late 1970s, the once powerful Iraqi Communist Party had been driven underground. Most elements of Iraqi society—trade unions, peasant societies, student groups, and youth organizations—were penetrated by the Ba'th and subordinated to the regime.[46] In their study of post-1958 Iraq, the Sluggletts write: "Everything that was authentically popular or even remotely critical came under suspicion and was ruthlessly suppressed."[47] The Ba'thization of society was complemented by the essential merger of the Regional Command of the Ba'th and the Revolutionary Command Council in 1977. At this point, the Ba'th Party and the Iraqi state virtually became synonymous. Within the ruling elite, power devolved onto Saddam Hussein, a process that concluded with the retirement (apparently for health reasons) of President al-Bakr in July 1979.[48]

Despite the Ba'thization of the Iraqi population, the regime faced substantial degrees of opposition from various social constituencies. What amounted to a civil war was fought with the Kurds throughout most of the 1970s. The regime also faced opposition from women's groups and the gathering Shi'i movement. A full appreciation of the regime's vulnerability requires that we examine each of these pockets of opposition in turn.

The Kurdish Struggle Against the Ba'th

Iraq is composed of two main ethnic groups: Arabs and Kurds. The latter ethnic group has been without political control of its destiny for most of the twentieth century. Under the Ba'th regime, moreover, the Kurds have been increasingly subjected to Arabization or Ba'thization policies aimed at extirpating their cultural distinctiveness and political identity. These policies have proceeded despite the fact that the Kurdish people constitute approximately 28 percent of the Iraqi population.[49]

The Kurdish people have struggled for political autonomy in their homeland (an area extending over Turkey, Iraq, and Iran, with smaller parcels in Syria and the former Soviet Union) for most of the twentieth century. Although the Kurdish people were assured statehood under the terms of the Treaty of Sèvres, these promises were deleted from the Treaty of Lausanne in 1923. Throughout Iraq's monarchic period, there were numerous Kurdish revolts and tribal uprisings against Baghdad's rule. The toppling of the Iraqi monarchy brought a brief period of hope to the Kurdish cause. Kurdish leader Mullah Mustafa Barzani triumphantly resurfaced in Baghdad after being exiled for most of the post–World War II period. By 1961, however, the relationship between the new republican regime and the Kurds had deteriorated greatly. By late summer, a new phase of the civil war had broken out and essentially continued until 1975.

A lull in the civil war occurred in 1970, when the Ba'th regime and the Kurds reached a tentative accord. The agreement gave the Kurds extensive political recognition and under Article 14 established the procedures for effecting "autonomy for the Kurdish people." Other aspects of the agreement included: (a) the recognition of the Kurds as one of the two main nations that make up Iraq (Article 10); (b) the recognition of the Kurdish language as an official language in regions where the Kurds formed a majority, with Kurdish designated as the language of instruction at schools in these regions (Article 1); (c) agreement that the Kurdish people could set up distinct organizations for youths, students, women, and educational workers (Article 5); (d) agreement that Kurdish workers that had participated in the war would be reinstated in their jobs unconditionally (Article 6); and (e) agreement that the Kurds would be afforded equal status with Arabs in running Iraq—i.e., in nominations for public, political, and military offices (Article 2). The size of the autonomous region was to be determined by a census. The Ba'th regime immediately undertook measures to insure that the census could be used to lessen the size of the autonomous region. Kurdish families were resettled in large numbers in order to alter the ethnic balance of specific areas, especially the contested oil-rich region of Kirkuk.[50] In following years, differences concerning the application of the agreement proved interminable. Despite the stipulations of the 11 March 1970 agreement, the Ba'th proceeded to issue its own declaration on Kurdish autonomy without consulting the Kurdish leaders. The size of the Kurdish autonomous area turned out to be considerably smaller than the total area of Kurdistan.[51] From the perspective of the Kurds, the declaration by the Ba'th regime was wanting in several respects and thoroughly violated the spirit of the 1970 accord: "In reality it [the Ba'th declaration] gave only limited self-rule in a region that excluded Kirkuk," wrote Christine Moss Helms.[52] Not surprisingly, the unilateral declaration by the Ba'th regime ushered in another phase of fighting between Baghdad and the Kurds.

The next phase of the 1961–1975 war between the Kurds and the central authorities in Baghdad proved particularly costly to both sides. The Kurds fielded an army of about fifty thousand *peshmergas* (insurgents).[53] Baghdad, committing the major proportion of its military capacity to the fight, fielded eight army divisions, most of its tanks, and the entire air force. An economic blockade was imposed on the region by the Ba'th regime. The war created serious hardships for the local population and caused severe social dislocation. Inside the war zone, a number of makeshift camps with inadequate facilities housed Kurdish families fleeing from Baghdad's bombing raids. Disease, poor supplies, and inadequate medical attention plagued the temporary settlements. The war sent over a quarter of a million refugees across the border into neighboring Iran. In the summer of 1974, the Iraqi army attempted to deliver a final blow to the peshmergas, but the offensive fell far short of its goal. The war continued throughout the winter and exacerbated the difficult living conditions of much of the northern population.

The stalemate was broken in favor of the Ba'th regime by virtue of the Algiers Accord between Iraq and Iran. Under the terms of the Algiers treaty, the shah agreed to suspend Iranian assistance to the Kurdish movement. In return for this termination of support, Iraq abandoned a long-standing policy on the Shatt al-Arab waterway, accepting the thalweg, or midchannel principle, as marking the southern border between the two countries. The Iraqi capitulation on the Shatt al-Arab attests to the drain that the civil war had on Baghdad. The rapidity with which the Kurdish struggle collapsed in the aftermath of the Algiers Accord cannot be over-stated. The Kurdish movement had become extremely dependent upon Iranian assistance, although the shah (along with the United States) had no intention of letting the Kurds prevail.[54] Within weeks of the Algiers agreement, the fourteen-year-old civil war came to an abrupt halt.

Between the collapse of the civil war in 1975 and the outbreak of the Iran-Iraq War in 1980, the condition of the Kurdish people continued to deteriorate. Ba'th policy against the Kurds had genocidal characteristics.[55] Large numbers of Kurds were resettled in central and southern Iraq in strategic hamlets reminiscent of Vietnam. Relocated Kurdish groups tended to fall into one of three categories, either: (1) those that surrendered to Iraqi authorities after the collapse of fighting in 1975; (2) the inhabitants of ethnically mixed areas (the regime was trying to de-Kurd strategically important regions, especially Kirkuk); or (3) the entire population of border villages along the Turkish and Iranian frontiers, creating for the regime *cordon sanitaires* to inhibit further insurgency.[56] Of the dispersal of Kurds from the oil-rich regions of Kirkuk and Khanaqin, the International League for Human Rights wrote: "The apparent goal of the Iraqi Government is to gain complete control of the petroleum resource in Kurdistan and then deny the Kurds any rights to the economic riches of their area."[57] Kurds were prohibited from purchasing land in Kirkuk and other important regions. So-called development strategies in Iraqi Kurdistan must be understood in the context of the Kurdish struggle. The plan to develop the region with urban-centered light industries, for example, had the underlying political goal of eroding Kurdish nationalism.[58] The Ba'th regime boasted about development of the Kurdish area during the 1970s, but much of the money went toward constructing strategic roads and building new villages in which to resettle Kurdish families.[59]

The Ba'thization and Arabization of the region was intensified in the post-1975 period. The language of instruction in the schools was Arabic rather than Kurdish.[60] Kurdish schools were given names from Arab history.[61] The new Kurdish villages included buildings for Ba'th Party headquarters.[62] Kurdish papers were closed by Ba'th officials. Kurdish faculty at Salaimaniya University were replaced by Arab teachers. The Faculty of Kurdish Studies at Baghdad University was abolished. The equivalent of U.S. $1,500 was offered to any Arab that took a Kurdish spouse.[63] During 1979, Saddam Hussein argued that Kurds and Arabs were ethnically linked by virtue of their common historical ties dating back to the Assyrians and the Babylonians. Consequently, in spite of the Aryan ethnic roots of the Kurdish people and the Indo-European lineages of their language, Hussein declared that "there was no contradiction between the 'Kurdishness of the Kurd' and his being a part of the Arab nation."[64]

With the collapse of the civil war, the Kurdish opposition again split into two antagonistic camps.[65] Mustafa Barzani's sons, Mas'ud and Idris, formed the KDP provisional command. This group tended to find more support among the Karmanji-speaking areas of Iraqi Kurdistan. The Patriotic Union of Kurdistan (PUK), headed by Jalal Talabani, was formed from three different groups, the Komala (Marxist-Leninist), the Socialist Movement of Kurdistan, and the General Line (followers of Talabani). In 1977, the PUK moved its headquarters from Damascus to Iraqi Kurdistan. The PUK tended to find more support among the Sorani-speaking areas of Kurdistan. Following intense fighting between the KDP and the PUK, a third group, the Socialist Party of Iraqi Kurdistan, also emerged.[66]

The Kurdish military struggle was gradually revived during the late 1970s, and in the summer of 1978 fighting between the Ba'th regime and Kurdish insurgents grew in intensity. The Ba'th regime responded by razing and evacuating more Kurdish villages.[67] The Ba'th also attempted to close off external support for the Kurdish insurgency. In November 1978, the Ba'th extracted a promise from Syria to halt aid to the PUK. A similar agreement was reached with Turkey in April 1979.

By the close of the 1970s, two separate facts were undeniable:

1. The Kurdish insurgency and the Kurdish people had suffered greatly after the collapse of the insurgency in 1975. Political opposition among the Kurds was openly split, and its operational latitude and effectiveness was greatly diminished. The Kurdish population was visibly suffering at the hands of the Ba'th regime. A little more than one year after the collapse of the Kurdish insurgency, for example, U.S. columnist William Safire lamented: "Here is a culture being systematically demolished, a people being destroyed. . . . What do the Kurds want? Not independence, not a new nation out of three existing nations. They want to be let alone, as an autonomous region of Iraq, loyal to Baghdad but living their own lives."[68]
2. The Kurdish struggle had indeed suffered a severe blow and was wrought with factionalism, but it was showing clear signs of reemerging. The Slugletts noted: "Although the Algiers Agreement had dealt a fearful blow to the Kurdish Movement, the brutal and repressive policies pursued by the regime in the area ensured that the spirit of the resistance was not completely crushed."[69] The latent Kurdish threat, especially in view of events in Iran in the late 1970s, was taken seriously by the Ba'th regime, which continued to deploy at least one-third of its army in the north of the country.[70]

The Women's Struggle Against the Ba'th

The condition of Iraqi women has historically provided some of the Middle East's starkest manifestations of oppressive conceptions of gender.[71] One telling example of women's subjugation was evident in the phenomenon of *fasl* that was practiced well into the twentieth century. In fasl, women could be exchanged with enemies in order to avoid the shedding of blood. The following account reveals the thoroughly oppressive conditions faced by Iraqi women:

> Those earmarked for later delivery to the aggrieved party were young girls that had not yet attained majority. They and the other women given in *fasl* or, to use the name by which they were known, the *fasliyyat,* led a particularly harsh life, their husbands normally oppressing them and holding them in contempt. Disposal by *fasl* was not the only system to which the peasant women were exposed. Sometimes, with a view to winning favour, her father offered her as a gift to one or other of the notables of the village. This went under the designation of *zawaj-ul-hibah* or "gift marriage". Moreover, often, when still a child, she was pledged to a personage or relative in *waqf* (literally, mortmain) marriage—*zawaj-ul-waqf.*[72]

By the late 1950s, it was apparent that the resilient views of men and women in Iraqi society were showing some strain in the face of change, particularly in the larger towns and cities. Nonetheless, many conventions that more clearly revealed the subordinate position of women in Iraqi society, such as *purdah* (segregation), were still widely practiced.[73]

The oppression of Iraqi women has been under increasing attack throughout the twentieth century. Along with the growth of the Western-exposed intelligentsia came the articulation of a clear feminist consciousness. Historical materialist precepts, for example, were initially employed to help account for the "ancient fetters" that enslaved Iraqi women. According to these arguments, the harem and veil, as examples, bore the mark of feudalism and would disappear with the evolution of society.[74] During the 1920s, women's organizations began to draw attention to the exploitation and oppression of women. Calls to educate Iraqi women and to drop the veil echoed within feminist literature and other political quarters such as the ICP. In 1952, the League for the Defense of Women's Rights was formed, although this organization did not obtain official sanction until the monarchy was toppled in 1958. The president of the league, Naziha Dulaimi, was appointed minister for municipalities in 1959, the first time that any woman had been assigned a cabinet portfolio in the Middle East. Perhaps the most notable achievement of the league was its contribution to new legislation on marriage and the family. The law enacted under Qasem was based on a draft submitted by the league. It was designed to protect women from a number of oppressive practices, especially marriages arranged at an early age. The feminist struggle in Iraq was brought to an abrupt halt following the first Ba'th coup in 1963. The offices of the league were closed and many of its members were arrested and tortured.[75]

Following the Ba'th's second accession to power in 1968, the regime refused to tolerate autonomous women's groups. The Ba'th proclaims itself as the only body capable of correctly and meaningfully guiding the emancipation of women. "The liberation of women cannot be done through women's societies alone," stated a party report in 1974. "It can be done through the complete political and economic liberation of society. The Arab Ba'th Socialist Party has a leading role to play in the liberation of women since it leads the process of social and cultural change."[76] The Ba'th program is extremely modest in its emancipatory ambitions. It identifies the strengthening of the family unit as a primary goal of the "revolution."[77] In other places, the Ba'th report was even more restrictive in its outlook: "Whilst women are incapable of performing permanent service on a wide scale in the armed forces, especially in the combat unit, men are likewise incapable of looking after children as women do in general." "Therefore, if men are better suited than women in the army, women are better suited than men in childcare."[78]

By the late 1970s, despite the repression of grassroots women's movements, there were changes in the condition of Iraqi women. These developments must be seen in the context of Iraq's evolving economy under the Ba'th regime. The Ba'th itself tends to rationalize the need to address the condition of women in terms of the economic direction of the July 17–30 revolution. The same 1974 party report declares that the party must be indefatigable in its efforts to achieve "legal equality and the provision of equal opportunities of work" for women. It goes on to attack antiquated views of women as "alien and harmful" and as inconsistent with the "needs of modern times." In short, the regime's concern for Iraqi women appears to be subordinated to the imperatives of the Ba'th economic program. To these ends, legal reforms have granted women the right to own their own land and to be full members of agricultural cooperatives. Other reforms have sought to grant women equal pay, equal allowances, equal leave, equal opportunities for promotion, maternity leave, and nursing breaks. In 1978, the regime introduced amendments to the Personal Status Law that allowed women the right of divorce in cases of persistent dispute, adultery, incurable disease, or prolonged spousal absence. The amended law also requires men to register their marriages in court, a change designed to lessen the opportunities for illegal polygamy.[79]

These changes have been complemented by modest advances in educational opportunities for women. A greater percentage of women could be detected at all levels of education on the eve of the war with Iran. During the 1970s, for example, the percentage of females in elementary school rose from 29 to 45 percent. Increases for secondary education remained considerably lower; that is, from 29 to 31 percent for the same period. The percentage of women in professional programs such as medicine and engineering also increased during the 1970s. In medicine, female enrollment rose from 7 percent to 22 percent; in management and economics, enrollment rose from 17 percent to 38 percent. These changes in the educational opportunities for women underlined the growing participation of women in the Iraqi workforce. By the end of the 1970s, women could be found working as gas station attendants, bus conductors, and traffic guides.[80] Women formed 19 percent of the Iraqi workforce by the turn of the decade. They had also managed to break further into prestigious occupations such as accounting, medicine, engineering, and high-level government.[81]

In an attempt to coopt any genuine women's struggle and to placate the international community, the regime has sponsored its own women's organization, the General Federation of Iraqi Women (GFIW). This body is undoubtedly hindered by the limited aspirations of the Ba'th regime regarding gender equality. The GFIW is widely viewed as catering to the needs of the regime, and to an extent serves as the regime's mouthpiece on issues concerning women. The GFIW has cooperated with the security forces of the Ba'th regime—behavior that "makes a mockery of their propaganda about women's liberation."[82] Despite the political restrictions that govern all social constituencies in Iraq, a number of organizations aimed at the genuine emancipation of Iraqi women have been active, including the Iraqi Women's League. The activities and social critique of these groups contributed to the delegitimation of the Ba'th regime, especially among segments of the Iraqi intelligentsia. Although the women's struggle did not confront the regime militarily, its importance should not be discounted. At a minimum, by helping to sustain a genuine feminist consciousness, women's groups further narrowed the social base of the Ba'th and impeded its efforts to achieve a social and political hegemony in the country.

Emerging Shi'i Opposition to Ba'th Rule

The gravest threat to the Ba'th regime in the late 1970s appeared to emanate from Iraq's Shi'i population. The Shi'i challenge manifested itself in increasingly popular marches and protests. It contributed to the overall image of the Ba'th regime as illegitimate, especially when considered alongside the activities of the ICP, the Kurds, and women's groups. The Shi'i opposition was engaged in a wholesale attack upon the secular ideology of the Ba'th. But in the late 1970s, the Shi'i threat was still in its latency, compared with events in neighboring Iran.

Nonetheless, the number of sporadic protests and riots grew, notably in the ath-Thawra township of Baghdad and the holy cities of Najaf and Karbala. The most visible protests took place in February 1977, on the occasion of Ashura, when thousands of Shi'is, including some who were well armed, called for the overthrow of the Ba'th regime.[83] When the police attempted to intervene during a procession from Najaf to Karbala, the angry crowed shouted: "Saddam, remove your hand! The people of Iraq do not want you!"[84] In June 1977, Saddam Hussein warned against the linking of religion and politics.[85] The occasion precipitated a crisis within the ruling coterie of the Ba'th, and Shi'is were included in the revamped Revolutionary Command Council later that year.[86] In 1979, further Shi'i demonstrations followed the overthrow of the shah. A Shi'i political leadership more clearly emerged, with at least two and perhaps as many as five groups appearing on the periphery of the Iraqi political stage.[87] With the decline of the ICP in many of its traditional strongholds, the Shi'i groups, especially the ad-Da'wa (the Islamic Call), were uniquely positioned to mobilize large segments of the Iraqi population.[88]

The regime immediately moved to contain any Shi'i uprising, both through conciliatory gestures and outright repression. Batatu commented: "In practice, Saddam Husayn pursued two tactics: *tarhib* and *targhib,* as Iraqis would say. He terrorized with one hand and offered rewards with the other."[89] In public appearances, leaders of the Ba'th regime did all they could to accommodate Ba'th ideology to the tenets of Islam. The regime promised to disburse funds for the maintenance and construction of holy sites and mosques.[90] In the aftermath of the Iranian revolution, the Ba'th regime was seriously alarmed by the prospect of a Shi'i uprising. Seeing the manner in which the Islamic regime in Iran was fuelling rebellious sentiments, the Ba'th tended to regard the Shi'i struggle and the wider Islamic movement "as a challenge to its very existence."[91]

State Repression—The Primary Pillar of the Ba'th Regime

The emergence of fundamental political opposition to the Ba'th regime is revealing, reflecting as it does the sweeping changes in the texture of Iraq's social canvas as it was drawn into the global economic fold. New social constituencies, including the modern middle class and working class, emerged in the urban centers, especially Baghdad. Other social groups, among them the landed class, noticeably declined. In the 1960s and 1970s the Kurds showed much greater signs of overcoming local tribal identities: they were becoming a coherent and highly politicized nationalist force. The influx of Western ideas contributed to a heightened political consciousness with respect to the condition of women in Iraq. At the same time, in the face of the pressures of modernization and secularization, the traditional clerical class consolidated its opposition to the regime and articulated an Islamic ideology that stood diametrically opposed to the pan-Arab worldview extolled by the Ba'th.

Political opposition to the regime was undoubtedly nurtured by the stunning degree of poverty that plagued much of Iraq. Migration from the countryside had placed enormous stress upon urban centers.[92] In 1947, the ratio of rural population to urban was about two to one; by 1977, the ratio had reversed, with the urban population totalling almost two-thirds of the population.[93] As a result of this pressure on urban areas, living conditions deteriorated, particularly in Baghdad, a city that came to contain more than one-quarter of Iraq's total population. The Baghdad district of Madinat ath-Thawra inflated to a population of at least 1.5 million in the late 1970s. It was originally designed to house only 300,000. Iraq's annual abstract of statistics for 1978 records that 0.5 million people were still living in reed huts (sarifas), 4 million in mud houses, and 0.25 million in tents. Thus, out of a population of some 15 million, almost one-third of the Iraqi population was inadequately housed during the 1970s.[94] In 1977, at least 1.5 million Iraqis lived in absolute poverty.[95] A study of income distribution in Iraq for 1971 reveals wide disparities. Among urban households, the bottom 40 percent received just 17.7 percent of the national income; the top 30 percent received 57.1 percent of the income. The top 10 percent alone received almost 30 percent of the income. Among rural households, the bottom 40 percent received 19.4 percent; the top 10 percent received 42.2 percent.[96]

The privation and hardship faced by many Iraqis created pools of potential support for the well-developed poles of political opposition to the Ba'th regime. By the late 1970s, opposition social forces, molded by Iraq's particular development, had been aggressively shunted onto the margins of the system or forced completely underground. Political dissent was not permitted. The Ba'th regime was unwilling to allow genuine political demands to be aired and worked through. The Ba'th state hovered precariously over the people. As a ruling bloc in the Gramscian sense, the Ba'th had utterly failed to forge a political hegemony. Its social foundations were tenuous in the extreme.

By the late 1970s, the regime came to rest on one essential pillar: state repression. The policing apparatus of the Iraqi state had been consolidated during the mid-1970s. Party difficulties with the first chief of internal state security, Nadhim Kzar (involving a bungled coup attempt and an embarrassing series of bizarre hatchet murders in Baghdad led by a fictional character named Abu al-Tubar and former members of Kzar's police service), led to the revamping of the security apparatus.[97] The response to the Kzar affair and the Abu al-Tubar crimes transformed a potentially inconsequential episode in contemporary Iraqi history into a pivotal political juncture of the Ba'th revolution. Internal crime became inextricably linked to "counter-revolutionary imperialist plots by subversive forces." The affair was used to justify the expansion of the police state. "All that we hear and read about, including those crimes which have taken place recently," Saddam Hussein claimed in a speech in September 1973, "are new devices to confront the Revolution and exhaust it psychologically. These are not sadistic crimes as some imagine; they are crimes committed by traitorous agents."[98] The crimes were not addressed in criminal terms but rather on grounds of treason. The transgressions were conceptualized as attacks against "the people" in the service of counterrevolutionary forces. As Samir al-Khalil writes of Saddam Hussein's September 1973 speech, it was "designed to make treason grow more vague and abstract; now it could be found in people's thoughts, not only in their deeds. At the same time its monstrousness was made palpable and concrete through Abu al-Tubar's sadism. . . . Treason in his hands was a much larger offense, directed at the whole people, and a much less specific one. Once treason was ensconced in this fashion, police work logically became the substitute for all politics."[99]

Iraq's security apparatus was revamped and brought under the more immediate control of the Ba'th Party. The Ba'th Party's political report for 1974 made the following sobering observation:

> The security force was inoculated on all levels by Party elements and other patriotic and qualified men. This force, however, was difficult to reform and rebuild because of its longstanding rotten structure. During the past few years, this force has reflected badly on the Party in many aspects. We must confess that the leadership was wrong in not tightening control further over this very important apparatus. The leadership had full confidence in the Party members in this force which caused some of them to abuse it and conspire against the Party as was shown in the June 30th criminal conspiracy. This conspiracy, however, sounded the alarm, and the leadership made extensive changes.[100]

Three separate institutions comprised the new security institutions: the Amn, or State Internal Security; the Estikhbarat, or Military Intelligence; and the Mukhabarat, or Party Intelligence. All three agencies were independently responsible to the Revolutionary Command Council. Of the three wings, the Mukhabarat became the most feared.[101] The growth of the policing apparatus in Iraq was reflected in the proportion of public sector workers employed in the Ministry of the Interior, the main department responsible for internal security. According to the abstract of statistics for 1978, the Ministry of the Interior employed 22.8 percent of all government employees. This was more than the combined figure for the ministries of health, finance, justice, education, labor and social affairs, housing and reconstruction, and higher education and scientific research.

By the latter part of the 1970s, the features of Iraqi politics that would characterize the decade of war had begun to emerge:

> Fear is the cement that holds together this strange body politic in Iraq. All forms of organization not directly controlled by the party have been wiped out. The public is atomized and broken up, which is why it can be made to believe anything. A society that used to revel in politics is not only subdued and silent, but profoundly apolitical. Fear is the agency of that transformation; the kind of fear that comes not only from what the neighbours might say, but that makes people careful of what they say in front of their

children. This fear has become a part of the psychological constitution of citizenship. Fashioned out of Iraqi raw material, this fear is ironically the mainstay of the country's national self-assertiveness in the modern era. The violence that remained buried as a potential in the subconscious culture of society's groups surfaced as this new kind of fear drove through all private space that once existed on the peripheries of families, boundaries of communities, or by virtue of status or class origin. The result was a true regime of terror whose deepest roots lay in the growing fear that people now had of each other.[102]

But forced silences can always be broken. The Ba'th regime was well aware of this possibility.

The Sociopolitical Struggle and War

By the end of the 1970s a fundamental rift had developed between the political and social spheres in Iraq. Changes within Iraqi society had created new social forces with political agendas that diverged from the Ba'th worldview. Political channels capable of accommodating Iraq's emerging social forces were closed. Political dissent in any form was aggressively quieted. It was a political offense punishable by death to leave the Ba'th and join an alternative party, or to coax others to do the same. The regime had systematically insured that political opposition would be driven underground or exiled. One was either with the Ba'th regime or potentially traitorous and forever suspect.

It is this context that gave events in Iran their heightened importance. The Islamic Revolution reverberated within the artificial political atmosphere in Iraq. It insistently reminded the Ba'th regime of its susceptibility and suggested to the Iraqi people that repressive political orders could unravel. It struck fear into the regime and, possibly, hope into the people. The theocratic project in Iran, moreover, appeared to be doing all it could to intensify Iraq's political fissures, especially with respect to the Shi'i struggle. Tensions between the two states inevitably escalated.

At the same time, the turmoil of postrevolutionary Iran meant that Iraq's traditional rival in the Gulf was substantially weakened. Only five years earlier, Iraq had been forced to acquiesce to Iranian strength and accept the capitulatory terms of the Algiers Accord. A mere six years later, the Ba'th regime was suddenly handed the opportunity to emerge as the dominant power in the Gulf and enhance its prestige in the Arab world. Greater regional leverage would go a long way toward stabilizing oil revenues—revenues that were increasingly crucial for the maintenance of the repressive state. The temptation proved too much for the Ba'th.

These domestic and regional dynamics bore the strains of the rapid social transformation that accompanied Iraq's insertion into the global economy. Neither the internal opposition against the Ba'th nor the regime's quest for stable oil revenues can be adequately addressed outside of this evolving socioeconomic tapestry. In other words, the political conflicts that impelled the Iraqi regime to attack Iran were inscribed with Iraq's rudimentary sociopolitical struggles. The analysis of the origins of the Iran-Iraq War can now be completed by devoting closer attention to the socially grounded interstate conflicts that enveloped both regimes in the aftermath of the Islamic Revolution.

Notes

1. For a brief and comprehensive survey of these developments see Fran Hazelton, "Iraq to 1963," in *Saddam's Iraq: Revolution or Reaction?*, ed. CARDRI, (Zed Books, 1985).

2. Roger Owen, *The Middle East in the World Economy: 1800–1914,* (Methuen, 1981), pp. 180–181.

3. See discussion in Charles Issawi, *The Economic History of the Middle-East, 1800–1914: A Book of Readings,* (University of Chicago Press, 1966), Chapter 3, "Steam Navigation on the Tigris and Euphrates, 1961–1931," especially pp. 146–147.

4. See discussion in Phebe Marr, *The Modern History of Iraq,* (Westview Press, 1985), pp. 22–24.

5. See Issawi, *Economic History,* op. cit., pp. 163–164.

6. Discussion extracted from Marion Farouk-Sluglett and Peter Sluglett, "The Transformation of Land Tenure and Rural Social Structure in Central and Southern Iraq, c. 1870–1958," in *International Journal of Middle East Studies,* 15, (1983), pp. 493–495.

7. Figures from Roger Owen, *The Middle East in the World Economy: 1800–1914,* p. 182, 275. For a detailed discussion of the changes in the quantity and quality of Iraq's trade behavior, see Mohammed Salman Hasan, "The Role of Foreign Trade in the Economic Development of Iraq, 1864–1964: A Study in the Growth of a Dependent Economy," in *Studies in the Economic History of the Middle East from the Rise of Islam to the Present Day,* ed. M. A. Cook, (Oxford University Press, 1970).

8. Hanna Batatu, *The Old Social Classes and the Revolutionary Movements of Iraq: A Study of Iraq's Old Landed and Commercial Classes and of its Communists, Ba'thists, and Free Officers,* (Princeton University Press, 1978), p. 24.

9. Mohammad Salman Hasan, "The Role of Foreign Trade," in *Studies,* op. cit., p. 350.

10. Statistics from Mohammad Salman Hasan, "The Growth and Structure of Iraq's Population, 1867–1947," in *Bulletin of the Oxford University Institute of Economics and Statistics,* (1958).

11. Batatu, *Old Social Classes,* op. cit., pp. 86–114, 119–132.

12. Ibid. Discussion based on pp. 224–318.

13. Ibid., pp. 209–210.

14. See discussion in Marr, *Modern History of Iraq,* op. cit., pp. 137–141.

15. See discussion in Elie Kedourie, "The Kingdom of Iraq: a Retrospect," in *The Chatham House Version and other Middle-Eastern Studies,* (University Press of New England, 1984). Quote from p. 269.

16. On the specific nature of the sharecropping arrangements, see Saleh Haider, *Land Problems of Iraq,* (unpublished dissertation, London University, 1941) cited in Issawi, *Economic History,* op. cit., pp. 177–178.

17. Sluglett and Sluglett, "Transformation of Land Tenure," op. cit., p. 505.

18. See discussion and statistics in Hasan, "The Growth and Structure of Iraq's Population: 1867–1947," in *Studies,* op. cit., pp. 344–345.

19. See discussion in Marr, *Modern History of Iraq,* op. cit., p. 142.

20. Doris G. Phillips, "Rural Migration in Iraq," in *Economic Development and Cultural Change,* 7, (1959), p. 409.

21. See discussion in Marion Farouk-Sluglett and Peter Sluglett, "Labour and National Liberation: the Trade Union Movement in Iraq, 1920–1958," *Arab Studies Quarterly,* 5:2, (1981).

22. See discussion in Marion Farouk-Sluglett, "Contemporary Iraq: Some Recent Writings Reconsidered," *Review of Middle East Studies,* 3, (1978), pp. 91–92.

23. See discussion in Hazelton, "Iraq," in *Saddam's Iraq,* op. cit., p. 8.

24. Batatu, *Old Social Classes,* op. cit., pp. 28–29.

25. The social foundations of the ICP forms one of the central concerns in Batatu's, *The Old Social Classes and the Revolutionary Movements of Iraq,* op. cit.

26. See discussion in Hazelton, "Iraq," in *Saddam's Iraq,* op. cit., pp. 20–22.

27. The most thorough account of this period may be found in Uriel Dann, *Iraq Under Qassem: A Political History, 1958–1963,* (Praeger, 1969).

28. On the period between 1958 and 1968, see Majid Khadduri, *Republican Iraq: A Study in Iraqi Politics Since the Revolution of 1958,* (Oxford University Press, 1969).

29. Sluglett and Sluglett, *Iraq Since 1958: From Revolution to Dictatorship,* (I. B. Tauris and Co. Ltd., 1990), p. 85.

30. See the discussion in U. Zaher, *Political Developments in Saddam's Iraq: 1963–1980,* (Zed Books, 1989) p. 32.

31. *Sunday Times,* 10 February 1963, quoted in Zaher, *Political Developments,* op. cit., p. 31.

32. See discussion in Zaher, "Political Developments" op. cit., pp. 40–41.

33. Sluglett and Sluglett, *Iraq Since 1958: From Revolution to Dictatorship,* (I. B. Tauris, 1990) p. 217.

34. Batatu provides the most thorough discussion on the middle-class nature of the regime. See *Old Social Classes,* op. cit., Quote from p. 1133.

35. Marr, *The Modern History of Iraq,* p. 247.

36. See discussion in Batatu, *Old Social Classes,* op. cit., pp. 1127–1129.

37. Doreen Warriner, *Land Reform and Development in the Middle East: A Study of Egypt, Syria, and Iraq,* (Greenwood Press, 1957), p. 172.

38. Khadduri, *Republican Iraq,* op. cit., p. 151.

39. Statistic quoted in Robert Springborg, "Iraq's Agrarian Infitah," *MERIP Middle East Report,* 17:2, (March–April 1987), p. 16.

40. Discussion from Sluglett and Sluglett, *Iraq Since 1958,* op. cit., pp. 226–227.

41. See the discussion in Celine Whittleton, "Oil and the Iraqi Economy," in *Saddam's Iraq,* op. cit. The following outline is primarily based upon pp. 61–64.

42. See discussion in Edith Penrose, "Industrial Policy and Performance in Iraq," in *The Integration of Modern Iraq,* ed. Abbas Kelidar, (Croom Helm, 1979).

43. Marr, *Modern History,* op. cit., pp. 249–250.

44. See 'Isam al-Khafaji, "The Parasitic Base of the Ba'thist Regime," in *Saddam's Iraq,* op. cit.; Sluglett and Sluglett, *Iraq Since 1958,* op. cit., Chapter 7;

and Joe Stork, "State Power and Economic Structure: Class Determination and State Formation in Contemporary Iraq, in *Iraq: The Contemporary State,* ed. Tim Niblock, (Croom Helm, 1982).

45. Statistics from Marr, *Modern History,* op. cit., pp. 273–281.

46. See discussion in U. Zaher, "Political Developments," op. cit., pp. 48–49.

47. Sluglett and Sluglett, *Iraq Since 1958,* op. cit., p. 229.

48. For some of the reasons behind al-Bakr's gradual withdrawal from the ruling apex, see Marr, *Modern History,* op. cit., pp. 228–229.

49. See calculations in Ismet Sheriff Vanly, "Kurdistan in Iran," in *People Without a Country: The Kurds and Kurdistan,* ed. Gerard Chaliand, (Zed Books, 1980), pp. 154–158.

50. See discussion in Peter Sluglett, "The Kurds," in *Saddam's Iraq,* op. cit., pp. 195–196.

51. See discussion in Vanly, "Kurdistan in Iraq", in *People,* op. cit., pp. 176–178.

52. Christine Moss Helms, *Iraq: Eastern Flank of the Arab World,* (Brookings Institution, 1984), p. 30.

53. Figures from Vanly, "Kurdistan in Iraq," in *People,* op. cit., pp. 181–182. Other figures are comparable with these numbers. Sluglett and Sluglett add that some fifty thousand irregular fighters can be added to estimates of the Kurdish strength (see *Iraq Since 1958,* op. cit., pp. 168–169).

54. The realpolitik that characterized both Iranian and U.S. support for the Kurdish movement was made clear in the Pike Report (on Central Intelligence Agency activities) to the U.S. House of Representatives. In writing of U.S. assistance to the Kurds, the report states that:

> It is clear that the project was originally conceived as a favor to our ally (the Shah) who had cooperated with the United States secret services and felt threatened by his neighbors. . . . The Shah's own aid could not but make ours seem insignificant by comparison. Our contribution must thus be considered as largely symbolic. . . . Neither the foreign Head of [the Iranian] State nor the President and Dr. Kissinger desired victory for our [Kurdish] clients. They merely hoped to ensure that the insurgents would be capable of sustaining a level of hostility just high enough to sap the resources of the neighboring [Iraqi] state.

55. For a general discussion of human rights abuses in the face of the collapse of the Kurdish insurgency, see *Human Rights in Iraq,* compiled by Middle East Watch, (Yale University Press, 1990), pp. 73–74.

56. Sluglett and Sluglett, *Iraq Since 1958,* op. cit., p. 188.

57. The International League for Human Rights, *Statement to the Members of the United Nations Committee on the Elimination of Racial Discrimination,* 14 January 1977.

58. One analysis of the relationship between development and the assault on the Kurds as an ethnic group is made by contributors to *Middle East Contemporary Survey,* v. 1, (1976–1977), p. 410. They write: "Industrialization speeds urbanization, which in turn dissolves tribal affinities which have always been the backbone of Kurdish ethnocentricity—if not necessarily of organized nationalism." v. 1 (1976–1977), p. 410.

59. Ofra Bengio and Uriel Dann, *Middle East Contemporary Survey,* v. 2 (1977–1978), p. 521.

60. See discussion in *Middle East Contemporary Survey,* v. 3 (1978–1979), p. 569.

61. Vanly, "Kurdistan in Iraq," in *People,* op. cit., p. 195.

62. Ibid., p. 197. Ismet Sheriff Vanly, who was invited by the Ba'th to inspect the Kurdish region after the collapse of the Kurdish struggle and who was subsequently the victim of an attempted assassination by the Ba'th, writes: "The first thing which struck us in Arbil, the capital of 'autonomous' Kurdistan, was a banner stretched right across the town hall, proclaiming, first in Arabic, then in Kurdish, that 'The Baath way is our way'. . . . In all the Region's larger settlements, as in other parts of Kurdistan, the Arab Baath had prosperous looking local branch offices." See also *Middle East Contemporary Survey,* v. 3 (1978–1979), p. 569.

63. Submission to the UN by the International League for Human Rights, 14 January 1977. This information corroborates submissions by Kurdish leaders. See letter to Kurt Waldheim, Secretary-General of the United Nations, 18 May 1978 by Mustafa Barzani, chairman, Kurdistan Democratic Party, including appendices A through K.

64. *Middle East Contemporary Survey,* v. 3 (1978–1979), p. 569.

65. Conflicts among the Kurds were common, owing in part to tribal differences and attempts by Baghdad to divide the Kurdish movement. Open conflicts, for example, had appeared in the late 1960s between Jalal Talabani and forces faithful to Barzani.

66. Discussion extracted from Martin van Bruinessen, "The Kurds Between Iran and Iraq," in *MERIP,* 16:4, (July–August 1986).

67. *Middle East Contemporary Survey,* v. 2 (1977–1978), p. 521.

68. William Safire, "Of Kurds and Conscience," *New York Times,* 13 December 1976.

69. Sluglett and Sluglett, *Iraq Since 1958,* op. cit., p. 187.

70. *Middle East Contemporary Survey,* v. 3 (1978–1979), p. 570.

71. Gender in this study refers to the historical-cultural conceptions of men and women, including ideas of masculinity and femininity. On gender in the Arab world, see Nawal El Saadawi, *The Hidden Face of Eve: Women in the Arab World,* (Zed Press, 1980).

72. Ibid., p. 146.

73. One revealing narrative on the situation of women in Iraqi society, especially with respect to conventional rituals and practices and the differences between town and country, may be found in Elizabeth Warnock Fernea, *Guests of the Sheik: An Ethnography of an Iraqi Village,* (Anchor Books, 1969).

74. Batatu, *Old Social Classes,* op. cit., pp. 395–396.

75. This summary is based primarily upon Deborah Cobbet, "Women in Iraq," in *Saddam's Iraq,* op. cit.

76. Report of the Eighth Regional Congress of the Arab Ba'th Socialist Party, 8–12 January 1974, (Baghdad, 1974), p. 185.

77. Ibid., p. 35.

78. Ibid., pp. 46–47.

79. Outline of legal changes extracted from Amal al-Sharqi, "The Emancipation of Iraqi Women," in *Iraq: The Contemporary State,* ed. Tim Niblock, (Croom Helm, 1982), pp. 83–84.

80. Education and employment statistics extracted from General Federation of Iraqi Women, *The Working Program of the Iraqi Republic to Improve the Woman's Status*—national papers presented to the international congress for the United Nations Women's Contract, Copenhagen, 14–30 July 1980, pp. 21–45.

81. See discussion in Marr, *Modern History,* op. cit., pp. 272–273. Marr's assessment of the changes is cautiously optimistic: "Women in 1980 still had a long way to go to achieve equal status with men, but the trends were clear, and the progress, especially in the 1970s, impressive." "Women," in *Saddam's Iraq,* op. cit., p. 273.

82. Cobbett, p. 129.

83. See discussion in Bengio, *Middle East Contemporary Survey,* v. 1 (1976–1977), pp. 405–408.

84. Hanna Batatu, "Iraq's Underground Shi'i Movements," in *MERIP Reports,* 12:1, (January 1982), p. 6.

85. Bengio, *Middle East Contemporary Survey,* v. 2 (1977–78), p. 522.

86. See discussion in Ofra Bengio, "Shi'is and Politics in Ba'thi Iraq," in *Middle Eastern Studies,* 21:1, (January 1985), pp. 3–8.

87. Ibid. Bengio, in her 1985 article, identifies five groups, one of which was not formed until 1982. The five include the Organization for Islamic Action, the Iraqi Mujahidin, the Movement of the Mujahidin Ulama in Iraq (founded in Iran in 1980), Al-Da'wa, and (1982) the Supreme Council of the Islamic Revolution. Batatu, writing three years earlier in "Iraq's Underground Shi'i Movements," identifies two main political groups, Al-Da'wa, formed in 1969, and the Mujahidin, formed in Iraq after the Islamic Revolution in Iran.

88. See discussion in Marion Farouk-Sluglett and Peter Sluglett, "Some Reflections on the Present State of Sunni-Shi'i Relations in Iraq," in *Bulletin of the British Society for Middle Eastern Studies,* 5, (1978), pp. 79–87.

89. Batatu, "Iraq's Underground Shi'i Movements," in *MERIP Reports,* 12:1, op. cit., p. 7.

90. See discussion in Bengio, *Middle East Contemporary Survey,* v. 3 (1978–1979), pp. 570–571.

91. Bengio, *Middle East Contemporary Survey,* v. 4 (1979–1980), p. 513.

92. For a discussion of some of the concrete problems that forced migration, particularly after the heralded land reforms of the postrevolutionary period, see Atheel Al-Jomard, "Internal Migration in Iraq," in *The Integration of Modern Iraq,* ed. Abbas Kelidar, (Croom Helm, 1979).

93. Joseph Stork, "Class, State and Politics in Iraq," in *Power and Stability in the Middle East,* ed. Berch Berberoglu, (Zed Books, 1989), p. 34.

94. See discussion in 'Isam al-Khafaji, "The Parasitic Base of the Ba'thist Regime," in *Saddam's Iraq,* op. cit., Figures on housing and population from p. 82.

95. Alan Richards and John Waterbury, *A Political Economy of the Middle East: State, Class, and Economic Development,* eds. Alan Richards and John Waterbury, (Westview Press, 1990), pp. 282–283.

96. Statistics extracted from Shakir M. Issa, "The Distribution of Income in Iraq, 1971," in *The Integration of Modern Iraq,* op. cit., pp. 132–133.

97. These paragraphs draw upon the illuminating discussion in Samir al-Khalil's *The Republic of Fear: The Politics of Modern Iraq,* (University of California Press, 1989), pp. 6–12.

98. Ibid., p. 8.

99. Ibid., pp. 9–10.

100. *Revolutionary Iraq: 1968–1973,* political report adopted by the eighth regional congress of the Arab Ba'th Socialist Party, January 1974, p. 172.

101. The most detailed discussion of the Ba'thist security apparatus may be found in al-Khalil, *Republic of Fear,* op. cit., Chapter 1, "The Institutions of Violence."

102. Samir al-Khalil, *Republic of Fear,* op. cit., pp. 275–276.

4

The Drift to War

Between the signing of the Algiers Accord in 1975 and the fall of the shah in 1979, Iraqi-Iranian relations were at their warmest. After the insurrection, Iraq quickly expressed the desire to continue cordial relations,[1] but despite these initial gestures the friendly atmosphere quickly dissolved. By the fall of 1979, Iran's foreign minister, Ebrahim Yazdi, appropriately summarized Iranian-Iraqi relations as "very cool."[2] Over the next year, Iran and Iraq gradually became each other's primary security concern.[3] Official government statements, interviews with political leaders, newspaper commentaries, and radio broadcasts frequently addressed the growing tensions between the two countries. Interviews with political leaders and official policy organs routinely provided lengthy and elaborate expositions on the reasons for the growing hostility. In the fall of 1979, for example, the Iranian foreign minister, in an effort to account for the deteriorating relations, detailed the logical flaws of Ba'th ideology, drew attention to the undemocratic nature of the Ba'th regime, and expressed concern over the stark repression in Iraq. The blunt contrast between the misguided, undemocratic, repressive Ba'th regime in Iraq and the flowering Islamic Revolution in Iran, the listener was led to conclude, lay at the root of the growing tensions.[4] Expositions of a similar nature often appeared on the Iraqi side. The Ba'th party organ *ath-Thawrah*, for example, reviewed Iraqi-Iranian relations under the shah and the Islamic government in a series of articles during the spring of 1979. The final piece in the series expressed a desire for friendly relations but maintained that Iraq had a "natural" concern for the Arab population in Arabistan (Khuzestan). The series concluded with the accusation that the Iranian regime was inventing "illusory" enemies in order to justify the expansion of the Iranian army.[5]

This rising attentiveness and mutual concern was closely bound up with a growing conflict between the two countries. This conflict manifested itself through a calumnious rhetoric, especially in the state-controlled media of both countries, that extended far beyond the bounds of normal diplomatic dislike or disapproval. Iraq was nothing short of contemptuous of the revolutionary leadership in Iran. Khomeini was variably referred to as a "Pahlavi," as that "mummy Khomeini," as a "shah wearing a turban," and as being "too petty" to carry out the revolution. The revolutionary leadership was alternatively characterized as Khomeini's "gang," as a cluster of "sick politicians," as "lunatics," as "frenzied charlatans and imposters," as the "racist Persian clique," as a "criminal gang," and as "murderers" displaying "animosity, despicable racism, and empty vanity." The following Baghdad commentary in response to border clashes with Iran was typical:

> The charlatans and tricksters of Iran will pay a heavy price for their reckless line. The reckless and misguided Khomeyni group knows more than anyone else—because it experiences this daily—the type of answer it gets from the Iraqis across the border. It is a price which this deviate group will continue to pay.[6]

Iran was equal to the rhetorical task. The Iraqi regime was described as the "Takriti gang," as the "gangster regime," as a "regime of tyrants," as "Satans," as "traitorous" to the Gulf region, as "subservient" to American imperialism, as "inhumane," and as "fascist butchers." Saddam Hussein was characterized as "mentally ill" and as the "puppet of Satan." In its response to clashes with Iraqi-supported Kurdish groups in August 1980, Iran's Interior Ministry offered the following diatribe:

> As the dear compatriots may well know, mercenary elements of bloodthirsty Saddam Husayn—this obedient servant of the United States—have not yet renounced their antihuman and bestial conduct. Saddam Husayn—this autocratic and legitimized dictator—without learning a lesson from the malevolent and black past of his erstwhile, deposed, executed collaborator, the traitorous Mohammad Reza, is resorting to crimes and treachery similar to that of his friend. . . . Little does he know that the ramshackle and shaky bases of the oppressive regime which relies on gunpowder and the bayonet of the Iraqi Ba'th will soon be destroyed thanks to the wakefulness and positive efforts of the dedicated and revolutionary Iraqi Muslims, and that the roots of oppression and cruelty will soon dry up and will consign nefarious Saddam to the trash heap of History.[7]

Ayatollah Khomeini himself drew on a colorful repertoire of adjectives when characterizing the Ba'th regime, using the words "despicable," "criminal," and "murderous."

As tensions and the conflict escalated, Iraq resurrected several of the interminable territorial disputes, particularly with respect to the Shatt al-Arab waterway and the three Gulf islands of Greater Tunbs, Lesser Tunbs, and Abu Musa. On 30 October 1979, Iraq demanded that the Algiers Accord be revised. From the Iraqi perspective, the treaty had been extracted in the face of the "mercenary mutiny" of the Kurds, leaving the regime with no choice but to accept its unfair terms. The 1975 treaty had been political-ly expedient and nothing more. In the spring of 1980, the territorial ante was upped: Iraq demanded the return of the islands (mentioned above), which had been seized by Iran in 1971. Both countries continued their war of words over the disputed lands and became increasingly intransigent. Their positions were mutually incompatible. The territorial issue reached its peak on 17 September 1980 when Saddam Hussein unilaterally abrogat-ed the Algiers Accord. In a speech delivered to Iraq's National Assembly, Hussein declared that Iranian noncompliance with the provisions of the 1975 agreement now forced the move on Iraq, despite Iraq's best efforts. Triumphantly, Hussein declared: "This Shatt shall again be, as it has been throughout history, Iraqi and Arab in name and reality, with all rights of full sovereignty over it."[8]

The heightened insecurity and growing conflict between Iran and Iraq was capped by a series of military clashes along their common border. The clashes generally involved exchanges of fire, border-post raids, air incur-sions, and limited military operations. Each country repeatedly claimed to be the victim of gratuitous aggression by the other. Border provocations provided both countries with an opportunity to fire additional rhetorical salvos. Iraq described border clashes in late May, for example, as "aggres-sion [that] comes as part of the criminal provocative acts committed by the agent Persian regime against Iraq and its struggling people."[9] In a similar vein, during the escalation of border incidents in February 1980, Iran sum-marized the clashes as "yet another confirmation of the Iraqi Ba'th Party's hostile stand against the Islamic revolution and the sons of the border vil-lages."[10] The border collisions, which began in earnest in February 1980, continued relatively unabated until the outbreak of war in September.

During the year prior to war, Iran and Iraq became each other's prima-ry concern. While other international political issues were important to both regimes, such as the accord between Egypt and Israel and the possible U.S. response to the hostage crisis, both countries became seriously alarmed by the other's posture and activities. Both regimes characterized these threats in politically inclusive terms. References to the integrity of the Arab *nation* or the Islamic *nation* were thus very common. It was not the more narrowly based regimes that were threatened, in other words, but rather the lofty principles and aspirations of nations. When probing beyond the mounting insecurity between the two countries, it is evident that it was threaded by three distinguishable political dynamics: the attempts by Iran to foment a Shi'i uprising in Iraq; the alarm that the potential Shi'i uprising created for the Ba'th regime; and the struggle by the Ba'th regime in Iraq to secure oil revenues. These dynamics, in turn, were signatured by the sociopolitical struggles that characterized each country. The slide to war, therefore, bore an intimate relationship to the evolving sociopolitical fields in both Iran and Iraq. They reflected the uplifting determinations of the social floor rather than the downward determinations of the eternal inter-state ceiling. Each political dynamic warrants examination in terms of the manner in which it is linked to the broader social fields in Iran and Iraq. Through this procedure, we can uncover the social foundations of the mounting security problems and thereby fully reveal the social origins of the Iran-Iraq War.

The Genesis of Iran's Aggressive Campaign Against Iraq

Both components of the Iranian middle class figured prominently in the revolution. The modern middle class, composed of urban-educated, salaried professionals, independently employed professionals, and intellectuals, set the revolutionary process in motion by demanding that the shah end state repression and democratize the political system. More importantly, the traditional middle class, composed of bazaaris and the ulama, provided the inspiration and revolutionary mobilization required to break the regime. Each element of the revolutionary opposition had been extensively conditioned by the extensive socioeconomic transformations of contemporary Iran. By the end of 1978, the monarchy was seriously faltering. The departure of the shah early in the new year and the arrival of Khomeini shortly thereafter marked the final episodes in the collapse of the monarchy. On 11 February, the army declared its neutrality. The provisional revolutionary government (PRG), headed by Mehdi Bazargan, proceeded to pave the way for the new Islamic Republic.

One key to the success of the Iranian revolution lay in the solidarity achieved among the diverse opposition. The shah provided the necessary focus that allowed the opposition to put aside its differences in order to topple the monarchy. Profound ideological cleavages among the revolutionary opposition were thus successfully concealed in the face of a common adversary. With the fall of the shah, the unity of the opposition quickly unravelled and their inherently different political agendas rapidly surfaced. Each element of the anti-shah coalition subscribed to a different interpretation of the political and economic nature of the revolution, and a different social and political outlook for post-Pahlavi Iran. The inevitable struggle for postrevolutionary hegemony in the months following the insurrection was intense. The ulama clearly had the upper edge going into the postrevolutionary period in view of the factors that combined to give the revolution its Islamic flavor, but their political position was far from unassailable. At a minimum, the prospect of being forced to soften their Islamic vision was very real.

At least three different ideological threads could be detected after the fall of the shah.[11] Each ideological stream was represented by a number of political parties and had a distinct social base.

1. The first ideological pocket consisted of the liberal-bourgeois parties of the modern middle class. There were dozens of political groups within the liberal cast. Among the prominent were the Teachers' Association, the Movement Group, the Democratic Union of the Iranian People, the Republican Party, the Radical Party, the Association for the Protection of the Constitution, the Society of Free Muslims, the Iranian Association of Jurists, and the Writers' Association. These groups tended to view events as a shift from an authoritarian regime to a liberal democracy, thereby emphasizing the political dimension of the revolution. One of their primary concerns was to protect private enterprise and property. Their base of support was concentrated within the judiciary, salaried professionals, educational workers, many of Iran's intellectuals, and the moneyed classes. The liberal groups lacked any mass social base and their mainstream economic program was unlikely to generate one. The most prominent liberal groups were the National Front and the Freedom Movement. The National Front, led by Karim Sanjabi of the Iran Party, emphasized the importance of Iranian nationalism. The National Front, predictably, characterized the revolution as a struggle of Iranian nationals rather than as an Islamic struggle. The Freedom Movement, headed by Mehdi Bazargan, voiced strong support for a parliamentary democracy and embraced the idea of a healthy economy driven by the private ownership of property. The liberal opposition was best situated to temper clerical ascendency in the postrevolutionary period.

2. The second ideological strain in postrevolutionary Iran was represented by the numerous parties on the left.[12] The driving force behind the radical left parties came from Iranian intellectuals (especially the students). The radical left in Iran was characterized by intense factionalism. It included the Fedaiyen-e Khalq, the Paykar Organization, the Tufan Organization (Maoist), the Organization for Communist Unity, the Communist Party of Iranian Workers and Peasants, the Party of Socialist Workers (Trotskyist), the Organization of the Militant Workers, the Communers Organization, the Marxist-Leninist Committee, and the Organization of Revolutionary Youth. The Tudeh Party was the main left-wing party.

   A collection of radical Islamic parties rounded out the political left. The radical Islamic parties, particularly the Mujahedin-e Khalq, were also centered in the modern intelligentsia. Despite their diversity, these groups can be summarized as advocating the radical transformation of Iran's socioeconomic structure, including the nationalization of key economic sectors and the removal of all imperialist ties. They tended to view the 1979 revolution as a necessary step toward these goals but believed that considerable work still lay ahead. Although these groups embraced the struggle of Iran's toiling poor, they lacked a broad social base. On the whole, the left stood little chance of commandeering the Iranian revolution. In view of this reality, the Tudeh Party, for example, supported the radical clergy and strove to guide revolutionary policy in a direction commensurate with their long-term agenda.

3. The third ideological faction contending for power in postrevolutionary Iran was made up of the fundamentalist ulama. Important differences among the clergy certainly existed. Among the three most prominent figures, for example, Ayatollah Taleqani and Ayatollah Sharia'at Madari emphasized the importance of establishing a democratic political system, a position that gave them greater compatibility with the liberals and some regional movements. In contrast, Ayatollah Khomeini and numerous mid- to lower-level ulama emphasized the importance of establishing an Islamic political system with the *marja'e taqlid* (most learned religious figure) at its apex. "Our nation gave its blood to create an Islamic republic," asserted Khomeini in a speech at Qom cemetery on 9 March 1979, "not a democratic republic."[13] The followers of Khomeini, including Ayatollah Beheshti, Ayatollah Mosavi Ardbili, and Ayatollah Mahdavi Kani, along with Hojjatolislams Khamenei, Bahonar, and Hashemi Rafsanjani, founded the Islamic Republican Party (IRP) during the insurrection. The Islamic parties, and particularly the IRP, came to figure most prominently in the policy directions of postrevolutionary Iran.

The political struggle of the postrevolutionary period evolved into a battle between the liberals and the fundamentalists, or radical clergy.[14] In broad class terms, this struggle could be summarized as a conflict between the modern and traditional segments of the middle class. The PRG under Bazargan was stacked with liberal representatives. Although the radical clergy did not exercise formal power within the old state apparatus, they tended to exercise de facto power by virtue of their strong links to the revolutionary institutions that spontaneously arose during the collapse of the monarchy. These revolutionaries included the Komitehs and the Revolutionary Guards. The radical clerics undermined the authority of the PRG, prompting Bazargan to describe the government metaphorically—"a knife without a blade." Major political events in the early postrevolutionary period, which included a referendum to decide the general political form of revolutionary Iran, the drafting of a new constitution, and the initial elections to the Majlis, revealed the growing political power of the radical clerics. The influence of the liberals was waning. The PRG was undermined further by its inability to address popular demands for far-reaching social change.[15] Bazargan resigned the day after students seized the U.S. embassy in the fall of 1979.

The decisive factor in the clergy's struggle to consolidate political power was rooted in its ability to sustain revolutionary fervor within the general population. These efforts were nourished by a theocratic-populist strategy that enlisted Islam to lend thematic coherence to a political discourse that concerned itself, first and foremost, with the protection of "the oppressed Iranian nation," especially its downtrodden masses. This linguistic atmosphere was heavily permeated with xenophobic motifs that helped to keep the population on guard against so-called foreign predators.[16] The symbolic world of theocratic-populism kept the population politically mobilized and effectively turned the ulama into revolutionary vanguards. By sustaining popular revolutionary fervor, clerical control of the revolution was insured. Theocratic-populism, in short, was instrumental in the accumulation of clerical power.

Within these parameters can be detected the germination of the aggressive campaign against Iraq. The first thing to notice in making a closer examination of the theocratic-populist discourse is that the "oppressed Iranian masses" were deemed to be the primary beneficiaries of the Islamic Revolution. Khomeini's address to the Iranian people from Qom in the immediate aftermath of the insurrection clearly reveals this discursive thrust:

> Apart from wanting to make your material life affluent, we want to see your moral life affluent as well. You need spiritual values. They have taken away our spiritual values. . . . We are going to make power and water free for the poor classes. We shall make buses free for the poor classes. Do not be satisfied with just this. We shall impart greatness to moral and spiritual values. . . . We shall develop both your world and your hereafter.[17]

Despite an apparent affinity with the impoverished masses of Iranian society, however, theocratic-populism tended to deny the political meaningfulness of social stratification and division. The Islamic social ideal nullified social division and cleavage. Islam performed a type of levelling function. The primary social constituency became "the devout nation." In an address to the Iranian people less than two months after the revolution, Khomeini propounded the following theme:

> I tell all the sections of society that in Islam there are no privileges recognized for one group as distinct from another, Sunni or Shi'a, Arabs or Persians, Turks or non-Turks. Islam recognized social distinction only for the just, for piety. Only those with piety enjoy social distinction. Those with the spirit of humanity enjoy social distinction. Social distinction is not governed by wealth and material possessions. All such privileges must be eliminated, and everybody made equal.[18]

In response to the heavy fighting between Kurdish insurgents and Tehran in August 1979, Khomeini succinctly reiterated this notion: "I proclaim to the honourable people of Kurdestan that we consider you to be our brothers and equals and that you will enjoy equal rights with your other Iranian brothers wherever you may be and that in the Islamic Republic there is absolutely no difference between Azarbayjanis, Kurds, Lors, Arabs, Persian or Baluchis."[19] According to the logic of the theocratic-populist discourse, the only meaningful social entity in postrevolutionary Iran was the pious nation. The individual or the group was inseparable from the nation, and individual interests were necessarily subordinated to it. "We regard the whole nation as part of us and ourselves as part of the nation," said Khomeini, speaking to a group of students and educational professionals from Sanandaj (in the Kurdish region), "and we all are servants of the nation."[20]

Social conflict and political discord, therefore, was incommensurate with Islamic society. Political opposition merely undermined the intrinsic unity of the Islamic nation. When the revolutionary Komitehs were criticized, Khomeini typically claimed in response: "The aim of the opposition is to discredit anybody who wants to serve the people."[21] There was, of course, an obvious disparity between the professed unity of the pious nation and the rampant political opposition within the country. In order to explain and discredit this opposition, the theocratic-populist discourse drew upon xenophobic themes and narratives. The spiritual unity and political coherence of Islamic society could only be punctured by the machinations of foreigners. This alleged link between internal discord and foreign elements is readily visible in Khomeini's address to the Iranian people shortly before his departure for Qom:

> We all know that the secret behind the great victory that the nation has scored lied *[sic]* in the unity of expression of all strata, from the capital to the remotest parts of the country, and that its sole objective was to overthrow the satanic rule and to get rid of colonial associates and international colonialists, and set up an Islamic republic. We are not in great need of maintaining this unity of expression and unity of objective. The great nation should beware of certain divisive elements that, by means of deceitful slogans, want to pave the way for the return of foreigners to our Islamic country and to restore the same old repression and looting in another form. By isolating them and refraining from participating in their gatherings, and by means of Islamic logic, the great nation will neutralize their harmful propaganda.[22]

The aim of the revolution was to "cut off the hand of foreigners." Social unrest and political discord was necessarily residual; that is, it lingered by virtue of imperialist design. Iranians were repeatedly cautioned to be on guard against foreign intruders: "Islam produces human beings, and this is what the foreigners, the superpowers, are afraid of. They are afraid of humans, so they attack Islam, for it is a religion which breeds humans."[23] According to the theocratic-populist discourse, colonialism had "done its homework" and knew where to foment unrest and sow disenchantment. Strikes, marches, protests, and sit-ins against clerical policy were dismissed as the work of foreign forces. The increasingly pejorative connotation that surrounded the terms *liberal* and *intellectual* was partly created by linking them to foreign groups. "Let these moribund brains drain away," Khomeini announced in response to criticism from Iraqi liberals. "These brains have worked for the aliens." The primary antagonist in the theocratic-populist calculus was the United States. Internal opponents were routinely branded as "lackeys" of U.S. imperialism. Iran was depicted as the natural prey of the United States.[24] The second storming of the U.S. embassy and the taking of U.S. hostages was therefore equivalent to capturing "the den of corruption" or "the nest of imperialism."

It is within this language that we can detect two separate leitmotifs that helped to initiate and sustain Iran's aggressive posture against Iraq. The first involved the so-called natural bonds that were created with other downtrodden nations. As the theocratic-populist project drew attention to the "oppressed Iranian nation," it expressed a natural affinity with other oppressed peoples, especially Muslim peoples, throughout the world. "As a Muslim nation," Iranian foreign minister Ebrahim Yazdi remarked in an interview in the spring of 1979, "we feel duty-bound to help all oppressed peoples."[25] Khomeini, in an address to Muslim's around the world, said: "Muslims and oppressed people of the world, hold each others' hands and turn your face toward the great God." "Take refuge in Islam and arise against the oppressors and those who usurp the rights of the nations."[26] Iran essentially found itself exporting revolution in order to consolidate the revolution at home. This did not necessarily demand direct assistance or confrontation. "The revolution's guidelines and courses will go to other places, whether we wish it or not," claimed newly elected president Bani-Sadr. "Basically, if we are able to build a model Islamic society, it will automatically go beyond our frontiers, for others would wish to copy it."[27] As a neighboring Muslim country, especially one with a history of conflict with Iran and, indeed, the only other Shi'i-dominated country in the world, Iraq was an inevitable target for Tehran's purple blasts.

The second motif was directly linked to the creation of external enemies. Within its nucleus, the theocratic-populist discourse generated a litany of potential counterrevolutionary threats. In this sense, the aggression against Iraq was a natural offshoot of the xenophobic leitmotif of postrevolutionary Iran's godly ideological cloak. The linkage between its aggression toward Iraq and the theocratic-populist dialogue was unmistakable:

The Iraqi people must get rid of the claws of this gang [Ba'th regime]. Like the Iranian Army which, after realizing that the deposed shah was fighting Islam, joined the people and contributed to making their Islamic revolution, the Iraqi Army must rise up. . . . The war that the Iraqi Ba'th wants to ignite is a war against Islam."[28]

Events in Iraq provided Iran with further opportunities to specifically draw the Ba'th regime into its rhetorical orbit. The execution of the eminent Iraqi Shi'i figure, Baqir as-Sadr, in April 1980 prompted Iran to declare a three-day period of mourning and a public holiday. Khomeini proclaimed: "Baqir as-Sadr . . . gained the exalted rank of martyrdom in a heart-rendering manner by the hands of the despicable Iraqi Ba'th regime."[29] Iraq's expulsion of citizens of Iranian origin provided additional fodder for the theocrats. A statement issued by the regime proclaimed: "The inhumane Iraqi Ba'th regime has forced thousands of Muslim brothers and sisters to leave that country in the most disgraceful manner on charges of being Shi'ite Muslims and opposing the bloodsucking regime of Saddam Husayn."[30] The campaign against Iraq was reinforced by linking it with U.S. imperialism. Iraq was depicted as the "U.S. agent in the region."[31] Thinly veiled references to U.S. "appendages and stooges" frequently appeared in Tehran's political commentary.

There was a direct link between the aggression against Iraq and the rhetorical world that sustained Iran's revolutionary zeal and consolidated clerical power. Within this discursive atmosphere, Iran's revolutionary identity was solidified, its external foes were defined, and the aggressive posture against Iraq derived its impetus and meaning. Through direct broadcasts and support for Shi'i groups in Iraq, Iran encouraged the overthrow of the Iraqi regime. Radio Tehran regularly broadcast messages by Islamic groups such as the Islamic Revolution Struggle of Iraq, the Islamic Movement of Iraq, and the Islamic Revolutionary Army for the Liberation of Iraq. Although the groups existed probably in name only, they routinely issued calls for the Shi'i population in Iraq to rise up and overthrow the Ba'th regime.[32] These wishes extended to Iran's top political leaders, with Khomeini unequivocally expressing the hope that the Ba'th regime would be "despatched to the refuse bin of history."

To recapitulate, the presence of the radical clerics within the postrevolutionary terrain of Iran generated and reinforced the aggressive campaign against Iraq. A small part of this process would have been sustained by what might be called pure or unadulterated ideology. Among the religious ideologues, for example, the Islamic narratives of overthrowing impious states *(futah)* were undoubtably operative.[33] The driving factor, however, was the theocratic-populist discourse that sustained revolutionary fervor and insured clerical ascendency. This rhetorical universe served as a constant reminder that the ulama were the pivotal force behind the revolution, and strongly suggested that they were the key to its continued success. The functioning of the revolutionary institutions, moreover, was greatly assisted by this symbolic cloak. Revolutionary fulfillment and the preservation of clerical leadership were virtually inseparable for Khomeini and the radical clerics. Theocratic-populism went a long way to help them achieve their hegemonic aspirations. Aggression against Iraq was the flip side of this xenophobia-laden rhetorical strategy. There was no cultural imperative unfolding in the Gulf region in the early 1980s; no correcting of the spiritual laws of history. The theocrats were motivated by the more temporal concern of consolidating their grip on the postrevolutionary state. The campaign against Iraq, however, gravely concerned the Ba'th regime.

The Ba'th State and Iraq's Shi'i Population

With the gradual insertion of Iraq into the world economy, initially as a supplier of agricultural goods and later as a supplier of crude oil, the Iraqi social field was radically altered. By the 1970s, Iraq's class fabric had come to include a growing, indigenous capitalist class, a modern middle class, an urban-centered working class, and a body of rural agricultural workers. The large and powerful landed class of the monarchy was eclipsed by the land reform policies of the revolutionary regimes. The evolving class structure of Iraq was accompanied by extensive demographic shifts. In addition to continually growing in size, the Iraqi population was becoming increasingly urbanized. By the late-1970s, two out of every three Iraqis lived in the cities. The most palpable manifestation of Iraq's shifting demographics was the growth of dense pockets of urban poor, especially in Baghdad.

As indicated in Chapter 3, on the eve of war an incongruity had emerged between the social and political spheres in Iraq. The Ba'th regime had developed into an island unto its own. Nourished by an unending, and for all intents and purposes unlimited, supply of oil revenues, the Ba'th state had systematically closed off independent avenues of political expression. Authentic and autonomous political activity was aggressively discouraged. In social terms, however, the evolving Iraqi tapestry had come to contain new constituencies, and these demanded a more open political system. In the closed world of the Ba'th, the opportunity for these constituencies to air their grievances and advance their interests was greatly circumscribed. Political life was increasingly incommensurate with the imperatives of society. The Iraqi people were thoroughly alienated from their political leaders. A disjuncture between the political and social worlds of Iraq, not unlike the contradiction that toppled the Pahlavi monarchy in neighboring Iran, had emerged clearly.

Within this volatile setting, Iraq's Shi'i opposition showed signs of emerging as a serious challenge to the Ba'th regime. Unlike the Kurdish struggle, which was tinged with nationalism, or the Marxist-inspired activity of the ICP, this movement sought to mask or house their activities within Islam and the mosque. Protests had occurred in the Shi'i holy cities of Najaf, Kazimiyyah, and Karbala and in the Shi'i-dominated Madinat ath-Thawrah district of Baghdad. Despite the Sunni-dominated state apparatus in a predominantly Shi'i society, the emergence of a Shi'i politics in Iraq should not be characterized as a religious struggle. It was not a sectarian conflict.[34] Nor can the Shi'i opposition be adequately understood as a struggle of the poorer Iraqis (who were predominantly Shi'i) rising up against the wealthy and those fragments of the middle classes that had fared well in postrevolutionary Iraq. The Shi'i movement cannot be reduced to a struggle for material betterment. Rather, the emerging Shi'i opposition was bound up with the sweeping changes of twentieth-century Iraq. The social transformation of contemporary Iraq created two distinct and highly disaffected social groups that combined to fuel the Shi'i struggle: the declining clerical class and the impoverished Shi'i masses. Both groups must be considered separately in order fully to comprehend the rise of the Shi'i challenge to the Ba'th regime.

Over the century prior to the outbreak of war, the social position and political influence of the Shi'i clergy was in continual decline. The forces of modernization, secularization, and—especially—economic satellitization were at the heart of these changing fortunes.[35] A series of pressures bore down upon the ulama. Pivotal was the waning attraction of the religious profession for many Iraqis. In 1918, more than six thousand students attended the theological seminaries in Najaf. By the twilight of the monarchy, the number had fallen by two-thirds—a decline that can largely be attributed to the growing tendency toward secular education and new opportunities for employment in the modernizing economy and the expanding civil service. The thinning of the ranks of the ulama went hand in hand with their declining prestige and authority. This net effect was exacerbated by falling income, due to the loss of tithes, taxes, and fees. The ulama were thus inspired to form political associations to protect their social standing. Batatu noted: "They were moved by a growing sense that the old faith was receding, that scepticism and even disdain for traditional rites were rife among the educated Shi'is, that the belief of even the urban Shi'a masses was not as firm, and their conformism to ancient usages not as punctual or as reverent as in past time, and that the *ulama* were losing ground and declining in prestige and material influence."[36]

The Shi'i men of religion, moreover, were concerned with the growing attraction of the Iraqi Communist Party among the urban Shi'i population. During the 1940s and 1950s, communist influence even managed to penetrate Iraq's holy bastion of Najaf. Clerical alarm at ICP activity ran particularly high in the aftermath of the 1958 revolution as the latter's profile grew under Qasem. In the fall of 1958, leading clerics in Najaf founded a political organization called the Association of Najaf Ulama. The organization aimed to raise the religious consciousness of Iraqis and combat atheism. In view of the nominal influence of Ba'thism or Nasserism at the time, the goal of combating atheism was synonymous with combating communist influence throughout the country. In 1960, for example, a decree was issued by a prominent cleric forbidding membership in the ICP. As further testimony to the concerns of the ulama, a younger cleric, Muhammad Baqir al-Sadr (who was executed by the Ba'th regime just prior to the Iran-Iraq War), wrote an extensive and widely-read critique of European philosophy entitled *Iqtisaduna.* It is significant that almost one-third of this text was devoted to refuting Marxism and historical materialism.

The general decline of the ulama in the face of the secular path of contemporary Iraq contributed to their political cohesion. Iraq's secular tendencies became even more visible with the accession to power of the Ba'th regime in 1968. The Ba'th, which has traditionally been dominated by Sunnis, adopted an avowedly nonreligious platform. This posture, along with Ba'th contempt for autonomous organizations, "helped to alienate the conservative religious groups of both Sunni and Shi'i."[37] Despite the Ba'th's nonsectarian posture, the Shi'i religious establishment was aggressively targeted by the party. This has been enumerated in detail by Ofra Bengio:

> The brunt of secularization or the breaking of the power of religion was directed in the main against the Shi'is. Thus, in the summer of 1969, the Ba'th unleashed a campaign of repression against Shi'i men of religion and institutions which included: the closure of Islamic institutions including a theological college in Najaf; the imposition of strict censorship on religious publications; the authorization of the sale of alcohol in the Shi'i holy places reportedly for the first time in Iraqi history; and persecution of Shi'i Ulama in general.[38]

The accession and consolidation of the Ba'th in the late 1960s encouraged the nucleus of the Shi'i Association of Najaf ulama to form the Da'wa al-Islamiyyah (the Islamic Call). The Da'wa stood opposed, first and foremost, to the secular tendencies of modern Iraq. "It is important to recognize," writes Michael Hudson, "that the Islamic opposition to the Ba'th regime led by Saddam Husayn eschews defining the conflict in sectarian terms; thus the Da'wa Party and other groups do not see themselves as Shi'is fighting the oppression of a Sunni government, but as spokesmen for all the Muslims of Iraq—Shi'i and Sunni, Arab and Kurd, against an evil secular government."[39] As the 1970s progressed, the Da'wa became the most prominent and most active religious group resisting the Ba'th regime.

The potential strength of the Shi'i clerics did not lie in their relative political cohesiveness or in their resolute opposition to the secular policies of the Ba'th. Rather, this small but politically vibrant fraction of Iraq's middle echelon was in a unique position to mobilize the Shi'i masses. This potential for mobilization, however, must also be seen in the context of the social transformation of modern Iraq. In fact, for a number of reasons it would have been possible to expect that the Shi'i masses would not have been disposed favorably to the efforts of the ulama. Throughout the southern Shi'i-populated region of Iraq, religion tended to be loosely organized. Religious institutions were uncommon for a number of reasons: extreme poverty, the nomadism of much of the population, the marshlands of the region, and the susceptibility of much of the area to seasonal flooding. In 1947, there were only thirty-nine religious institutions in the Shi'i areas. This translates into one institution for every thirty-seven thousand persons. Moreover, many of the rural Shi'i were of bedouin origin. Since Islam has traditionally "sat lightly on the bedouins," one could reasonably have expected that they would not eagerly embrace the Islamic movement.[40] Moreover, many Shi'is were of relatively recent conversion. They tended still to be governed as much by ancient tribal customs as by Islamic law.

Nonetheless, there were forces at work that reinforced the religiosity of the Shi'i, favorably disposing them toward the activities of the Da'wa and other Shi'i groups. In particular, the shifting land-tenure structures associated with the initial phases of Iraq's insertion into the world economy turned the Shi'i tribesmen into peasants. The condition of the rural Shi'i became deplorable. In these wretched circumstances, the southern population found the traditional Shi'i narratives particularly appropriate to their lives. As Batatu writes: "Shi'ism's anti-governmental motif, its pre-occupation with oppression, its grief-laden tales, and its miracle play representing Husayn's passion accorded with the instincts and sufferings of tribesmen-turned-peasants and must have eased the tasks of the travelling Shi'a mu'mins."[41] The miserable conditions of the countryside, moreover, encouraged massive migration to the urban centers. As a result, the shifting land-tenure structures had indirectly created large pools of Shi'i poor in Iraq's urban centers:

> As the Shi'i inhabitants of the southern provinces began to migrate to Baghdad in increasing numbers, they also came to constitute the majority of the urban poor in the slums that grew up around Baghdad and other cities after the Second World War. Naturally, the Shi'i poor, both those still living in villages and those who had migrated to the cities in search of work, were poor not because they were Shi'is but because, in the comparatively recent past, the great tribal diras (estates) of the South on which they lived had been appropriated by powerful tribal leaders, and the tribesmen had been left either entirely without land or with insufficient land for their subsistence.[42]

In keeping with their modest religiosity, the Shi'ism of the new city dwellers was centered less around the rituals of prayer and fasting and more with the Shi'i festivals and processions—venues that readily lent themselves to political exploitation.

It was the Iraqi Communists who first succeeded in mobilizing the poorer city dwellers. The efforts of the ICP to cultivate support among the urban poor was undoubtedly abetted by the narratives and promises of the Marxist discourse. In particular, the poor's aspirations for a better life and their sense of a politically corrupt regime meshed well with the egalitarian motifs and concrete political critiques disseminated by the ICP. The Slugletts emphasized this, writing: "Of course, it would be wrong to suggest that the rural migrants had any profound understanding of the theories of Marxist/Leninism: the appeal of the Communist Party lay in its uncompromising calls for the overthrow of a regime that was self-evidently controlled by foreign strategic and economic interests, and for an end to the exploitation and poverty of which this particular constituency was only too well aware."[43] Considerable support for the ICP continued in urban areas well into the 1970s, especially in Baghdad. As noted above, the ICP's growing popularity with the urban poor and members of the lower middle classes aroused the concern of the Shi'i clerics, prompting them to respond as early as the late 1950s. Clerical attempts to offset the growing influence of the Communists were eased by two important developments. First, put simply, conditions continued to get worse for the urban poor, despite the distributive policies of the postrevolutionary regimes. Secondly, the ICP fared poorly in the repressive postrevolutionary period. In the wave of violence after the first Ba'th coup in 1963, for example, many Communist cadres were brutally extirpated. By the late 1970s, after a brief and conditional flourishing under the Progressive Patriotic National Front, the ICP was decimated. The Communists were forced to take up arms in the north of the country, alongside the Kurds. This process freed up considerable ideological space among the urban poor. This space was unlikely to be filled by the pan-Arab ideologies of Nasserism and Ba'thism: both of these orientations generated concern among the Shi'i that, in the event of Arab unity, they might be consumed by Sunnism. With the progressive narrowing of permissible political discourse in Iraq to one of the Ba'th worldview, Shi'ism was uniquely situated to help the urban poor make sense of their world.[44] The Shi'i narratives, mentioned above, provided the have-nots with an important way to structure their social and political grievances.

The Baghdad district of Madinat ath-Thawrah epitomized the political latency of the Shi'i movement. Madinat ath-Thawrah was one of the urban centerpieces of Qasem's development policies. Qasem sought to address Baghdad's growing slum problem. To this end, the clearing of slums and the construction of brick housing proceeded together. The newly created area was renamed Madinat ath-Thawrah (City of the Revolution).[45] The district of Madinat ath-Thawrah, understandably, was one of the main centers of resistance to the first Ba'th coup in 1963.[46] The constant pressures of urban migration taxed its capacities, and by the late 1970s the City of the Revolution was swelling uncontrollably. Living standards were appalling, especially when contrasted with the more affluent parts of the capital.[47] Within Madinat ath-Thawrah could be found some of Baghdad's most deplorable slums. The area provides a large proportion of the city's unskilled labor force. Inflation, incessant migration from the rural areas, the influx of foreign labor, and generally poor labor representation further eroded the living standards of the area's inhabitants throughout the 1970s. Once a solid center of support for the Communists, in the postrevolutionary period it evolved into a strong base of Shi'i support. Indeed, Madinat ath-Thawrah came to be identified as "the stronghold of heroes" in militant Shi'i literature.[48]

The potentially powerful social force created by this confluence of circumstances occasionally manifested itself throughout the 1970s. Shi'i processionals in 1974 and again in 1977 turned into political marches against the Ba'th regime. The potential momentum of a divinely inspired political movement seriously alarmed the Iraqi leadership. Events in Iran had established an unsettling historical precedent. In the aftermath of the Iranian revolution, further stirrings among the Shi'i community transpired. Iran, as already noted, was doing its part to agitate the Shi'i population. The Ba'th regime sensed that growing numbers of Shi'i were attracted to the Islamic cause. In the spring of 1980, Iraq's interior minister admitted: "The number of misguided supporters and religious sympathizers is considerable."[49] The clearest testimony to the regime's alarm was evident in its execution of Iraq's most learned Shi'i figure, Baqir as-Sadr, in the spring of 1980. The Ba'th regime (this, too, is discussed above) characterized the Shi'i threat in politically inclusive terms. It was not the regime that was under attack but rather the Arab nation. The Ba'th presented themselves as defenders of the Arab homeland against the "racist Persians." The main Shi'i organization, Da'wa, was linked to "official and unofficial Iranian circles."[50] Internal agitation was attributed to Iranian nationals. Khomeini was accused directly of inciting "Iranians living in Iraq."[51] The regime deported thousands of Iraqi citizens of Iranian origin who were accused of having connections to ad-Da'wa, even though many of these citizens were from families that had been living in Iraq for generations.

Had it been even for their inspirational effect alone, events in Iran would have been disconcerting to the Ba'th leadership. But the direct efforts by Iran to foment a Shi'i uprising were horrifying to the regime. It is difficult to assess the degree to which the potential Shi'i uprising was responsible for the decision to invade Iran in September 1980. Most commentators have accorded it considerable weight. Joseph Stork's observations are exemplary: "The difficulty of insulating Iraqis from the contagion of revolution and mass politics persuaded Baghdad to eliminate the threat at its source."[52] Whatever the merits of assigning strength to this motivation, the developing tensions between Iran and Iraq were undergirded by a third political dynamic: the politics of oil.

The Ba'th Regime and the Politics of Oil Revenues

It would be an oversimplification to contend that oil interests caused the war. Such a claim invariably invokes the image of the oil classes or a venal political elite pushing for war in order to advance their narrow interests. Nonetheless, the struggle of the Ba'th regime to secure oil revenues figures prominently in the outbreak of war. Throughout the 1970s, oil revenues had become critically important to the survival of the Ba'th regime, and it felt increasingly vulnerable to any long-term drop in oil income. This vulnerability was compounded by Iraq's limited capacity to export its abundant oil. In the late 1970s, Iraq had three ways to get the oil out. The first (less profitable) was through terminals off the Iraqi coastline in the Gulf. The second and third were pipelines through Syria and Turkey. This rendered the Ba'th regime vulnerable to international political conditions. Indeed, the flow of Iraqi oil via the Syrian pipeline was subject to numerous interruptions prior to the war. Iraq, therefore, shared many of the problems facing landlocked countries. Its growing reliance on oil revenues, along with this situational vulnerability, manifested itself in a regional policy designed to reduce the likelihood of hazardous shifts in oil policy and pricing. Iraq struggled to acquire as much influence as possible over regional oil production and pricing policies. The postrevolutionary turmoil in Iran, Iraq's long-time rival in the Gulf region, infected the Ba'th regime with the sense of opportunity. By further weakening its traditional Gulf rival, Iraq could enhance its regional stature. Regional paramountcy and enhanced stature in the Arab world would go a long way toward giving the Ba'th regime the necessary influence to guide regional oil policy (in OPEC decisionmaking bodies) in predictable and safe directions.

Two frequently identified aspects of the war—Hussein's quest for regional hegemony and the dispute over the Shatt al-Arab waterway—are related to the struggle to secure and stabilize oil revenues. The quest for regional paramountcy and the territorial disputes must be considered in terms of Iraq's growing vulnerability to downward trends in its oil income. The claim here is not that the struggle for regional hegemony or the dispute over the Shatt al-Arab can be entirely reduced to the Ba'th's efforts to secure and stabilize oil revenues: Simple territorial grabs do undoubtedly animate policymakers and political leaders from time to time. Nonetheless, there is a sense in which these efforts were instrumentally related to the efforts to secure and maximize oil revenues. The oil imperative rested upon two related sociopolitical dynamics. First, the oil wealth allowed the regime to contain subordinate social forces. Oil money clearly enhanced the regime's prospects for political control. Secondly, the infusion of oil wealth helped trigger the development of Iraq's capitalist class, a process that allowed the regime to carve out a small social base. By turning attention to the Ba'th struggle to secure oil revenues in terms of each of these sociopolitical dynamics, the examination of the social foundations of the slide to war between Iran and Iraq can be rounded out.

Oil and Political Control

With the nationalization of the Iraqi Petroleum Company and its subsidiaries in 1972, the Ba'th regime acquired control over an almost unlimited supply of oil revenues. For the Ba'th, the nationalization of the ICP could not have come at a more propitious time. The huge rise in oil prices following the Arab-Israeli war in 1973 resulted in an equally huge rise in Iraq's oil revenues. Between 1972 and the outbreak of the war with Iran in 1980, the rise in Iraq's oil revenues far outstripped increases in production. Over the eight years prior to war, production did rise, to nearly double what it had been—growing from 72.1 million metric tons to 130.2 million metric tons. But oil revenues increased by more than 4,000 percent. By 1980, oil revenues had reached a staggering U.S. $26.5 billion, compared with $575 million in 1972.[53] The almost unlimited supply of oil revenues after 1973 created a wide array of options for the regime in its dealings with subordinate social classes and potentially explosive issues. A few examples adequately illustrate this fact:

1. The regime could grant periodic wage increases, allowing it to avoid direct confrontations both with state workers and the laboring classes. This was invaluable in an atmosphere in which labor was not allowed to organize freely.
2. A campaign of mosque constructions and generous grants to the Shi'i clerics in the late 1970s was similarly designed to ward off dangerous confrontations.
3. The absorption of surplus labor into the inefficient public sector of the Iraqi state was partly designed to avoid explosive social confrontations, minimizing urban pockets of bitterness and frustration. The state also acted as employer-of-last-resort for university graduates. By the end of the 1970s, the Iraqi state (excluding the armed forces) was by far the largest individual employer in the economy.[54]
4. The state distributed tens of thousands of television sets and cash donations to Kurdish families that had been forcibly resettled.[55]

These cooptive strategies were utterly dependent upon oil money. The use of oil money to thwart social unrest and coopt political opposition operated in lieu of genuine democratic exchange and political dialogue. The oil money allowed the regime to contain subordinate classes and groups, at least to some extent, by selectively responding to their demands. The Ba'th regime, in a sense, floated on the price of a barrel of oil.

If these cooptive strategies failed, the Ba'th could fall back upon the repressive apparatus of the state. Oil money had facilitated the expansion of the policing apparatus. By 1980, the repressive apparatus employed about one-fifth of the economically active labor force in Iraq. This extraordinary peacetime size of the security apparatus was considerably eased by the oil income. The political function served by the large policing apparatus was invaluable to the regime. Samir al-Khalil, whose *Republic of Fear* is devoted to assessing the effects of the policing apparatus, offers the following sobering assessment of the Iraqi police state:

> Authority used to be the butt of popular jokes, anecdotes, and satirical poems, cultural safety valves that provided relief from the traditional oppressiveness of the state. But all that is gone now. No one dare ridicule authority any longer in Iraq because everyone is afraid. The tone of political culture has become Kafkaesque: saturated with a sense of the impersonality of sinister and impenetrable forces, operating on helpless individuals, who nonetheless intuit that they are being buffeted about by a bizarre, almost transcendental kind of rationality.[56]

By the eve of war, the regime had managed to atomize much of its population through fear. Political life beyond the state was limited to the underground movements, whose aim generally was to destroy the regime. From the perspective of political autonomy, the Ba'th regime was a facsimile of the Bonapartist state. Ba'thi autonomy, however, was not created through the offsetting effects of countervailing social forces as it was in postrevolutionary France. Rather, the extreme wealth available to the Ba'th regime, especially after 1974, gave it powerful leverages that momentarily insulated it from the tug of Iraq's dissenting political spectrum. Society was temporarily captive of the Ba'th and its aspirations.

Oil Revenues and the Ba'th's Social Base

The second motive behind the regime's determination to secure oil money allowed the Ba'th to begin carving out a genuine social base of its own. As mentioned above, Baghdad's oil-fed development strategies contributed to the growth of an indigenous capitalist class. In order to understand this dynamic, we must briefly trace the nature of Ba'th "socialism" in the context of postrevolutionary development policies. Ba'thi economic policy revealed a continuity with Iraq's postrevolutionary regimes in that it expanded the indigenous bourgeoisie. Between 1958 and 1968, Iraq's private sector continued to expand. In the manufacturing sector, for example, private capital made considerable headway. Both smaller enterprises (those with less than ten workers) and larger firms flourished. The redistributive policies characteristic of the republican regimes tended to create lucrative opportunities for private capital. In short, although the Iraqi state became involved in the economy to a much greater degree in the post-1958 period, this involvement did not come at the expense of the private accumulation of capital.[57]

After its accession in 1968, the Ba'th trumpeted what it called a "revolutionary" economic and social program. It repeatedly boasted of being vigilantly anti-imperialist and stridently socialist. Section 2 of the Arab Ba'th Socialist Party's *Political Report* for 1974, for example, was entitled "Transformations on the Road to Socialism." The U.S. sense of the socialist character of Iraq, especially in the face of Iraq's comfortable relationship with the Soviet Union, figured prominently in U.S. decisions to destabilize the regime (by supporting the Kurds) in the early 1970s. The socialist rhetoric of the regime and the growing involvement of the state in the Iraqi economy managed to convince some scholars of the regime's socialist thrust. A study published by the Middle East Institute in 1978 stated:

> Following the Revolution of 1968, when the country was spared changes of regimes and rulers, grandiose schemes of development were initiated which marked a significant departure from the social and economic policies of previous regimes. Not only did the new rulers seek to transform the economic system from free enterprise to collectivism, but also to achieve the country's economic independence without which political independence cannot be long sustained. . . . Only after 1968, when the political system became fairly stabilized, did the government lay down a consistent policy correlating political, economic and social affairs and take steps to carry them out. The immediate objective of this policy was to increase production and raise the standard of living, but the ultimate objective was to establish a socialist society in which all injustices would be wiped out and all citizens enjoy the benefits of progress and prosperity.[58]

Other commentators subscribed to similar characterizations of the Ba'th. "Increasingly," Phebe Marr wrote in 1985, describing the post-1958 regimes, "they favoured socialism over laissez-faire economics and emphasized greater benefits to the lower classes."[59]

There is strong evidence to suggest that the socialist boasts of the regime were entirely contradicted by its practice. As the Slugletts maintained: "In spite of any appearances to the contrary, the Ba'th, like its predecessors, was not committed to 'building socialism' or to the radical transformation of existing relations of production, but to maintaining and sustaining the existing capitalist economic order."[60] These observations have been echoed by other writers: "The Ba'th ideology and slogans," stresses 'Isam al-Khafaji, "are an extreme expression of a political movement's efforts to give leftist form to a fundamentally rightist content."[61] The post-1968 period has been accompanied by the continual expansion of Iraq's capitalist class. This has been acknowledged by the Ba'th leadership itself. In 1983, for example, as he encouraged members of the contracting bourgeoisie to donate more money to the war effort, Saddam Hussein told of how the revolution had made millionaires out of barefoot men. Said Hussein:

> You know that there was only a handful of contractors before the revolution. . . . Now, this contractor owns not thousands [of Iraqi dinars] but millions. . . . I was informed that he had donated only a pittance. He did not ask himself: "Where did I get this fortune? Isn't it thanks to these new circumstances?"[62]

Even a much looser notion of socialism, as in the sense of a regime tending to side with workers and wage earners, is inappropriate for the Iraqi Ba'th. The regime offered its workers no opportunity to organize independently, and strikes were strictly forbidden; and low productivity in Iraq's manufacturing and service sectors in the mid-1970s was responded to with increased worker surveillance and discipline. Wage increases were directly tied to increases in productivity.[63]

In stark contrast to its professions, the Ba'th regime has cradled capitalist development since its accession to power in 1968. Through infrastructure work and megadevelopment projects, the state became the main generator of private wealth in the country. Although the Ba'thi state played an increasingly important role in the domestic economy, it was never at the expense of private capital. These trends accelerated after the massive influx of oil revenues toward the mid-1970s. This relationship between the Ba'thi state and the expansion of private capital was most visible with respect to the growth of the contracting bourgeoisie. Soaring investment expenditure by the state throughout the 1970s was paid out mainly to private contractors. By 1975, there were 2,788 contractors officially registered with the state; this compared with only 829 contractors in 1970/71. Between 1975 and 1981, the annual growth rate for the construction sector was 29 percent. By 1981, the construction sector accounted for 17 percent of the GDP, compared with 4 percent in 1975. Some of the large contractors have amassed huge fortunes. Elements of this class branched out into the industrial sector of the economy. Strong personal connections to the regime played an important role in the growing success of many of the contractors. The fact that many members of this class originated from relatively humble backgrounds testifies to the scale of capital accumulation in Iraq. This fraction of the bourgeoisie was thoroughly dependent upon the state, fully relying upon the state-sponsored development projects to advance its interests, and frequently receiving substantial concessions from the state through its generous tax and labor laws.

The industrial faction of the capitalist class also fared very well during the 1970s. As can be seen in Table 4.1, the private industrial sector continued to thrive alongside the public sector. The number of large industrial establishments owned by the state increased by 81 between 1973 and 1977; the number of private industrial establishments increased by 192. After the oil boom, there was a large increase in the number of small industrial establishments—a rise of 13,000 between 1974 and 1975. Between 1970 and 1975, the Industrial Bank's credits and loans totaled a little over 10 million ID (Iraqi dinars). In the next two years alone, credits and loans totaled more than 22 million ID. In some cases the contributions of the regime obviated the need for the private sector to front any capital of its own. One writer revealed: "The Industrial bank was committed to granting loans of up to 80% of the total cost of construction projects, while loans for other projects were given up to 40% of cost in the three central provinces and of up to 50–60% of cost in the other provinces. In other words, the industrialist had only to inflate the cost of his project (a device regularly resorted to) in order to obtain a loan which would cover the total cost."[64]

Table 4.1   Growth in Number of Industrial Establishments in Iraq

| Year | Large Establishments (employing more than ten workers) | | Small Establishments |
	Publicly Owned	Privately Owned	
1973	185	1090	26,377
1974	198	1043	26,332
1975	204	1145	39,275
1976	225	1254	37,669
1977	266	1282	41,719

Source: Annual Abstract of Statistics, Ministry of Planning, Republic of Iraq, 1978.

Despite the rhetorical posture of the Ba'th regime, therefore, it is clear that the capitalist class in Iraq was flourishing. The regime went far beyond merely creating the conditions for the expansion of Iraqi capitalism (for example, by establishing an industrial infrastructure). The state became the lifeline for a parasitic fraction of the Iraqi bourgeoisie—contractors, brokers, upper-level bureaucrats, and speculators.[65] The degree to which this fraction relied on the state is evident in the following excerpt from a memo sent by a member of the planning council to the Iraqi president in 1977:

What does the contractor need? He needs the capital, which he obtains from the state; the machinery, which he also obtains from the state; the raw materials, which are supplied by the state at subsidized prices; and technical expertise, which is available by depleting the state sector of its technicians. When all these facilities are made available to him, he has nothing left but to open an elegant office; and even this may not be necessary.[66]

State-sponsored development created important new fractions among Iraq's capitalist class during the 1970s. Their interests demanded that state coffers be constantly replenished by oil revenues so that they could be used for "development." The capitalist class was understandably "developing a vested interest in the maintenance of the system."[67] The complement to this was that part of the bourgeoisie was forming an important social base for the regime. The Ba'th elite, sensitive to potential constellations of support, was thus provided with an additional motive to pursue its economic policies.

Ba'th interests in nursing the nascent capitalist class (along, of course, with the other political benefits of oil money) created a powerful incentive to secure and stabilize oil revenues. A regime disposed toward enhancing its international influence for political gain was destined to sense the opportunity created by Iran's postrevolutionary turmoil, especially the widely reported disarray within the regular military. The Ba'th Party organ, *ath-Thawrah,* had spoken disparagingly of "ragged" Iranian forces.[68] Social unrest and uprisings among Iran's ethnic minorities added to the image of revolutionary fragility. The Iraqi regime, in effect, tasted blood. Attacking the pariah Islamic state was an extremely safe and potentially rewarding move in international political terms. Iraq, in short, was presented with a golden opportunity to decapitate the revolution for extensive political gain.[69]

It is in this sense that the developing security problems between Iran and Iraq were bound up with inter alia the Ba'th struggle to stabilize oil revenues. The Iranian revolution created a unique opportunity for Iraq. It was certainly not "natural" or "inevitable" that Iraq would capitalize on the momentary disarray in Iran. No inexorable imperative inspired the Ba'th regime to fill the regional power vacuum in the Gulf region. Had the oil imperative been absent in Iraq, the turbulence of postrevolutionary Iran might have gone unnoticed; at least it would not have evoked a significant response. But the importance of oil revenues, combined with Iranian efforts to foment a Shi'i revolution, proved to be too compelling. By the spring of 1980, the slide to war appeared to be irreversible. On 22 September, amidst mounting tensions, Iraqi forces launched a full-scale invasion of Iran.

Eight Years of War

In the years leading to war, the growing conflict between revolutionary Iran and Iraq was, as we have seen, undergirded by three distinguishable political dynamics: the efforts by Iran to incite a Shi'i uprising in Iraq; the alarm created by the potential Shi'i rebellion for the Ba'th regime; and the Ba'th struggle to secure and stabilize oil revenues. Each of these political dynamics was closely related to the transformed social fields in both countries. Iran's aggressive policy was linked to the struggle among contending social forces in the aftermath of the February insurrection—forces that had been tailored profoundly by the Pahlavi modernization drives. Theocratic-populism entered into this struggle and played an important role in the ascendency of the ulama. Theocratic-populism, moreover, cradled an aggressive campaign targeted at the Shi'i population in Iraq. The Ba'th regime was seriously alarmed by this prospect. The potential Shi'i uprising in Iraq, however, was itself linked to the social evolution of Iraq's clerical class and the Shi'i masses, an evolutionary trajectory taking place within a society thoroughly transformed as the region was inserted into the global economy. The Ba'th regime, moreover, was tenuously poised above an alienated and increasingly fractionated society, and was determined to secure its oil revenues in order to contain Iraq's authentic social forces and cultivate its growing capitalist base.

Ultimately, the Ba'th regime was sufficiently motivated to attack Iran. In examining the social foundations of the developing security problems between Iran and Iraq, and by demonstrating that these dynamics were in turn rooted in the evolutionary socioeconomic path of both countries, we have uncovered the social origins of the Iran-Iraq War. These origins *caused* the war in the sense that they laid its foundations: they nourished the hostilities that led to war. The emerging conflict between the two regimes still had to be mediated through leading political figures. The etiological program of war, I submit, is necessarily subjectivized and contingent. The personalities within the decisionmaking coteries of Iran and Iraq, especially Saddam Hussein and Ayatollah Khomeini, were certainly immediately relevant to the outbreak of war. The war was never inevitable, just increasingly likely.

According to all indications, Saddam Hussein expected the war to be short. As it dragged on through the 1980s, it was clear that he had miscalculated grossly: it would take almost eight years for the belligerents to accept a ceasefire. Despite the immense costs of the war, however, the theocrats in Tehran and the Ba'th regime in Baghdad came out on top. Both regimes, that is, consolidated their political control over rival contenders and subordinate social forces. The emancipatory struggles of subordinate social groups (of primary concern in the critical study of war and peace) relapsed over the course of the war. These social and political dynamics help to account for its near-decade length. We now turn to a discussion of these dynamics as they pertain to each country.

Notes

1. For a detailed account of the message conveyed by Iraq to the provisional government in Iran, see *Iraqi News Agency,* 13 February 1979, *FBIS (Foreign Broadcast Information Service): Daily Reports,* 14 February 1979.
2. Beirut, *An-Nahar,* 1 October 1979, *FBIS: Daily Reports,* 4 October 1979.
3. Iraq, for example, figured front and center in a discussion of Iran's security problems by Iranian president Abolhasan Bani-Sadr in May 1980. Tehran Domestic Radio Service, 5 May 1980, *FBIS: Daily Reports,* 6 May 1980.
4. Tehran Domestic Radio Service, 15 October 1979, *FBIS: Daily Reports,* 16 October 1979.
5. *Ath-Thawrah,* 12–14 June 1979, *FBIS: Daily Reports,* 14, 15 June 1979.
6. Baghdad Voice of the Masses, 4 September 1980, *FBIS: Daily Reports,* 5 September 1980. My emphasis.
7. Tehran Domestic Radio Service, 26 August 1980, *FBIS: Daily Reports,* 27 August 1980. My emphasis.
8. Speech to National Assembly, 17 September 1980, *FBIS: Daily Reports,* 18 September 1980.
9. Iraqi News Agency, *FBIS: Daily Reports,* 28 May 1980.
10. Tehran International Radio Service, 26 February 1980, *FBIS: Daily Reports,* 26 February 1980.
11. Some writers have identified as many as five ideological currents, adding the nationalist and monarchist trends. See Eric Hooglund, "Iran in the 1980s," in *The Iranian Revolution and the Islamic Republic,* eds. Nikki R. Keddie and Eric Hooglund, (Syracuse University Press, 1986), pp. 17–20.
12. For a detailed survey of the forces on the Iranian left at the outset of the postrevolutionary period, see *MERIP Reports,* 86, (March–April 1980).
13. From *FBIS: Daily Reports,* 12 March 1979.
14. One of the clearest discussions of this period of revolutionary Iran may be found in Shaul Bakhash, *The Reign of the Ayatollahs: Iran and the Islamic Revolution,* (Basic Books, 1984), pp. 52–91. Detailed accounts of this period may also be found in *Middle East Contemporary Survey,* v. 3 (1978–1979), pp. 514–527, and v. 4, (1979–1980), pp. 438–456.
15. Hossein Bashiriyeh's discussion on the inability of the PRG to address "the social question" provides an interesting analysis of the declining influence of the liberals in the immediate aftermath of the revolution. See *The State and Revolution in Iran: 1962–1982,* (St. Martin's Press, 1984), pp. 139–149.
16. For a discussion on theocratic populism in Iran, see Kambiz Afrachteh, "The Predominance and Dilemmas of Theocratic Populism in Contemporary Iran," in *Iranian Studies* 14:3–4 (summer–autumn 1981).
17. Tehran Domestic Radio Service, 1 March 1979, *FBIS: Daily Reports,* 5 March 1979.
18. Tehran Domestic Radio Service, 1 April 1979, *FBIS: Daily Reports,* 2 April 1979.
19. Tehran Domestic Radio Service, 22 August 1979, *FBIS: Daily Reports,* 23 August 1979.
20. Tehran Domestic Radio Service, 28 April 1979, *FBIS: Daily Reports,* 30 April 1979.

21. Tehran Domestic Radio Service, 19 April 1979, *FBIS: Daily Reports*, 20 April 1979.

22. Tehran Domestic Radio Service, 28 February 1979, *FBIS: Daily Reports*, 1 March 1979.

23. Tehran Domestic Radio Service, 1 March 1979, *FBIS: Daily Reports*, 5 March 1979.

24. Tehran Domestic Radio Service, 19 May 1979, *FBIS: Daily Reports*, 21 May 1979.

25. Tehran Domestic Radio Service, 10 May 1979, *FBIS: Daily Reports*, 14 May 1979.

26. Tehran Domestic Radio Service, 30 October 1979, *FBIS: Daily Reports*, 1 November 1979.

27. Tehran Domestic Radio Service, 13 June 1980, *FBIS: Daily Reports*, 16 June 1980.

28. Address by Khomeini to national mobilization representatives, Tehran International Radio Service, 17 April 1980, *FBIS: Daily Reports*, 18 April 1980.

29. Tehran Domestic Radio Service, 22 April 1980, *FBIS: Daily Reports*, 23 April 1980.

30. Tehran Domestic Radio Service, 6 April 1980, *FBIS: Daily Reports*, 7 April 1980.

31. Tehran International Radio Service, 10 March 1980, *FBIS: Daily Reports*, 11 March 1980.

32. *Middle East Contemporary Survey,* 4 (1979–1980), pp. 514–515.

33. As Bernard Lewis writes: "These [futuh] were not seen as conquests in the vulgar sense of territorial acquisitions, but as the overthrow of impious regimes and illegitimate hierarchies, and the 'opening' of their people to the new revelation and dispensation. The notion of a superseded old order is vividly expressed in the invocation of an ultimatum said to have been sent by one of the Muslim Arab commanders to the princes of Persia: 'Praise be to God who has dissolved your order, frustrated your evil designs and sundered your unity.'" From *The Political Language of Islam,* (University of Chicago Press, 1988), p. 93.

34. The characterization of the Shi'i opposition as a religious conflict between the Sunni and the Shi'i has been critically assessed in P. Sluglett and M. Farouk-Sluglett, "Some Reflections on the Sunni/Shi'i Question in Iraq," *Bulletin of the British Society for Middle Eastern Studies,* 5, (1978), pp. 79–81.

35. The following discussion primarily draws upon two excellent discussions of the Shi'i population and struggle in Iraq: Marion Farouk-Sluglett and Peter Sluglett, *Iraq Since 1958: From Revolution to Dictatorship,* (I. B. Tauris and Co., 1990), especially pp. 190–200; Hanna Batatu, "Iraq's Underground Shi'a Movements: Characteristics, Causes and Prospects," in *Middle East Journal,* 35, (1981). Statistics drawn from Batatu.

36. Batatu, "Iraq's Underground," in *Journal,* op. cit., 35, p. 586.

37. Sluglett and Sluglett, "Some Reflections," in *Bulletin,* op. cit., 5, p. 87.

38. See discussion in Ofra Bengio, "Shi'is and Politics in Ba'thi Iraq," in *Middle Eastern Studies,* 21:1, (January 1985). Quote from p. 2.

39. Michael C. Hudson, "The Islamic Factor in Syrian and Iraqi Politics," in *Islam and the Political Process,* ed. James Piscatori, (Cambridge, 1983), p. 87.

40. See the discussion in Hanna Batatu, *The Old Social Classes and the Revolutionary Movements of Iraq,* pp. 41–42.

41. Batatu, "Iraq's Underground," in *Journal,* op. cit., 35, p. 585.

42. Sluglett and Sluglett, *Iraq Since 1958,* op. cit., pp. 190–191.

43. Ibid., p. 193.

44. Samir al-Khalil has described the narrowing of political discourse in Iraq rather aptly as the "end of politics." See *Republic of Fear: The Politics of Modern Iraq,* (University of California Press, 1989), pp. 235–236.

45. See the discussion in Phebe Marr, *The Modern History of Iraq,* (Westview Press, 1985), pp. 169–170.

46. See discussion in Samir al-Khalil, *Republic of Fear,* op. cit., pp. 58–59.

47. Ibid. See figures, pp. 283–284.

48. See discussion in Batatu, "Iraq's Underground," in *Journal,* op. cit., 35.

49. *FBIS: Daily Reports,* 16 May 1980.

50. *FBIS: Daily Reports,* 10 April 1980.

51. *FBIS: Daily Reports,* 21 April 1980.

52. Joseph Stork, "Class, State and Politics in Iraq," in *Power and Stability in the Middle East,* ed. Berch Berberoglu, (Zed Books, 1989), p. 51.

53. Celine Whittleton, "Oil and the Iraqi Economy," in *Saddam's Iraq: Revolution or Reaction?* ed. CARDRI, (Zed Books, 1985).

54. See discussion in Joseph Stork, "State Power and Economic Structure: Class Determination and State Formation in Contemporary Iraq," in *Iraq: The Contemporary State,* ed. Tim Niblock, (Croom Helm, 1982), p. 38.

55. See discussion in *Middle East Contemporary Survey,* 3, (1978–1979), p. 569.

56. See discussion in al-Khalil, *Republic of Fear,* op. cit., Chapter 1. Quote from p. 45; figure on employment from p. 38.

57. It is in view of these processes that Hanna Batatu's claim (in *The Old Social Classes,* op. cit.) that the social power of private property was uprooted by the revolutionary regimes must be heavily qualified. See also discussion in Hanna Batatu, "State and Capitalism in Iraq," in *MERIP Middle East Report,* 16:2, (Sept.–Oct. 1986).

58. Majid Khadduri, *Socialist Iraq: A Study in Iraqi Politics Since 1968,* (Middle East Institute, 1978), pp. 111–112.

59. Phebe Marr, *Modern History,* op. cit., p. 247.

60. This is the main contention of the conceptual chapter of Sluglett and Sluglett, *Iraq Since 1958,* op. cit. They stress that the growth of the public sector of Iraq's economy has been easily matched by the growth of the private sector and the clear development of a moneyed class in Iraq. Quote from p. 228.

61. The following discussion, including statistics on the growth and nature of the parasitic bourgeoisie, is indebted to 'Isam al-Khafaji, "The Parasitic Base of the Ba'thist Regime," in *Saddam's Iraq: Revolution or Reaction?* ed. CARDRI, (Zed Books, 1989). Quote from p. 85.

62. Quoted in 'Isam al-Khafaji, "State Incubation of Iraqi Capitalism," in *MERIP,* 16:5, op. cit., p. 4.

63. See the discussion in Joseph Stork, "State Power," in *Iraq,* op. cit., p. 43.

64. Discussion indebted to 'Isam al-Khafaji, "The Parasitic Base," in *Saddam's Iraq,* op. cit. Quote from p. 78; figures extracted from pp. 74–77.

65. Ibid. This is one of al-Khafaji's main contentions.

66. 'Isam al-Khafaji, "State Incubation," in *MERIP,* 16:5, op. cit., p. 6.

67. Sluglett and Sluglett, *Iraq Since 1958,* op. cit., p. 250.

68. *FBIS: Daily Reports,* 14 April 1980.

69. Iraq's net opportunity has been straightforwardly summarized by al-Khafaji: "If the Iraqi regime could exert a dominant role in the region it would then be able to insure its control over all decisions of OPEC. . . ." See al-Khafaji, "The Parasitic Base," in *Saddam's Iraq,* op. cit., p. 86.

Part II
THE SOCIAL FOUNDATIONS OF THE PROTRACTED WAR

5

The War and Clerical Consolidation in Iran

The Islamic Revolution arose as the social forces carved out by the Pahlavi modernization drives struggled to achieve their goals. For the modern middle class, this largely meant attaining an acceptable level of democratization within the political system; for the embattled traditional middle class, it meant trying to reverse the economic and social trends of twentieth-century Iran. Both forces were joined by millions of Iranians, especially the urban poor, who had been economically and politically marginalized by the shah's development policies. The revolutionary opposition united in the face of a common adversary despite their divergent political orientations. With the fall of the shah, however, the cohesiveness of the revolutionary opposition quickly dissolved. The ulama had gained the upper hand by virtue of their control of the state apparatus and the revolutionary institutions. The postrevolutionary struggle to control the direction of the new republic now intensified.

This struggle lay at the heart of the aggressive foreign policy of the new Iranian government, especially its truculent campaign against the Ba'th regime in Iraq. Ultimately, the Ba'th regime, itself hovering precariously over a deepening social crisis, was sufficiently motivated to attack the Islamic state. The Iran-Iraq War was rooted in the sociopolitical turmoil of both Gulf states. It began as a war of societies in crisis. And so the war would continue for almost eight years. As surely as the war's outbreak bore the imprint of the evolving social fields in Iran and Iraq, so was its continuation also propelled by them.

In Iran, the war directly entered into the continuing postrevolutionary struggle. It was prolonged because it contributed to the extension of the radical clerics' hegemony: the war assisted the ulama in their bid for total control of the revolution. A number of related dynamics linked the war to this consolidation of clerical power. First, it intensified the conflict between Bani-Sadr and the clergy, and hastened a resolution in favor of the

117

latter. Second, the war lent itself perfectly to the populist strategy of the ulama. Third, it provided a blanketlike pretext for the containment and elimination of remaining opposition to the clergy. Fourth, the war created an opportunity for the growth and extension of revolutionary organizations. And lastly, it provided the clergy with a permanent excuse as to why the revolution had failed to deliver on its promises to Iran's destitute masses. Ultimately, the war proved to be so valuable that the clerics refused seriously to entertain efforts to end it. Consolidation of radical clerical power allowed the clergy to implement their political and social agenda with minimal opposition—a process that had far-reaching consequences for Iran's disempowered social groups, especially its working classes, the ethnic minorities, and Iranian women.

The Ulama Find a Blessing in War

The process of revolutionary consolidation by the ulama encountered determined resistance from the center of Iran's political spectrum (that is, from its liberal factions, which included the National Front and the Freedom Movement) and from the left (especially the Mujahedin Khalq).[1] Each element of the revolutionary opposition held a different interpretation of the collapse of the monarchy; and each subscribed to a different agenda regarding Iran's revolutionary future. The center, undergirded by the modern middle class, tended to view the revolution as a straightforward political change, usually characterized in terms of the replacement of the repressive monarchy with an open, democratic system; accordingly, they emphasized the nationalistic character of the revolutionary opposition, not its religious nature. On the left, both secular and religious forces tended to view the revolution as a necessary, or at least unavoidable, step in the creation of a truly egalitarian, classless society. Cautious support for the radical ulama by the left was forthcoming only because the clerics adopted stridently antiimperialist stances: the left, especially the Tudeh Party, believed that a strong revolutionary front had to be maintained in the face of counterrevolutionary forces. Both the center and the left clashed sharply with the clerical view of the revolution, which emphasized the upheaval's organic Islamic temper and aspired fully to Islamicize Iran's social and political fabric.[2]

The ulama recognized the difficulty of sustaining popular support in the face of mounting criticism from antagonist elements. The growing conflict between the liberal-center and the radical ulama manifested itself in several ways: in Bazargan's Provisional Revolutionary Government (PRG), in the referendum on the nature of the new Iranian republic, in the debate over Iran's new constitution, and in the work of the Council of Experts. The resignation of Bazargan in the aftermath of the hostage affair signaled an important victory for the radical clerics over liberal forces. The ulama prevailed by virtue of their close contact with the revolutionary institutions, and by the continuing importance of the mosque network and the untainted figure of Ayatollah Khomeini. Perhaps most fundamentally, clerical ascendency was nurtured by the rhetorical pale they erected. This sustained revolutionary fervor and kept the population mobilized against perceived counterrevolutionary elements.

With the ousting of the shah, the ulama were acutely aware of the potential for a decline in revolutionary momentum. To the delight of the clergy, the prolonged U.S. hostage crisis had obvious ramifications for mobilization.[3] During the escalation of the conflict with Iraq, it was evident that some ulama viewed the potential for war in similar terms.[4] Indeed, some of the clergy preferred to see the hostilities intensified.[5] Their rudimentary calculus was presciently summarized by Ervand Abrahamian well before the Iraqi invasion. He wrote: "The clergy are unlikely to find another public enemy as unpopular as the shah against whom they can rally the whole population—unless, of course, a foreign enemy invades the country and threatens the existence of the entire nation."[6] Enter Iraq! The possibility that an Iraqi invasion could work in favor of the theocrats, a possibility recognized by some ulama and scholarly commentators, did not appear to have influenced Saddam Hussein's thinking: "Ignorant of the history of revolutions, Saddam and his allies failed to understand that external aggression has often contributed to the consolidation of revolutions as it did in the Russian and French revolutions."[7]

There are a number of reasons to suppose that a military attack might have been debilitating for the theocrats. Regular reports were emerging that Iran's postrevolutionary conflict had left its military in a shambles, and the fighting prowess of the revolutionary bodies was at best an unknown quantity. Saddam Hussein might at least have banked upon the passive support of the Arab population of Khuzistan, and strongly have expected the war to rekindle opposition from other ethnic minorities in Iran, especially the Kurds. But in keeping with historical precedent, the radical clergy proved adept at exploiting the war in order to extend their political hegemony. The Ba'th invasion provided the ulama with Iran's axiomatic common enemy. Xenophobic themes were fully enlisted to arouse popular sentiments. The war was presented as nothing less than a war against the "Great Satan" incarnate. The regime extolled Iraq as the embodiment of all that was antithetical to Islam. The defense of Islam, by political implication, became the defense of the theocratic regime. Over time, with its mobilizational potential fully exploited, the war was widely recognized as a "blessing" for the theocrats. "War, war until victory" became the hardened battle cry of the clergy.

The War and Bani-Sadr's Decline

The relationship between the war and the process of clerical consolidation was multifaceted. In the initial months of the war, this relationship intensified the conflict between the liberals and the radical clerics. Although the continuing decline of the liberals was the political corollary of clerical ascendency in Iran, the war offered the liberals a chance to arrest their slide. At the time of the Iraqi invasion, the political battle between the radical clergy and the liberals manifested itself in a struggle between the newly elected Iranian president, Abolhasson Bani-Sadr, and clerical figures who were strategically located throughout the organs of government. Bani-Sadr had first appeared in the company of the revolutionary opposition as Khomeini's adviser in Paris, during the fading days of the monarchy. Although he was an extremely religious man (his father was an ayatollah and close associate of Khomeini), his political views contrasted sharply with those of the radical clerics. Bani-Sadr emphasized the democratic nature of the new state. His support for personal rights and freedoms gave him political affinity more with the liberal camp than the radicals. Khomeini, in his ongoing effort to appear to be aloof from the postrevolutionary struggle, endorsed Bani-Sadr's bid for the presidency, and in January 1980, Bani-Sadr garnered more than 75 percent of the popular vote. It was a resounding electoral victory.

It was clear that Bani-Sadr attached considerable importance to the presidential office. But he lacked an independent power base. De facto political control was increasingly in the hands of the radical ulama, especially through their command of the revolutionary institutions. Subsequent elections to the Majlis, moreover, gave the Islamic Republican Party (IRP) political control within the official state apparatus, which had the effect of reproducing the broader conflict between Bani-Sadr and the radical ulama within the republic's formal institutions. In accordance with his liberaltechnocratic approach to governance, Bani-Sadr sought significantly to reduce the influence of the clergy and, perhaps fatally, to subordinate the revolutionary institutions to the executive/legislative apparatus.[8] A conflict arose between the IRP and Bani-Sadr over the right to nominate the prime minister. Bani-Sadr's first three nominations were rejected by the IRP and the president was forced to capitulate—the prime minister's office going to Rajai. Bani-Sadr publicly voiced reservations about the latter's administrative competency. Subsequent struggles over the composition of the cabinet (where the president exercised veto power) continued to reveal the growing strains between Bani-Sadr and the IRP. A frustrated Bani-Sadr ventured to attack the IRP publicly, declaring that they were trying to monopolize the revolution and exercise "despotic" control over the government.

The conflict between Bani-Sadr and the ulama momentarily subsided in the face of the Iraqi invasion. The president's public profile was greatly enhanced through his role as commander in chief of Iran's forces. As Shaul Bakhash documented it:

> The front provided an escape from the frictions and frustrations, from "that poisoned atmosphere and those barren conflicts," of the capital. It allowed Bani-Sadr to give priority to the war effort. . . . It also made for excellent public relations. Newspaper photographs often depicted the president in army fatigues, peering down gunsights, sharing a humble tray of rice with the troops, or touring the battle zone from the rumble seat of a motorcycle, his arms wrapped tightly around the waist of the driver and, except for a bristling black mustache, his face lost beneath a fierce-looking pith helmet.[9]

These initial benefits, however, could not be turned into permanent gains for the president. "For Bani-Sadr," wrote Robin Wright, "the war was almost a blessing."[10] But, on the whole, the war intensified the conflicts between the two sides, and ultimately the "blessing" was for the radicals. The war hastened the removal of Bani-Sadr.[11] Members of the Majlis and the president engaged in a battle for authority over the war effort, and the dispute was at least partially responsible for the fact that while Bani-Sadr was in power Iran failed to present its case in UN deliberations on the war.[12] In his capacity as supreme commander of the armed forces, Bani-Sadr began spending most of his time at the front. He believed from the outset that the bulk of the war should be prosecuted by the military (rather than the Revolutionary Guards) and that appropriate military training should be the primary consideration. As time passed, Bani-Sadr spent increasing amounts of time with the military (even moving to Khuzestan), and suspicion grew among the ulama that he was cultivating an independent base of support for his broader political cause. From the perspective of the ulama, the military—their loyalty uproven—was perceived as a possible threat. Thus, as their main political rival forged stronger ties with the armed forces, this fear was compounded. Clerical suspicions were well-summarized by Eric Rouleau: "Some IRP leaders are wondering why Bani-Sadr is 'assiduously courting' the military, why he is spending most of his time at the armed forces headquarters, why he is making constant tours of the various fronts and the officers' mess, and why he has nothing but extravagant praise for the army. The head of state, they concede, is commander-in-chief of the armed forces, but does he have nothing else to do?"[13] The conflict became overtly public with the publication of Bani-Sadr's letter to Khomeini in which he accused the cabinet of "running the army" and of "putting obstacles in the path of the Commander-in-Chief in the middle of a raging war." Ultimately, Bani-Sadr claimed that the cabinet was "more disastrous than the war" and urged their dismissal.[14]

The ulama, however, proved capable of using the war to politically neutralize Bani-Sadr. State radio and television, controlled by IRP support-ers, tended to focus on the achievements of the Revolutionary Guards at the expense of the military and Bani-Sadr. IRP leaders repeatedly voiced strong criticism of the president's handling of the war. Bani-Sadr undoubt-edly felt pressured to launch Iran's first counteroffensive against Iraq pre-maturely, and when it failed, early in 1981, new fodder was added to the clerical cause. The president's absence from Tehran, furthermore, provided the mullahs with unique opportunities to drive wedges between Khomeini and Bani-Sadr.[15] Bani-Sadr fought back against the clerical onslaught. One of his most frequently employed tools was his newspaper column, "The President's Diary." In the column—which was published regularly—Bani-Sadr tackled subjects as diverse as his war plans and Erich Fromm.[16] The president also attacked the ulama in public speeches. The growing con-frontation prompted Khomeini to urge both parties to bury their differences in the overall interests of the revolution.

The beginning of the end for Bani-Sadr can be traced to his public address on 5 March 1981. The occasion turned into a clash between sup-porters of the president and supporters of the IRP. Bani-Sadr's vitriolic attack on the radical ulama was greeted with an equally virulent response. Opposition groups, still stinging from their relatively poor showing in the elections to the first Majlis, threw their support behind Bani-Sadr. Increasingly, the conflict emblematized the struggle between the liberal center (the modern middle class) and the radical clergy. As the confronta-tion intensified, a three-man committee was appointed to resolve the impasse. In its report issued on 1 June 1981, the committee found that Bani-Sadr had unnecessarily inflamed the political situation. On 21 June, the Majlis declared that the president was incapable of discharging his duties. Bani-Sadr had already gone underground and later he fled the coun-try.

With the removal of Bani-Sadr, political power was fully concentrated in the hands of the radical ulama. Bani-Sadr's removal merely confirmed a trend in evidence since the formation of the PRG in 1979; that is, during the first two years of the revolution, liberal political elements wielded only nominal authority in the executive and legislative organs of the state. Their presence created an illusion of political pluralism, one undoubtedly useful to Khomeini and the ulama. De facto political power, however, was accu-mulating in the hands of the clerics. With the ousting of Bani-Sadr, appar-ent and real power merged in the hands of the radicals. Subsequent presi-dential elections put the ulama firmly in control of the executive, legislative, and judicial branches of government. Within the legislative apparatus, clerical control was assured by the establishment of the Shura (Council of Guardians), a body with ultimate veto authority.[17]

The War as an Islamic Cause

The manner in which the ulama presented the war to the Iranian public greatly assisted their full ascendency to power. Iraq's aggression easily played into the theocratic-populism of the Islamic government and thus helped to sustain Iran's revolutionary fervor. The ulama presented the war as part of the historical struggle of Islam. Shortly after the Iraqi invasion, Imam Khomeini characterized the war as a battle between "the glorious Koran and the pagans."[18] In the words of Iranian President Khameni'i, the conflict with Iraq was "a tug of war between Islam and blasphemy."[19] The Ba'th leaders were described as "enemies of Islam and the Koran."[20] The atheistic character of Saddam Hussein was placed beyond public doubt: "The infidel Saddam commits these monstrous acts to prove that he does not believe in Islam and humanity."[21] The Iranian nation was thus continuing the centuries-old struggle of Islam:

> The difference between us and them [the Ba'th] is that our motivation is Islam. Those who from the early days of Islam have served Islam and have fought and have shown self-sacrifice are recorded in history. The holy prophet faced many more hardships than we have. For many months, for many years, he was imprisoned and confined. . . . Nevertheless, he resisted and had to resist; and the Iranian nation will resist and has to resist.[22]

The choice was simply between Islam and glory or abysmal defeat and failure. In Khomeini's words: "O you great Islamic nation, you are now at a two-way junction: The road to eternal happiness and honour under the most honourable shadow of *jihad* for God and the defense of the Islamic nation or the road to abjectness and eternal shame should you, God forbid, show laxness and coolness in this *jihad*."[23] On other occasions, the nature of the war as a *jihad* (holy war) was clarified: "War means aggression against other countries to obtain their resources and wealth . . . *jihad,* in its Islamic context means defending one's freedom, border, honour, Islam and the Koran, and helping the oppressed and crushing the oppressors."[24] The military thrust into Iraqi territory was explained and justified in similar terms: "From the outset, our war began in a defensive manner; it is still a defensive one so far. The reason being that even our crossing into Iraqi soil was an extension of our holy defense."[25] The ulama, understandably, presented themselves as integral to the war effort: "The mosque is Islam's trench and the mosque altar is the place for war."[26]

The official depiction of the war in terms of the historical struggle of Islam was often held out as the primary reason that Iran could not accept the Iraqi ceasefire offers:

> Saddam does not believe in even a single tenet of Islam and we want to
> defend it. Saddam is carrying out atrocities against his own nation, a
> Muslim nation that is asking us for help. We want to defend them. We did
> not attack, we are on the defensive now too. Are you expecting us to
> shake hands in friendship with a person who would crush Islam under his
> feet and would destroy it if he had the power? You want us to sit with him
> and wish him health and peace? What sort of logic is this? Is this the logic
> of Islam? Do you . . . believe that this is the logic of Islam? May God cor-
> rect you, God willing.[27]

Earlier in the war the same rationale was in evidence: "How can we reconcile? And with whom? This is most ridiculous. It is like someone telling the
prophet to reconcile with Abu Jahl (Quraishi infidel in early Islamic writing)."[28] Similarly: "There is no way we can compromise with these people,
because we have one aim and that is Islam. Our entire nation wants Islam.
Saddam's aim is an anti-Islamic one. It is impossible for Islam to compromise with its opponents."[29]

The casting of the conflict in Islamic terms was reinforced by the idea
of martyrdom. The theme of martyrdom appeared at the outset of the war:
"No doubt, all of the resistance, arising from pure hearts committed to
Islam, stem from the mentality of martyrdom which continues growing in
the Muslim nation"; and the Islamic victory would be a victory "of blood
over the sword" and "faith over arms."[30] As Khomeini stressed during the
third week of the war: "If war is imposed upon us, everyone in our nation
becomes a fighter and we encounter with everything in our power even if
all the superpowers are behind it [Iraq]. This is so because we regard martyrdom as a great blessing, and our nation also welcomes martyrdom with
open arms."[31] Death in Iran's struggle against Iraq was given an ethereal
hue:

> Think about the fact that the best of the people at his own time, His
> Holiness the Lord of the Martyrs [Imam Husayn], peace be upon him, and
> the best youths of Bani-Hashim [the tribe of the Prophet and Imam
> Husayn], and his best followers were martyred, leaving this world through
> martyrdom. Yet when the family of Imam Husayn was taken to the evil
> presence of Yazid [the Ummayid ruler in whose time Imam Husayn was
> killed], Her Holiness Zeynab [Imam Husayn's sister] peace be upon her,
> swore saying: "What we experienced was nothing but beautiful. The
> departure of a perfect person, the martyrdom of a perfect person is beauti-
> ful in the eyes of the saints of God—not because they have fought and
> been killed, but because their war has been for the sake of god, because
> their uprising has been for the sake of God." Regarding martyrdom as a
> great blessing is not because they are killed. People on the other side also
> get killed. Their blessing is due to the fact that their motivation is Islam.[32]

Martyrdom was held out to the population as a blessed sacrifice. In com-
menting on fallen soldiers, Khomeini claimed that "they have been sacri-

ficed for Islam, and they have achieved eternal martyrdom and permanent honour thanks to His boundless blessings."[33]

A further dimension to the Islamic portrayal of the war involved the creation of a strong sense of continuity with Islam's past. "You should not fear war," said Khomeini. "The most blessed prophet has waged war for the sake of Islam. His holiness amir [Imam 'Ali, the first imam of the Shi'ites] has waged war for the sake of Islam. There were several wars in the course of a few years during the early days of Islam."[34] Martyrdom assisted in establishing this link:

> This anniversary coincides with the anniversary of the martyrdom of the most noble martyr Husayn ibn 'Ali, God's peace be upon him. He taught us to be neither subservient nor obsequious to those who perpetrate injustice. He recorded in his pure blood, and in the blood of his scion and companions in Karbala, the lessons of resistance, steadfastness, and sacrifice. These lessons map out, for the generations to come, the road of dignity, freedom, and pride. Our defensive resistance to the unjust war which is being imposed on us receives its profundity from the blood of martyrs for Islam, foremost of whom is the most noble martyr, Husayn ibn 'Ali, God's peace be upon him.[35]

An address by Khomeini to the families of fallen Iranian soldiers once again illustrates this tendency: "You people in the west and south . . . have stood against the oppressors and those who are attacking Islam and have offered martyrs like the martyrs in the early days of Islam."[36]

The ulama also presented the war as part of a counterrevolutionary conspiracy bent on defeating the Islamic Revolution. In the words of Ayatollah Beheshti: "We are preparing ourselves for a protracted struggle against . . . the Islamic revolution."[37] Iraq was often depicted as a puppet regime within the counterrevolutionary scenario. According to Iran's Foreign Ministry: "The war imposed on Iran was not planned by the Saddam regime. He is only a tool for implementing it. Behind him stand the enemies of the Islamic Revolution of Iran, who want to destroy our popular regime and our revolutionary model."[38] Similarly, the war provided crude confirmation of the xenophobic motifs of theocratic-populism. According to Beheshti: "The Ba'thist government serves as representative and agent for this superpower [the United States] in the area."[39] Ayatollah Khomeini pithily described Saddam Hussein as "this wretched servant" of the United States.[40] Saddam had fallen into the trap of "deceit practiced by its instigators."[41] Iran had stood fast in the face of "world-devourers and their dependent lackeys."[42]

The official presentation of the war helped the regime to mobilize the people in two ways. First, it created a large pool of volunteers for the front. In 1985, Heshemi-Rafsanjani illuminatingly dwelt upon Iran's wartime success: "The fact that there are still so many volunteers so long after the war has started shows that not only are the people not tired but that fighting the enemy and martyrdom has become sweeter for them."[43] On another occasion, Islam writ large was held out as the principal force behind Iran's successful mobilization at the front: "A great many countries claim that they can mobilize the people, but we have not witnessed such a situation in the world whereby the movement and mobilization for participating in the front can be carried out as a religious canonical duty. Indeed, such a method of dispatching forces to the fronts is unprecedented in history."[44]

Second, the Islamicization of the war helped to sustain revolutionary fervor, keeping the population politically mobilized against enemies of the revolution. This in turn reinforced the "Islamic nature" of the revolution, and tended to reaffirm clerical leadership. It created unity and a sense of focus that eased the way for the clerics to concretize their power. Clerical glee at this effect of the war sometimes could not be contained. In an address to the clergy, Khomeini said: "Even when a war begins, our nation begins to be awakened, becomes more mobilized, and you should know that as a result of this imposed war on Iran, the war which has been launched by the people who betrayed Islam, the arch opponents of our Islam, Iran has been united. What other event could unite our people to such an extent? This war has mobilized our people."[45]

The Elimination of Internal Opposition

The ulama were able to use the war as a blanketlike pretext to silence their critics and marginalize all internal opposition. "The war with Iraq," noted Tahmoores Sarraf, "had from its initial stages created a condition of emergency for the regime which was used to full advantage to justify aggressive moves against all opponents."[46] In an atmosphere in which all internal opposition was branded as "traitorous" and automatically linked to foreign elements, the war made these alleged linkages appear all the more tangible. Dilip Hiro has written: "With a war raging along 300 miles of its border with Iraq, the government convincingly labelled those creating disorder at home as unpatriotic agents of Iraq."[47] Speaking in 1985, the Iranian president, Khameni, claimed that the war was the first strike in the conspiratorial activities of the "liberals and enemies of the Islamic revolution." The opposition, according to Khameni'i, had tried to used the war to throw the revolution into a "position of defeat."[48]

With the elimination of Bani-Sadr, clerical entrenchment had moved a step closer to completion. Opposition to the regime was increasingly shunted to the periphery of Iran's political terrain. The war was figuring prominently in this trend. In the spring of 1981, for example, five nonclerical newspapers were closed down under the pretext that they had been "printing provocative materials during the time of war."[49] As the repression accelerated, the regime's detractors operated less and less in the open. Their activities increasingly manifested themselves in hit-and-run attacks against members of the clerical regime. The most dramatic attack was against members of the IRP as they gathered for a meeting on the evening of 28 June 1981, just days after the fall of Bani-Sadr. A powerful blast ripped through IRP headquarters, killing more than seventy party members, including co-founder and general secretary Beheshti. Bombings and attacks continued over the summer. On 30 August, the newly elected president, Rajai, and the newly appointed prime minister, Javad Bahonar, were killed when the prime minister's office was bombed. Throughout the remainder of the war, attacks by groups operating at the margins of the political system continued, although none achieved the sensation of the initial killings.

The theocrats attributed many of the attacks to the Mujahedin (the Islamic Mujahedin as opposed to their secular counterparts, the Marxist Mujahedin, which later became Paykar). The Mujahedin was influenced by the writings of Shari'ati and had generated a wide following among Iran's youth. Their leader, Mas'ud Rajavi, escaped to France on the same covert flight as Bani-Sadr. As the radical clergy consolidated their grip on power, the Mujahedin stepped up their opposition.[50] Once the Mujahedin had been implicated in the initial round of bombings, the ulama retaliated ferociously. Over the year following the blast at IRP headquarters, thousands of Mujahedin supporters were killed or imprisoned. By the time 1982 drew to a close, the operational capacity of the Mujahedin had been severely weakened. The bulk of its leaders inside Iran had been either incarcerated or killed, and disillusionment had set in within the rank and file. Many of its members had appeared on television to repudiate the Mujahedin and denounce its leader.[51] The faithful Mujahedin had been driven underground. Their decline (especially shown in public toleration of the government's backlash) has been directly linked to the circumstances of war. One commentator wrote in 1984: "During the height of the Mujahedin uprising, Iraq still occupied approximately one-third of Khuzistan province, including the important city of Khorramshar; the city Abadan was besieged and in danger of being captured; and the cities of Ahvas and Dizful were in range of Iraqi artillery guns. Thus, the Mujahedin's assault upon the government coincided with a grim phase of the war. This made it easy for the IRP to portray the Mujahedin as traitors and agents of foreign enemies at a time when popular anger against Iraq was high."[52]

As the ability of the Mujahedin to strike at the regime waned, the theocrats turned their attention to the last remaining stream of potential opposition: the Tudeh Party. From the outset of the revolution, the Tudeh cautiously offered its support to the regime. Their choice of position was influenced by the staunch antiimperialist line of the ulama.[53] With the progressive containment of the liberals and the Mujahedin, the regime's need to tolerate the secular left greatly diminished. Predictably, on 18 July 1982 the Tudeh Party's paper, Mardum, was banned amid allegations of its opposition to Islamic principles. Toward the end of 1982, the Tudeh Party itself became the subject of harsh criticism by the Iranian media. The Tudeh was painted as a political front for the Soviet Union, at a time when anti-Soviet sentiments were high because of Soviet arms sales to Iraq. The theocrats also obtained a detailed list of Tudeh members, courtesy of the British cabinet, following the defection of a KGB official from the Soviet Union.[54] Beginning in February 1983 and continuing into the spring, extensive operations were carried out against Tudeh Party leaders. Over the next year, high-ranking members of the Tudeh were forced to appear on television to confess to "crimes" said to have been committed by the party and to extol the virtues of Khomeini and the clerical regime. On 21 January 1984, eighty-seven Tudeh Party members were given prison terms ranging from one year to life.[55] With the bulk of the Tudeh's leadership incarcerated, the party was driven underground and its effectiveness was considerably emasculated.[56]

Much of the original opposition to the shah was now in exile. The largest exiled group was lumped together under an umbrella organization named the Council of National Resistance (CNR), established a few months after the flight of Bani-Sadr. It included the Mujahedin, the National Front, Bani-Sadr, and the Kurdish Democratic Party. In exile, however, the opposition was beset by factionalism, personality clashes, and fundamentally differing world views that significantly obstructed their ability to present a coherent and sustained critique of the regime.[57] By 1984, the CNR had fallen apart. Support for its member groups, moreover, continually weakened during the course of the war, and the ulama never lost the opportunity to brand them as counterrevolutionaries in the service of Iraq and the United States.

In short, the political corollary of clerical consolidation was the progressive enfeeblement of the opposition. Seven years after the grand coalition had toppled the monarchy, the ulama stood alone atop the postrevolutionary totem. The opposition was "divided and sterile"; "a growing helplessness became noticeable in their ranks."[58] The war had played a prominent role in their demise. Writing in 1987, Eric Hooglund lucidly summarized this dynamic: "The war with Iraq is the main Achilles' heel of the opposition. Attacks against the Islamic Republic permit the government to paint the opposition fairly easily with the brush of treason."[59]

The Extension of Clerical Control

The war strengthened the revolutionary organizations and helped to extend clerical control over the traditional apparatus of the Iranian state. The war was integrally related to a three-pronged policy to prevent counterrevolutionary activities within the military. This policy was partly inspired by two failed coup attempts by military personnel in the spring of 1980. The policy specified:

1. that the pasdaran (the Revolutionary Guards) should be enlarged and trained for the dual task of fighting Iraq and keeping a check on the military,
2. that a militia known as the basiijis (mobilization of the oppressed) should be developed and put under the control of the pasdaran, and
3. that the military should be fully Islamicized, enlarged, and equipped to fight the invading Iraqi forces.[60]

The expansion of the Revolutionary Guards created a countervailing armed force against the traditional military. Prior to the war, the pasdaran monitored and controlled rival elements of the postrevolutionary power bloc. They also helped to enforce many clerical decrees. By the conclusion of the war with Iraq, the pasdaran had swelled to over a quarter of a million active troops.[61] The establishment of the Ministry of Revolutionary Guards institutionalized the pasdaran. The basiijis at times reached a strength of one million volunteers.[62] Aside from providing an important balance against the distrusted regular military, the ranks of the pasdaran and the basiijis tended to draw heavily from the young urban poor and to lower middle classes, which had the effect of shoring up support for the regime.[63]

Another wartime move was the acceleration in the Islamicization of the regular military. In the fall of 1980, the Ideological-Political Directorate of the Armed Forces (IPD) was created in order to purge the military of suspected opponents. Different branches of the IPD aggressively indoctrinated the Ministry of Defense, the ground forces, the air force, the navy, and the general staff. As the war continued, the regime's confidence in the regular forces was slowly restored. Toward the middle of the war, for example, this growing trust was evinced in Hashemi-Rafsanjani's Army Day address: "This is a most remarkable event that has taken place in the Islamic Republic of Iran. An army on which world and regional arrogance and the Shah's regime had pinned its hopes as the guardian of the interests of arrogance and the policemen for the interests of regional reaction has, with today's developments, been transformed into the policemen of Islam and the interests of the deprived."[64]

The expansion of revolutionary organizations at the military level was complemented by a growth in the number of civilian organizations. The civilian counterpart to the pasdaran—the Jahad-e Sazandeghi, or Reconstruction Crusade—was commandeered early by the IRP in order to concretize rural support for the regime.[65] Designed to promote rural development, its function continually expanded throughout the war, especially in areas heavily damaged by fighting. Damage caused by the war provided the opportunity for the continual expansion of regime-directed organizations such as the Housing Foundation and the Foundation for the Affairs of the War Immigrants.[66] In conjunction with the popular revolutionary bodies, especially the Komitehs, these organizations helped to reconstruct wartorn areas. Their efforts were overseen by a central headquarters. Other wartime measures had the effect of enhancing the visibility of the clergy. For example, ration cards were distributed by the local mosques, which placed the mullahs at the center of a nationwide rationing network. Milani commented: "The mosques thus became a powerful economic and political force at the community level."[67]

The War and Iran's Poor

The Iran-Iraq War provided the clergy with a tidy excuse for the glacial pace at which economic reforms were introduced during the 1980s. Revolutionary promises of a better life for the *mostaz'efin* (the dispossessed), a primary social base of the radical ulama, remained unfulfilled throughout the war. This sluggish pace reflected the rudimentary conflict between those ulama advocating radical economic reforms and the more conservative clergy favoring the economic status quo. The latter stressed Islam's sanction of private property.[68] Far-reaching reform measures with respect to the nationalization of foreign trade, land reform, and the distribution of exiles' property, for example, were vetoed by the Council of Guardians (controlled by the conservative clergy).[69] In effect, the basic conflict between the reform-minded clergy and the conservative clergy effectively stalled the implementation of palliative socioeconomic measures.[70] By the end of the decade, these conflicts having failed to resolve themselves, signs were emerging that both clerical factions were cultivating more defined social bases. The conservative camp received growing support from the bazaaris, the landowners, and the modern bourgeoisie, and the reformist clerics drew increased support from the urban poor and the rural peasantry.[71]

The war with Iraq provided a powerful argument for lowering the expectations of Iran's destitute masses. In disregard of the underlying sociopolitical reasons that led to the impasse on socioeconomic reforms, the war could be held out as the primary factor behind the delay.[72] The following excerpt from Manasheri's detailed survey of the first revolutionary decade identifies this connection:

> The revolution had not yet eased the burdens of the *mostaz'efin*. For Khomeini's regime, which pledged to serve the *mostaz'efin,* this was not

only frustrating but also potentially dangerous. . . . Responding to these problems, Khomeini occasionally instructed the Government to mitigate the burden of the *mostaz'efin*. At the same time, he set out to explain, or explain away, the economic problems, presenting hardship as the price that loyal believers should pay in their struggle for Islam and the revolution. Similarly, he tried to lower material expectations, urging the *mostaz'efin* not to expect quick gains and advising them against consumerism.[73]

As the Islamic Revolution entered its "Thermidor," the war, in short, allowed the ulama to avoid alienating one of their primary bases of support.

Propulsion for the Clerical Political Agenda

The Iran-Iraq War entered directly into the process of revolutionary consolidation in Iran. It helped to insure the full accession of the radical clergy and the concomitant marginalization of Iran's remaining revolutionary opposition. Free from the fetters of legitimate dissension and critique, the ulama were able to implement their political agenda virtually unencumbered. In practice, this meant the thorough desecularization and Islamicization of Iranian society. To the considerable extent that the prosecution of the war played a role in Iran's postrevolutionary clerical entrenchment, it therefore had a profound bearing on the general policy direction of the country throughout the 1980s. In the absence of a protracted war, the balance of power between the clergy and its opponents would have been altered, and as a result the clerical agenda would have been tempered by dissenting visions of Iran's future. As it was, the clergy achieved political exclusivity: Iraq's invasion inadvertently cemented the theocracy. Iran's postrevolutionary vision was inseparable from the revolutionary vision of the mullahs.

In view of these dynamics, the Iran-Iraq War can be said to have indirectly resulted in a deterioration in the condition of Iran's subordinate social groups. By assisting the radical clergy in their agenda—a process that insured the implementation of a string of policies detrimental to women, the working classes, and Iran's ethnic minorities—the war played a critical role in solidifying and even intensifying social oppression. At times, this chain of causality was strikingly linear: war insured clerical ascendency; clerical ascendency insured the full Islamicization of Iranian society; the Islamicization of Iranian society further eroded the social power of already disempowered groups. Moreover, the clergy often appealed to the circumstances of war in order to justify specific policies, thus bringing the war to bear directly upon social conditions. It is valuable to address briefly each prominent social constituency in turn.

The Mullahs and Women

Hand in hand with the desecularization of Iranian society went the rein-
forcement of oppressive conceptions of gender. It is insufficient, however,
to paint the contrast between the position of women in prerevolutionary
Iran and the position of women in postrevolutionary Iran as one between
emancipation and reaction.[74] Although meaningful progress in the
women's struggle was made during the Pahlavi era, many of the changes
had a cosmetic character and were top-heavy (or state-heavy). In 1936,
Reza Shah banned the veil and allowed women to attend Tehran
University. These gains were tempered by the fact that only a relatively
small number of upper and upper-middle class women could safely aban-
don the veil during the Pahlavi monarchy. The banning of the veil, moreover, was a directive from on high and did not surface as a genuine expression of a women's movement. Indeed, under Reza Shah any independent
organization among women was forbidden. Guity Nashat's discussion of
Reza Shah's policies elaborates this crucial observation:

> The force and repression that accompanied the enactment of his policies
> hurt the cause of women's advance because it stifled the development of a
> political culture and experience among women. The fate of the Patriotic
> Women's League illustrates this point. The League was formed in 1922
> by a group of women with socialist tendencies who had been active in the
> Constitutional Revolution. . . . The women's league was affiliated with
> the Socialist Party, which had resumed its activities in the 1920s. Reza
> Shah used the various political groups at the beginning of his rise to
> power to consolidate his hold over the political system. However, once he
> had established firm control, he began to eliminate and disband any
> groups with any semblance of independence. Although the aim of the
> Women's League was merely to "emphasize respect for the laws and ritu-
> als of Islam, to promote the education and moral upbringing of girls, to
> encourage national industries, to spread literacy among adult women, to
> provide care for orphaned girls, etc.," it was not allowed to survive and
> was closed in 1932.[75]

This trend was partly reversed during the interregnum and into Mohammed
Reza Pahlavi's reign. In particular, there was a flowering of women's orga-
nizations, which included the Council of Women of Iran, the Women's
League of Supporters of the Declaration of Human Rights, and the Women
Teachers' Association.[76] The efforts of these groups achieved some
reforms in the 1960s. One of the six features of the shah's White
Revolution was the extension of female suffrage. The passage of the
Family Protection Law of 1967 marked another achievement for the
women's movement, a law that circumscribed the unilateral prerogatives of
husbands regarding divorce and polygamy.[77] These legal changes were
complemented by a significant expansion in educational opportunities and
a much greater role for women in the growing Iranian economy.[78]

Two conclusions can be drawn with respect to the situation of women under the Pahlavi monarchy. First, there was the development of a clear feminist consciousness.[79] Second, there were some modest legal and social gains for women, especially during the modernization drive of the post-1953 period. Both of these trends were dramatically reversed in the aftermath of the revolution. Under the authority of a *fatva* (religious decree), women were forced to observe the *hejab,* a practice that includes wearing the *chador* (veil) in public. The 1967 Family Protection Law was quickly suspended. The theocrats replaced this with a system that sanctioned polygamy.[80] One of the most striking changes was the encouragement of the *sigeh* or *mat'a* (practice of temporary marriages).[81] According to this practice, a man could take a wife for as short a time as an evening. Critics of the practice have widely characterized it as a form of legalized prostitution. As the following critique of sigeh reveals, the regime justified its policy with reference to the war:

> What motive, other than the satisfaction of lust, is there when a women for two hours becomes *sigeh* of a man, or a man for one or two hours enters into a *sigeh* contract with a woman? The difference here is that we camouflage such corruption with *Shar'iah.* The justification that *sigeh* is an instrument to take care of extra women caused by the war is ill-founded. *My question is, how many men who died in war left their wives behind?* I don't think there were many. Besides, how is a sigeh arrangement, a temporary arrangement, a panacea for such women's problems?[82]

The legal changes were frequently enforced by roving officers directly linked to the Komitehs, and women not wearing the chador were often dealt with very harshly by the authorities. Observation of the hejab effectively became universal.

The theocrats unswervingly promoted a conception of women that would relegate them to family care and childrearing.[83] The following exposition from one of the leading publications of the regime is revealing:

> A woman in the environment outside the family would lead to the propagation of corruption and permissiveness, which itself would lead to the weakening of the marriage bond and absence of warmth and cordiality within the family circle. . . . The women of our society through their work inside the family and the fulfilment of the essential duty of motherhood, teach their children the lesson of faith in god, piety and sacrifice.[84]

In other words, women were encouraged to preoccupy themselves with the "precious function of motherhood, rearing alert and active human beings."[85] This position was partly premised on the belief that women are not physically or intellectually equipped to deal with many of the roles in society. The following interview between journalist John Simpson and Mrs. Barzin Maknoun, who is both a faculty member at Tehran University and an Iranian official attached to a literacy program of UNESCO, reveals the extent of this view within the theocracy:

> Maknoun: The things that concern women in Iran are often misunder-
> stood, purposely so, in the rest of the world. It is our task here
> to show what Islam says about these things, and about what
> the real Islamic women should be. You have to study the Holy
> Koran, which shows that only Islam gives true rights to
> women—and more rights to women than men. But women are
> not fit to have every kind of responsibility. A woman cannot
> become what Imam Khomeini is, for instance.
> Simpson: You mean that women aren't the intellectual equals of men?
> Maknoun: No, I don't mean that at all. What we believe is than men and
> women are actually equal, but that they're made differently.
> Men are stronger in some things and women are stronger in
> others. A woman can get as close to Allah as a man can, but in
> a different way. A man can use his intellect to get there, and a
> women will use her high emotions. But they are both equal in
> the sight of God. You see, there are big differences physically
> between men and women, and these differences make it diffi-
> cult for them to do the same things. A woman can be a mother
> and care for a child, because of her high emotions. A man can-
> not do that. His duties are to support his wife and his family,
> because he's made that way.[86]

The ideological links between the "natural inferiority of women" and the prevailing Islamic definition of a woman's role within society are clearly evident in the above excerpt. As could be expected, there was a growing practice of segregation, especially in public places. Enrollment by women in higher education declined.[87] The theocratic sense of a woman's natural capacity and inherent social function, combined with the turmoil of the war-stressed economy, greatly constricted employment opportunities for women.[88]

Under the Islamic program of the radical clerics, the social power of women appreciably slipped. The modest gains of the Pahlavi era were erased. Autonomous women's organizations did not function in any mean-ingful political manner. The lives of women were entirely subordinated to the task of creating a better Islamic society, as defined by the fundamental-ists. Traditional conceptions of women as corrupters of men, as naturally inferior beings, and as male possessions were reinforced in the postrevolu-tionary period. The Iran-Iraq War, by providing the ulama with an excuse that could be used to justify almost anything—"there's a war on"—greatly contributed to the deteriorating circumstances for women.

Repression of Ethnic Groups: Kurdish Resistance

In the aftermath of the revolution, demands for regional autonomy and self-rule were advanced by Iran's numerous ethnic groups—among them the

Baluchis, Arabs, Azerbaijanis Turks, Qashqa'i Turks, Turkomanis, and the Kurds.[89] From the outset, the radical clerics adamantly refused to accept the demands voiced by Iran's ethnic minorities. Among other things, such an acceptance would have been entirely inconsistent with the basic theocratic premise of a unified Islamic nation. Thus the stage for confrontation was quickly set. The initial phases of the war distracted the regime's attention and diverted its resources. This gave ethnic groups the political space to acquire partial control of their affairs.[90] In the long run, this ephemeral benefit was greatly outweighed by the fact that the war hardened the intolerance of the theocratic regime, strengthened its security apparatus, threw a large section of the population firmly behind it, especially in the central region, and frequently took Tehran's armed forces into the ethnic zones.

Of these ethnically tinged struggles, the Kurdish resistance was by far the most active and aggressive. The Kurdish opposition was traditionally less organized than its counterpart in Iraq.[91] In the aftermath of the Iranian revolution, the Kurdish opposition consolidated itself into two primary groups, the Komala and the Kurdish Democratic Party of Iran (KDPI). Komala claimed—and still claims—to be acting directly in the interests of the Kurdish peasantry. The KDPI, however, gradually emerged as the stronger of the two. The new Islamic regime and the Kurdish groups oscillated between periods of dialogue and periods of armed confrontation, with the most violent encounters taking place in August 1979.[92]

The Kurdish groups continued to operate throughout the Iran-Iraq War. The KDPI initially managed to function as a de facto government in many areas of Kurdistan, constructing roads, building houses, organizing schools, and operating hospitals. Overall, however, their power declined. In part, this can be attributed to the fact that the war further divided the Kurdish opposition,[93] and by 1985 the Komala and the KDPI had declared war upon each other.[94] Also contributing to the decline was Tehran's movement of forces into the Kurdish region whenever possible.[95] From the outset of the war, Iranian forces, especially the Revolutionary Guards, fought intensely for control of the Kurdish towns, increasingly limiting insurgent operations to the mountain areas. By 1983, the KDPI was operationally ineffective. As the war progressed, the Kurdish region became thoroughly militarized.[96]

The Iran-Iraq War was a two-front conflict for Tehran. They were fighting Iraq along much of the common border and engaging the peshmergas in Iranian Kurdistan. For the Kurdish people, Tehran's counterinsurgency campaign was devastating. A report by a British health official who visited Iranian Kurdistan in 1982 was revealing:

> Overall, the war has caused a marked decrease in the provision of health care in Iranian Kurdistan. There has been total disruption of certain services in the rural areas for the past three to four years, including immunization programmes and vector control in those regions where malaria is

endemic. . . . The situation in the towns is difficult to assess, but the fact they are under Iranian control acts as a serious deterrent to people from the rural areas visiting them in order to attend those health services which are still functioning; for people actually fighting the war [i.e the peshmergas] such a visit is too dangerous to be considered. Thus, although it is possible for some people living in the West of Kurdistan to obtain medical care in Iraq (despite the high cost in terms of money and time) and for others to visit the towns in Iran, in general the overall access to medical services and the availability of health care has greatly declined as a result of the war.[97]

Throughout the counterinsurgency campaigns, many Kurds were indiscriminately arrested and incarcerated. In the words of one Kurd reported by a French group: "Khomeini thinks that everyone in Kurdistan, even the cats and dogs, are members of the KDPI and KOMALA."[98] Routinely, political prisoners were tortured.[99] Thousands of Kurds were forcibly relocated.[100] Perhaps the most dramatic cases of abuse involved those Kurdish prisoners whose executions were rushed so that their blood could be collected to fill shortages at the front.[101]

The Iran-Iraq War was a war against the Kurdish people: this was the war's hidden agenda. The position of the Kurds deteriorated throughout the 1980s. In an interview in 1988, KDPI leader Ghassemlou lamented that the Iran-Iraq War had "caused the total ruin of Kurdistan."[102] Indirectly, the war strengthened the theocrats' hard-line position on Kurdish demands for autonomy. More directly, it turned the Kurdish homeland into an interstate battleground, thereby enhancing Tehran's control of the region.

The Working Class and the War

The Islamic regime refused to tolerate any social action that interfered with the necessities of the war effort, a posture that encouraged the direct repression of labor. A portent of the relationship between the regime and Iranian workers came three days after the revolutionary insurrection: Khomeini ordered all workers to return to work.[103] In the face of worker resistance, Khomeini made the intention of the provisional government clear: "Any disobedience from, and sabotage of the implementation of the plans of the Provisional Government would be regarded as opposition against the genuine Islamic Revolution." Khomeini's threat came as a more fundamental transformation in labor relations was afoot. In the aftermath of the revolution, elements of the industrial working class frequently gained control over entire operations at the worksite, thus continuing historical trends established in the Paris Commune of 1871, the Russian revolutions of 1905 and 1917, the factory occupations of Italy and Germany shortly after World War I, and events in Spain in 1936, Hungary in 1956, Portugal in 1974, and Poland in 1981. The vehicle for these changes were known as *shuras* (workers' councils). The radicalization of many workers in the revolutionary aftermath, combined with the unique opportunity created by the fact that many factory owners and directors had fled the country, contributed to the rise of a period of "control from below." Workers often gained leverage over the financial, administrative, productive, and distributive operations of companies. At times, worker militancy included holding owners or managers hostage. The practical degree of control by the workers varied widely. In some cases, the workers acquired de facto autarchy within the operation. An example of extensive workers' control was the case of the Chit-e-Jahan textile factory in the industrial town of Karaj close to Tehran. The shura at Chit-e-Jahan symbolically occupied the former office of the factory's SAVAK agent that had been used to interrogate workers. The shura heavily influenced all elements of production, doubled the minimum wage, reduced top salaries by two-thirds, set up a workers' library, and distributed a daily liter of milk to each worker.[104]

The threat implied by extensive "control from below" was immediately sensed by the liberals and the ulama. Within a few months of the insurrection, the Bazargan government attempted to reassert authority at the top by appointing liberal professional managers. The pro-Khomeini clergy sought to counter the independent workers' shuras by setting up Islamic shuras and Islamic associations in the factories. Bayat's discussion of the clerical approach, usually dubbed as maktabi management, is illuminating:

> It is management by those whose position derives not from certain relevant skills (education or experience) but is based mainly on character and personal, or more importantly, ideological connections with the ruling clergy, especially the IRP. . . . They were in authority to preserve the presence of the ruling party in the factories, these being the most vulnerable parts of Iranian society. For them the policy of worker participation was limited to the corporatist shuras and Islamic Associations. In essence, their major policy was repressive one-man management; if they did not achieve this, they demanded workers' cooperation in a participatory management structure. Their strategy was hierarchical Islamic corporatism. Whilst profit maximization was their main objective, it was not the only one. By nature, maktabi management is committed to certain ideological and political measures, the implementation of which disrupts production or wastes working time. . . . This type of manager views the secularism of liberal managers as anti-Islamic. They use force and tight control instead of peaceful dispute settlement and reformist mediums—a policy of repulsion rather than incorporation.[105]

The Islamic associations had direct links to the ruling clergy within the Islamic Republican Party. "The Associations," notes Bayat, "were the vehicle for the consolidation of the clergy's power in the workplace in opposition to both liberal managers and the independent *shuras*."[106] Maktabi management acquired greater prevalence with the removal of Bani-Sadr and the waning influence of the liberals. To combat worker militancy, the theocrats also set up labor sections within the pasdaran and the basiijis. Although the working class may have been "the battering ram" of the Islamic Revolution, the theocratic regime clearly expressed early and immediate opposition to autonomous worker activity.

The gradual establishment of clerical control within the workplace was boosted by the outbreak of war with Iraq. Islamicization of the workplace continued throughout the war. The war was often directly used to justify theocratic policy and to minimize production disruptions. The regime proclaimed work as a duty comparable to fighting at the front. Khomeini admonished cement workers in Tehran, "To work itself is a jihad [crusade] for the sake of God; God will pay for this *jihad*—the *jihad* of labour which you [workers] are carrying out inside the barricade of the factory."[107] The theocrats paraded disabled soldiers around worksites in order to embarrass workers into accepting lower wages and poor working conditions. Under the stress of war, the regime refused to tolerate disruptions in production. In spite of the emasculation of genuine workers' organizations, strikes and protests did transpire, but usually they were put down with force. Labor legislation toward the end of the war offered little hope for the establishment and growth of truly independent trade unions.[108] The destruction of truly independent worker organizations significantly lessened the ability of laboring groups to resist the demands made upon them by the state.

The War Ends: "No Internal Threat"

Unilateral and multilateral efforts to bring the war to a close were wholly unsuccessful. Surveying the 1983–1984 period, one commentator appropriately summed up the efforts of the international community as "routine and in the main futile."[109] Indeed, the seemingly inexplicable length of the war, particularly in view of its obvious material and human tolls, created a popular conundrum among many observers, especially given Iraq's clear willingness to settle the war. How could such a costly war continue? What could the clerics possibly be gaining from the attrited affair? The key to the prolongation of the war rested in its relationship to the process of revolutionary consolidation in Iran, particularly in the advantages that accrued to the theocrats. The clergy, therefore, regularly refused seriously to countenance mediation efforts to end the war, or attached impossible conditions to prospective agreements. The war was simply too valuable for it to be ended. It sustained revolutionary fervor, allowed the theocrats to marginalize their critics, helped them to extend their grip on revolutionary and state institutions, provided a convenient explanation for failed revolutionary promises, and allowed the clergy to contain potentially disruptive social behavior. As long as these advantages were forthcoming, efforts to end the war would not gather significant momentum within clerical echelons.

This held good until 1986, when the severe drop in world oil prices significantly lessened the appeal of the policy of "war, war until victory." Growing war-fatigue among the Iranian population, especially in view of Iraq's military gains early in 1988, further softened Iranian resolve. Nonetheless, something much more fundamental had cleared the way for peace. The ulama had essentially cemented their control. As the war entered its final stages, the theocratic regime faced "no internal threat to its power."[110] The 1979 revolution unequivocally belonged to them. One of the clearest indications of this accomplishment came with the disbanding of the IRP in 1987. There was no need for the war to continue. Its blessings were waning. It had outlived its usefulness.

Notes

1. Ervand Abrahamian's "The Opposition Forces," written in February 1979, provides an illuminating outline of the different tendencies that inevitably surfaced in the postrevolutionary period. These he categorized as (1) religious conservatives (including Shariat-Madari), (2) religious radicals (especially the Mujahedin), (3) religious reactionaries, (4) secular reformers (the "liberals"), and (5) the secular radicals (including the Fedayi and the Tudeh Party). See Abrahamian in *MERIP Reports,* 9:2/3, (March–April 1979).

2. In this chapter, the terms *clerics* and *radical clerics* are used interchangeably. This employment does not overlook the fact that within the clerical fold there were considerable differences in political view. Most notably, among the grand ayatollahs (or *Ayatollah 'Uzman*) widely diverging political views could be detected. During the initial postrevolutionary period, the views of Shariat-Madari and Taleqani (who was also known as the Red Mullah) departed sharply from those of Khomeini. Some of these figures clearly sided with the liberals during the initial phase of the postrevolutionary struggle. The radical clerics, who commandeered the revolution as time went on and who tended to follow Khomeini's line, were drawn primarily from the middle ranks of the clergy. Their most prominent political figure during the initial period was Beheshti, and their main political organ was the Islamic Republican Party. These are the clergy that can appropriately be labeled as fundamentalist as opposed to traditional or progressive. See discussions by David Menasheri in *Middle East Contemporary Survey,* v. 3, pp. 506–510, v. 4, pp. 455–460, v. 5, pp. 525–526. For a discussion of different streams of Islamic political thinking, see Cheryl Benard and Zalmay Khalilzad, *The Government of God: Iran's Islamic Republic,* (Columbia University Press, 1984), pp. 30–34.

3. According to an interview conducted by Fred Halliday with Bani-Sadr after he fled to Paris, it was exclusively this potential for mobilization that appealed to Khomeini, even in the face of economic threats from the United States. Bani-Sadr's recollection of a discussion with Khomeini is revealing:

Once we were talking about the economic effects of the hostage crisis and I asked him, "What is the point in holding the Americans hostage?" He

[Khomeini] replied, "Our regime is consolidating itself. Our enemies are trying to make the Islamic constitution fail. We can use the hostages to get the constitution passed, then to get a president and a legislative assembly elected. Once we have done all that, we can think again. Our internal enemies will have been unable to move because to do so would expose them to the charge of being traitors.

Interview with Abol-Hassan Bani-Sadr by Fred Halliday, August 1981, published in *MERIP Reports,* 12:3, (March–April 1982), p. 6.

4. Kambiz Afrachteh goes so far as to suggest that the hostage crisis could not have been settled until it was superseded by an episode of similar, if not greater, mobilizing potential; namely, the Iran-Iraq War. See his "The Predominance and Dilemmas of Theocratic Populism in Contemporary Iran," in *Iranian Studies: Journal for the Society of Iranian Studies,* 14:3–4, (summer-autumn, 1981), pp. 194–195.

5. Eric Rouleau, *Le Monde,* 8 April 1980.

6. Ervand Abrahamian, *Iran Between Two Revolutions,* (Princeton University Press, 1982), p. 537.

7. Mohsen M. Milani, *The Making of Iran's Islamic Revolution: From Monarchy to Islamic Republic,* (Westview Press, 1988), pp. 285–286.

8. One of the most thorough accounts of the struggle between Bani-Sadr and the clerics may be found in Shaul Bakhash, *The Reign of the Ayatollahs: Iran and the Islamic Revolution,* (Basic Books, 1984), chapters 5 and 6. Detailed accounts may also be found in *Middle East Contemporary Survey,* v. 4., pp. 461–464 and v. 5, pp. 523–536.

9. Bakhash, *Reign of the Ayatollahs,* op. cit., pp. 130–131.

10. Robin Wright, *In the Name of God: The Khomeini Decade,* (Simon and Schuster, 1989), p. 93.

11. It has been argued that Bani-Sadr could have used the war to his advantage but that he failed to do so. See Sharif Arani, "The Toppling of Bani-Sadr," *The Nation,* 233:1, (4 July 1981), pp. 9–12.

12. See discussion in Waheed-uz-Zaman, *Iranian Revolution: A Profile,* (Islamabad: Institute of Policy Studies, 1985), pp. 258–260.

13. Eric Rouleau, "The War and the Struggle for the State," in *MERIP Reports,* 98, (July–Aug. 1981), p. 5.

14. See David Menasheri's discussion of Bani-Sadr's letter in *Middle East Contemporary Survey,* v. 5, p. 524.

15. See discussion in Sepher Zabih, *Iran Since the Revolution,* (Croom Helm, 1982), p. 128.

16. See discussion in Bakhash, *Reign of the Ayatollahs,* op. cit., pp. 131–133.

17. For a discussion of this council (in the context of economic policy divisions within the regime), see Fred Halliday, "Year IV of the Islamic Republic," in *MERIP Reports,* (1983), p. 4.

18. Tehran Domestic Radio Service, 24 September 1980, *FBIS: Daily Reports,* 25 September 1980.

19. Tehran IRNA, 8 January 1985, *FBIS: Daily Reports,* 9 January 1985.

20. Tehran Domestic Radio Service, 16 October 1980, *FBIS: Daily Reports,* 20 October 1980.

21. Prime Minister Raja'i, Tehran International Radio Service, 2 April 1981, *FBIS: Daily Reports,* 2 April 1981.

22. Ayatollah Khomeini's address to the Iranian nation, Tehran Domestic Radio Service, 30 September 1980, *FBIS: Daily Reports,* 1 October 1980.

23. Ayatollah Khomeini, Tehran Domestic Radio Service, 19 October 1980, *FBIS: Daily Reports,* 20 October 1980.

24. Tehran Domestic Radio Service, 5 February 1985, *FBIS: Daily Reports,* 6 February 1985.

25. President Khamene'i, Tehran Domestic Radio Service, 22 September 1986, *FBIS: Daily Reports,* 22 September 1986.

26. Ayatollah Khomeini, Tehran Domestic Radio Service, 18 November 1980, *FBIS: Daily Reports,* 19 November 1980.

27. Tehran Domestic Radio Service, 19 April 1985, *FBIS: Daily Reports,* 20 April 1985.

28. Tehran International Radio Service, 28 October 1980, *FBIS: Daily Reports,* 28 October 1980.

29. Ayatollah Khomeini's 'Id Ghadir Address, Tehran Domestic Radio Service, 28 October 1980, *FBIS: Daily Reports,* 29 October 1980.

30. Office of the Prime Minister, Tehran Domestic Radio Service, 4 October 1980, *FBIS: Daily Reports,* 6 October 1980.

31. Tehran Domestic Radio Service, 9 October 1980, *FBIS: Daily Reports,* 10 October 1980.

32. Khomeini's address on the eighth anniversary of the revolution, Tehran Domestic Radio Service, 10 February 1987, *FBIS: Daily Reports,* 11 February 1987.

33. Tehran Domestic Radio Service, 19 October 1980, *FBIS: Daily Reports,* 20 October 1980.

34. Ayatollah Khomeini, Tehran Domestic Radio Service, 3 November 1980, *FBIS: Daily Reports,* 4 November 1980.

35. President Khameni'i's Friday Sermon at Tehran University, Tehran International Radio Service, 27 September 1985, *FBIS: Daily Reports,* 27 September 1985.

36. Tehran Domestic Radio Service, 2 April 1981, *FBIS: Daily Reports,* 3 April 1981.

37. Tehran International Radio Service, 2 October 1980, *FBIS: Daily Reports,* 2 October 1980.

38. Foreign Ministry statement, Tehran International Radio Service, 11 December 1980, *FBIS: Daily Reports,* 12 December 1980.

39. Tehran International Radio Service, 2 October 1980, *FBIS: Daily Reports,* 2 October 1980.

40. Ayatollah Khomeini, Tehran Domestic Radio Service, 3 November 1980, *FBIS: Daily Reports,* 4 November 1980.

41. Khomeini, Tehran Domestic Radio Service, 1 April 1981, *FBIS: Daily Reports,* 2 April 1981.

42. Tehran Domestic Radio Service, 1 April 1983, *FBIS: Daily Reports,* 4 April 1983.

43. Tehran Domestic Radio Service, 9 January 1985, *FBIS: Daily Reports,* 9 January 1985.

44. President Khameni'i, Tehran Domestic Radio Service, 17 February 1984, *FBIS: Daily Reports,* 17 February 1984.

45. Khomeini was speaking on the eve of the month of Muharram. Tehran Domestic Radio Service, 5 November 1980, *FBIS: Daily Reports,* 6 November 1980.

46. Tahmoores Sarraf, *Cry of a Nation: The Saga of the Iranian Revolution,* (P. Lang, 1990), p. 186.

47. Dilip Hiro, *Iran Under the Ayatollahs,* (Routledge and Kegan Paul, 1985), p. 220.

48. Tehran IRNA, 5 January 1985, *FBIS: Daily Reports,* 7 January 1985.

49. Waheed-Uz-Zaman, *Iranian Revolution,* op. cit., p. 284.

50. For an outline of the Mujahedin outlook, see "We are an Islamic Movement separate from the ruling oligarchy," in *MERIP Reports,* 10:3, (March–April 1980). Interview conducted by Fred Halliday.

51. See the discussion by David Menasheri in *Middle East Contemporary Survey,* v. 5, pp. 537–538, v. 6, p. 556, and v. 7, pp. 535–536. Also see the chapter devoted to the Mujahedin in Tahmoores Sarraf, *Cry of a Nation,* op. cit., pp. 178–196. For a critical assessment of the Mujahedin, see Afsaneh Najmabadi, "Mystifications of the Past and Illusions of the Future," in *The Iranian Revolution and the Islamic Republic,* eds. Nikki R. Keddie and Eric Hooglund, (Syracuse University Press, 1986), pp. 154–156; see remarks and general discussion, pp. 162–170.

52. Eric Hooglund, "The Gulf War and the Islamic Republic," in *MERIP Reports,* 14:6/7, (July–Sept. 1984), p. 34.

53. See Tudeh Party report, *The Revolution, the Counterrevolution, and how we safeguard the People's Gain,* Tehran, July 1979. Reprinted in *As-Safir,* Beirut, 13 July 1979, *FBIS: Daily Reports,* 18 July 1979.

54. See discussion in John Simpson, *Behind Iranian Lines: Travels Through Revolutionary Iran and the Persian Past,* (Fontana, 1989), pp. 105–106.

55. *Middle East Economic Digest,* 27 January 1984.

56. See discussions by David Menasheri in *Middle East Contemporary Survey,* v. 6, pp. 555–556, v. 7, pp. 532–534, v. 8, pp. 442–444, and v. 9, pp. 440–441.

57. For a breakdown of the expatriate opposition, see Fred Halliday, "Year Three of the Iranian Revolution," in *MERIP Reports,* 12:3, (March–April 1982), pp. 4–5.

58. David Menasheri, *Middle East Contemporary Survey,* 10, (1986), p. 344.

59. Eric Hooglund, "Iran and the Gulf War," in *MERIP Middle East Report,* 17:5, (Sept.–Oct. 1987), p. 17.

60. Extracted from Sepehr Zabih, *The Iranian Military in Revolution and War,* (Routledge, 1988), p. 128.

61. From *The Military Balance,* 1987–88, p. 99.

62. Ibid.

63. See discussion of the pasdaran and state ministries in Halliday, "Year IV of the Islamic Republic," p. 7, especially note 10.

64. Tehran Domestic Radio Service, 18 April 1984, *FBIS: Daily Reports,* 19 April 1984.

65. See Emad Ferdows, "The Reconstruction Crusade and Class Conflict in Iran," in *MERIP Reports,* 13:3, (March–April 1983).

66. This discussion is indebted to Hooshang Amirahmadi, "War Damage and Reconstruction in the Islamic Republic of Iran," in *Post-Revolutionary Iran,* eds. Hooshang Amirahmadi and Manoucher Parvin, (Westview Press, 1988), especially pp. 142–146

67. See discussion in Mohsen M. Milani, *The Making,* op. cit. Quote from p. 287.

68. The best discussion of this tension during the initial phase of clerical consolidation may be found in Hossein Bashiriyeh, *The State and Revolution in Iran: 1962–1982,* (Croom Helm, 1984), pp. 111–185.

69. For a discussion of the different factions among the clergy and the role of the Council of Guardians see Dilip Hiro, *Iran Under the Ayatollahs,* op. cit., pp. 240–250.

70. For a description of the manner in which this conflict manifested itself with respect to land reform throughout the war, see Shaul Bakhash, "The Politics of Land, Law, and Social Justice in Iran," in *Iran's Revolution: The Search for Consensus,* ed. R. K. Ramazani, (Indiana University Press, 1990).

71. See discussion in Ahmad Ashraf, "There is a Feeling that the Regime Owes Something to the People," in *MERIP: Middle East Report,* 19:1, (Jan.–Feb. 1989), pp. 13–18.

72. See discussion in Fred Halliday, "The Revolution's First Decade," in *MERIP Middle East Report,* 19:1, (Jan.–Feb. 1989), pp. 19–20.

73. David Menashri, "Iran," *Middle East Contemporary Survey,* 9, (1984–1985), pp. 441–442.

74. Some writings speak glowingly of changes under the shah. For example, see Badr ol-Moluk Bamdad, *From Darkness into Light: Women's Emancipation in Iran,* (Exposition Press, 1977).

75. Guity Nashat, "Women in Pre-Revolutionary Iran: A Historical Overview," in *Women and Revolution in Iran,* ed. Guity Nashat, (Westview Press, 1983), pp. 27–28.

76. See discussion in Bamdad, *From Darkness,* op. cit., pp. 105–112.

77. See discussion in Gholam-reza Vatandoust, "The Status of Iranian Women During the Pahlavi Regime," in *Women and the Family in Iran,* ed. Asghar Fathi, (E. J. Brill, 1985), pp. 114–121.

78. See discussion in S. Kaveh Mirani, "Social and Economic Change in the Role of Women: 1956–1978," in Nashat, *Women and Revolution,* op. cit., pp. 69–86.

79. See discussion in Adele Ferdows, "Shariati and Khomeini on Women," in Keddie and Hooglund, *The Iranian Revolution,* op. cit., p. 141.

80. See discussion in "Women, Marriage and State in Iran," in *Women, State and Ideology,* ed. Haleh Afshan, (State University of New York Press, 1987).

81. See discussion in Shahla Haeri, "The Institution of Mat'a Marriage in Iran: A Formal and Historical Perspective," in Nashat, *Women and Revolution,* op. cit., pp. 231–251.

82. Cited in Tahmoores Sarraf, *Cry of a Nation,* op. cit., p. 126. My emphasis.

83. See discussion in Nira Yaval-Davis, "Women and Reproduction in Iran," in *Women, Nation, State,* eds. Nira Yaval-Davis and Floya Anthias, (St. Martin's Press, 1989).

84. *Keyhan International,* 5 February 1987, cited in Hamid R. Kusha, *Iran: The Problematic of Women's Participation in a Male-Dominated Society,* Sociology Department, University of Kentucky, Working Paper # 136, 1987.

85. Mohsen M. Milani, *The Making,* op. cit., p. 309.

86. Simpson, *Behind Iranian Lines,* op. cit., pp. 267–268.

87. See Shahizad Mojab, *The Islamic Government's Policy on Women's Access to Higher Education and its Impact on the Socio-Economic Status of Women,* Michigan State University, Working Paper # 156, 1987.

88. See Valentine Moghadam, *Women, Work and Ideology in Post-revolutionary Iran,* Michigan State University, Working Paper # 170, 1988.

89. For an interesting discussion on this, see Nikki R. Keddie, "The Minorities Question in Iran," in *The Iran-Iraq War: New Weapons, Old Conflicts,* eds. Shirin Tahir-Kheli and Shaheen Ayubi, (Praeger, 1983).

90. See discussion by David Menasheri in *Middle East Contemporary Survey,* 5, (1980–1981), pp. 552–554.

91. For a discussion of the Kurds in Iran, see A. R. Ghassemlou, "Kurdistan in

Iran," in *People Without a Country: The Kurds in Kurdistan,* ed. Gerard Chaliand, (Zed Books, 1980).

92. For the initial period of the Kurdish struggle in Iran after the revolution, see *Middle East Contemporary Survey,* v. 3, 1978–1978, pp. 527–528, v. 4, 1979–1980, pp. 467–469, v. 5, 1980–1981, pp. 554–556, v. 6, 1981–1982, pp. 550–551, and v. 7, 1982–1983, pp. 537–538.

93. See discussion by David Menasheri in *Middle East Contemporary Survey,* 5, (1980–1981), pp. 554–555.

94. See discussion in Martin van Bruinessen, "The Kurds Between Iran and Iraq," *MERIP Middle East Report,* 16:4, (July–Aug. 1986), p. 22.

95. Accordingly, the claim by Charles G. MacDonald that "the Gulf war has occupied and drained Khomeini's forces to such a degree that it limited Khomeini's ability to repress and defeat the Kurds" is overstated. See "The Impact of the Gulf War on the Kurds," in *Middle East Contemporary Survey,* 7, (1982–1983), p. 267.

96. According to one Kurdish figure, more that two hundred thousand soldiers were stationed in the region; and three thousand bases were set up by the theocrats. From a speech by Hassan Sharafi, general European representative of the Kurdish Democratic Party of Iran, Paris, 15 October 1989.

97. Bruce Dick, *Health Problems and the Provision of Health Care in Iranian Kurdistan,* paper of the Refugee Health Group Evaluation and Planning Centre, London School of Hygiene and Tropical Medicine, 1983.

98. Federation Internationale des Droits de l'Homme, Rapport de Mission, Iran: Mission au Kurdistan, 1983.

99. Ibid.

100. For example, see press release, 6 September 1984, "The Kurdish Program," New York.

101. See summary of report by Christian Rostoker, secretary-general of the Federation of the Rights of Man, Paris, France, Aug.–Sept., 1983.

102. Dr. Ghassemlou was interviewed by Ferdinand Hennerbichler for the Austrian newspaper, *Wiener Zeitung.*

103. Analysis here is based upon Assef Bayat's contributions. See "Workers' Control After the Revolution," *MERIP Reports,* 13:3, (March–April 1983) and *Workers and Revolution in Iran,* (Zed Books, 1987).

104. See discussion in Chris Goodey, "Workers' Councils in Iranian Factories," *MERIP Reports,* 88, (June 1980), pp. 6–7.

105. Bayat, *Workers and Revolution in Iran,* op. cit., pp. 175–176.

106. Ibid., p. 101.

107. Bayat, "Workers' Control," op. cit., p. 23.

108. Continuing reports on workers' activity and critical assessments of the clerics' labor policy may be found in *Tudeh News,* a publication of the Tudeh Party.

109. Uriel Dann, "The Iraqi-Iranian War," *Middle East Contemporary Survey,* 8, (1983–1984), p. 186.

110. Fred Halliday, "Iran's New Grand Strategy," *MERIP Middle East Report,* 17:1, (Jan.–Feb. 1987), p. 7.

6

The War and Ba'th Consolidation in Iraq

Saddam Hussein was bristling with confidence when Iraqi forces invaded Iran on 22 September 1980. He initially expected the war to be finished by the Eid al-Adha (Feast of the Sacrifice) on 20 October. The enormity of Saddam Hussein's miscalculation became increasingly evident as the war lengthened and its fortunes shifted. The war created monumental burdens for the Ba'th regime: steep yearly costs, sharp economic losses, and substantial declines in oil revenues. Nonetheless, the war was kind to Baghdad's rulers. Its prosecution provided the regime with special opportunities to consolidate political control and extend its grip on Iraqi society. The repressive arm of the regime operated alongside the war machine; meanwhile, a potentially solid base of support among Iraq's emerging capitalist class continued to develop. The regime was able to present itself as defender of the Arab homeland and protector of the Islamic faith against the Persian infidels. Saddam Hussein was depicted as standing valiantly at the helm of the Arab struggle. The war, moreover, was inversely kind to Iraq's political opposition. Ba'th political consolidation went hand in hand with the continuing repression of all non-Ba'thist forces, and the war added new sources of disagreement and frequently exacerbated older fissures among the fragile resistance. These dynamics exacerbated the conditions of Iraq's subordinated groups, an effect most visible with respect to the Kurdish population in the north.

Prosecuting the War

The war created steep economic costs for the Ba'th regime. Initially, it sought to keep the Iraqi population insulated from the burdens of the war, an approach widely dubbed as a "guns *and* butter" strategy. The financial strains of the war, however, quickly proved to be too great. Most of the strain emanated from the loss of oil export revenues. Attacks on Iraq's

145

southern port facilities of Mina Bakr and Khor Amaya resulted in heavy damage and closure early in the war. Before the attacks, almost 3 million barrels per day (b/p/d) were being exported through the Gulf terminals. Moreover, this damage nullified the effect of the so-called strategic pipeline, which could move crude oil from the northern oil fields to the southern oil fields or vice versa, depending upon whether it was preferable to export crude via the Gulf or the Mediterranean Sea. (Premiums were usually received if Iraq could get the oil to the Mediterranean.) This left Iraq with access to the Mediterranean terminals of Yumurtulik, through the Turkish pipeline, and Banias, through the Syrian pipeline. The Turkish pipeline had frequently been sabotaged. Iraq's precarious export situation was greatly exacerbated with the closing of the Syrian line, for political reasons, in April 1982. The regime immediately set about overcoming this vulnerability by constructing new pipelines and exploiting other means of export. The possibilities were examined for laying new pipelines through Turkey, Jordan, and Saudi Arabia. The regime employed antidrag chemicals on its Turkish pipeline to increase transit capacity.[1] At the same time, it began exporting crude oil and petroleum products by truck through Turkey and Jordan. By July 1983, it was estimated that 12,000 tonnes of fuel oil and 25,000 tonnes of other refined products were being exported by truck through Turkey and Jordan each day.[2] Shipments through the Jordanian port of Aqaba were so important to Iraq that it was partially financing Jordanian road construction, in addition to constructing its own six-lane expressway, in order to link Baghdad with Jordan's Red Sea terminals.[3] In 1985, Iraq began pumping oil around Kuwait and through Saudi Arabia to the Red Sea port of Yanbu' al-Bahr. These efforts resulted in modest increases in Iraq's oil export output. For the first three years of the war, Iraqi oil production stood at one-third of its 1980 levels. This corresponded with a drastic reduction in oil revenues. Iraq's annual oil revenue fell from U.S. $26 billion in 1980 to just $10 billion in 1981, $9.5 in billion 1982, and $8.5 billion in 1983.[4] Over the next three years, however, oil exports began to creep up, reaching 45 percent of the 1980 level in 1984, 53 percent in 1985, and 61 percent in 1986.[5] Small revenue recoveries in 1984 and 1985, however, were more than offset in 1986 by the sharp decline in oil revenues from U.S. $27 per barrel to $10 per barrel.[6]

At the outset of the war, the regime had more than U.S. $35 billion in foreign reserves. As the war passed through its third year, however, Iraq faced an increasingly precarious financial situation. Its foreign reserves were effectively depleted and oil revenues were insufficient to finance the war. As its financial situation deteriorated, Iraq negotiated payment deferments between contractors, foreign governments, and financial institutions. The extent of these deferments was revealed by the foreign affairs minister, Tariq Aziz, toward the end of 1984:

> In 1982–83, when we found ourselves in financial difficulty, we approached these [foreign] companies and told them: "If you want to continue these projects, then let's agree on a different pattern of payments." Accordingly, we reached agreement with everybody—with all the West European firms, with firms belonging to East Europe and the Soviet Union, and with other Third World countries. We had about 900 foreign companies working in Iraq at that time—and they are still working. We did it in 1983 and in 1984.[7]

Iraq also solicited trade credits from foreign governments, receiving a $230 million credit from the U.S. Department of Agriculture in 1983. Loans were also negotiated with foreign creditors, including a Euroloan of U.S. $500 million.[8] The most extensive financial assistance, however, came from Iraq's neighboring Gulf states—Kuwait, Saudi Arabia, Qatar, and the United Arab Emirates. These countries, especially Saudi Arabia and Kuwait, provided large quantities of cash, credit, and oil exchanges that helped to underwrite the costs of the war. By the end of 1987, Iraq's external debt was widely estimated to be more than U.S. $50 billion.

The financial burdens of the war forced the regime quickly to curtail its extensive development plans.[9] Many scheduled projects were postponed. Development contracts were generally limited to infrastructural and strategic ventures directly linked to oil production and the prosecution of the war. Beyond these developmental constrictions, however, the war had a much more enduring effect on the very nature of the Iraqi economy. Its fiscal burdens accelerated the expansion of Iraq's private sector, thus continuing a trend well under way prior to 1980.[10] Saddam Hussein, recognizing that an explicit endorsement of private enterprise was inconsistent with Baghdad's socialist posture, rationalized the move toward private enterprise with a typical Ba'th foray into social theory:

> Private enterprise must not control life. Similarly, the socialistic enterprises must not control life. If any one of them controls life alone, it will not realize its objectives, and the socialistic enterprises will not realize their human objectives. Private enterprise, if it monopolizes life, has its well-known disadvantages. In this regard I will not try to flatter anybody. However, coexistence between the two sides realizes man's happiness. Those who want to profit can profit, but man will be happy in carrying out such activities, be it a socialistic or a private activity. I will go so far as to say that both will end up realizing a socialistic objective because both of them meet human needs in a general and acceptable framework from the standpoint of socialist principles.[11]

The encouragement of the private sector reflected an overall strategy to increase economic production in a war-stressed economy.[12] Complementary reforms were also undertaken in the state sector, including efforts to reduce bureaucratic drag and interference.[13] Law 35, enacted in 1983, increased the private exploitation of land in the countryside.[14] By the end of the war, Iraq's economic restructuring included the selling of state land, farms, and factories to the private sector, a greater emphasis on the quality of productive output, the introduction of an export drive, and the encouragement of private enterprise.[15] The cluster of policies designed to encourage privatization included an easing of legal restrictions and investment ceilings, tax exemptions, relaxed credit lines, state-subsidized building materials, and closer cooperation with state officials.[16]

The high economic costs of the war made Baghdad open to a peaceful settlement for most of its duration. This inclination contrasted rather sharply with the regime's confidence at the war's outset. Saddam Hussein's initial optimism had led him to attach impossible conditions to the first United Nations ceasefire resolution of 28 September 1980. At that time, the Ba'th regime demanded that Iraq's "rights and sovereignty" be fully recognized—a demand implying Iraqi control over the entire Shatt al-Arab waterway, and one that was destined to be rejected by Iran. By the end of 1982, however, Iraq was clearly prepared to search for a compromise to end the war.[17] Iraq's strategy was often aimed at forcing Iran to sue for peace, rather than at prevailing militarily. Baghdad's determination to internationalize the war by attacking Gulf shipping, for example, was designed to bring international pressure on Iran. The speed with which Iraq accepted Security Council resolution 598, a full year before Iran, reflected the radically differing inclinations toward peace by the two regimes.

Living with the War's Positive Political Fallout

Although the war was economically draining for the Ba'th regime, it still created unique political opportunities. It is safe to say in summary that the political effects of the war were much more benign than its economic effects. The war provided the regime with opportunities to enhance its profile and extend its political control. The political atmosphere of Ba'th Iraq is closely guarded and hard to penetrate, but it would be difficult to overestimate the extent of these political benefits. Perhaps most importantly, the war provided the regime with an opportunity to engage in populist strategies. The regime used the war to expound cultural motifs and mythologies suggestive of a common Iraqi identity. Ideas of Arabness and Iraqiness were trumpeted throughout the decade, helping to de-emphasize the vast differences among the Iraqi people. Although Baghdad would have ended the war much earlier in the decade, it could at least live with its positive political fallout.

The first collection of themes contained in Baghdad's war-populism involved the characterization of the war as part of a broader Arab struggle.

The Arab-Persian dimension to the war was widely heralded by the regime, as clearly evident in the name given to the war by Iraq—Qadisiyat Saddam—a naming that conjures up Arab-Persian struggles of the seventh century. The regime recalled military commanders from the original Qadisiyah in order to create a sense of historical continuity. An exhortation broadcast in September 1980 stated: "O descendants of Al-Muthanna, Sa'd Ibn Abi Waqqas, Al'Qa'aq' and Khalid Ibn al-Walid. It is the banner of al-Qadisiyah and the honour of the mission once again which Iraq and the Arabs have placed in your hands and upon your shoulders."[18] Iraqi soldiers were described as "ancestors of the heroes of the first al-Qadisiyah, and heroes of the second al-Qadisiyah [the 1980 Iran-Iraq War]."[19] Iraq was presented as the defender of "the Arab nation's independence, sovereignty and territorial integrity."[20] Saddam Hussein, speaking in 1980, said:

> Brethren, O masses of the glorious Arab nation. When Iraq waged this honourable and valiant battle [against Iran], it had a strong belief that it was defending the Arab nation's sovereignty, honour and rights. Iraq's lands and waters are part of the Arab sovereignty and Arab honour. . . . He who threatens Iraq's sovereignty threatens the entire Arab sovereignty. He who usurps part of the Arab homeland in its eastern or western section, in its centre or in any of its parts is a foe that must be deterred; and the territory must be liberated from his grasp. We do not distinguish between one usurper and another.[21]

Nearly two years later, in another radio broadcast, Iraq was characterized as "an impregnable dam protecting the eastern flank of the Arab homeland."[22] And toward the end of the war Saddam Hussein asked: "How would Iran's aggressiveness and evil affect the Arab if Iraq did not act as a wall?"[23]

The war was presented as part of the continuing struggle of the Arab nation to purge its land of "aggressors" and to free itself from "slavery and exploitation."[24] Saddam Hussein proclaimed early in the war: "The Arabs have waged many wars and battles in the modern age. They were forced to enter all these wars including this war which was begun by Iran and in which Iraq was the Arab side."[25] Iran thus threatened the freedom and independence of the Arab nation. "If the Turks managed to rule the Arabs for hundreds of years, the Iranians can do likewise," said Hussein in a 1988 interview.[26] According to the regime, the integrity of the Arab people was at stake: "Some people say he [Khomeini] wants to take the nations back to the Middle Ages," declared Tariq 'Aziz, then deputy prime minister, during the third year of the war, "[but] his aim is in fact much more dangerous—he wants to divide the body of the Arab nation."[27] Hence, the entire Arab nation should celebrate the fruits of military victory: "It is indeed significant that the Arabs should consider the *al-Faw* battle to be their own," claimed Saddam Hussein shortly after Iran had been driven from the peninsula in 1988, "and in fact it is their own battle."[28] At the pinnacle of the

Arab struggle stood the figure of Saddam Hussein—the other side of Qadisiyat Saddam. When the war was carried into Iraqi territory, Hussein's position as defender of the Arab nation was fully exploited. Bomb-damaged shops in Basra were strewn with posters hailing Hussein as "the second great conqueror of the Persian Army."[29]

A second body of themes centered around Iraqi nationalism. A heroic, modern "Iraqi man" became the national symbol, transcending class, religious, and ethnic divisions within Iraqi society.[30] This new "Iraqi man" was blessed with "uniqueness," graced with "boundless energy," and was "a disciplined and patient citizen, capable of coping with all critical conditions."[31] Iraqis were told on the radio:

> Our modern man is developed and is completely different from the one who existed before. Our modern Iraqi is more enduring, more precise, more energetic, and better prepared to meet responsibility. The base of the revolution's faithful men has expanded and covers all Iraq. The base of reserve of leaders—both in civilian and military life—has increased. . . . It is all the Iraqis who have now passed the tests and who have sincerely and certainly proved to be loyal through their sacrifices by carrying the gun in defense of Iraq and in building Iraq in an exemplary manner.[32]

The modern Iraqi was presented as the product of a rich and illustrious past: "You are the sons of the Tigris and Euphrates. You are the sons of Adam's tree and Noah's ark, which came to rest on your land. You are the sons of the civilization of Mesopotamia, which illuminated the world when the rest of mankind was living in darkness."[33] The war was held to have "renewed the ancient Iraqi history and culture, which extends thousands of years."[34] Resistance against Iran was necessary for the preservation of the Iraqi character: "This new character constitutes new ground for glory, pride, happiness and prosperity. This new character must not be conquered."[35] Iraq's successes in the war were directly linked to the power of the Iraqi spirit: "The strong Iraqi will and the creative Iraqi genius have completely reversed the situation on the enemies. . . . Last year, the solid Iraqi will, the deep-rooted Iraqi unity, and the great Iraqi ability were tested. Last year, the enemy tried to move from one sector to another on the front, looking for any military or political loophole. . . . On every section of the Iraqi borders, the enemy found the Iraqis alert, unified, and ready to sacrifice in order to defend their dear, lofty Iraq."[36] In his address on Army Day in 1986, Saddam Hussein reiterated the link between Iraq's wartime successes and the special qualities of Iraqi men and women:

> O glorious Iraqi men and women, the great achievements we attained in our steadfastness in the face of aggression and in the field of construction and prosperity, the achievements that are admired by the nation and appreciated by the world, are the result of bravery, ability, and patience

expressed by the brave Iraqi men in this long and honourable battle. . . .
This war has become one of the major events in modern history. This is
the result of the Iraqi women and men's patience as well as the result of
their sacrifices, persistence, and their strong insistence on facing evil and
aggression.[37]

Iranian attacks on the besieged city of Basra frequently provided occasion
for Iraqi virtues to be extolled: "The Iraqi citizen is standing on the borders
of our Basra more lofty and with greater dignity and pride, knowing only
continuous offering which embodies the value, ethics, and nobleness in the
full sense of the word."[38]

A third collection of themes sought to present Iraq as a beleaguered
nation, plotted against by foreign forces, thus exploiting and reinforcing
xenophobic motifs embedded within Iraqi culture. "The battle being waged
by Iraq today against the ruling clique in Iran is no mere dispute between
two Third World states," declared Saddam Hussein in 1982, "but a result of
the wide scheme planned by known international sides and implemented
both directly and indirectly in order to force Iraq to give up its independent
stands."[39] Similar themes were in ample evidence in the following address
by Hussein to the Iraqi people in 1987:

> O Iraqis, you have destroyed the great conspiracy at its most serious
> phase. You have destroyed the conspiracy against your present, future,
> hopes, security, honour, and sovereignty and conspiracy against the secu-
> rity, honour, and sovereignty of the Arab nation by your heroic confronta-
> tion. The conspiracy has been destroyed and defeated, and its evil wind,
> which was feared by our righteous people, has receded. . . . This conspira-
> cy is now wallowing in the bitterness of defeat. The parties to this con-
> spiracy are cursing one another, and all of them are cursing their bad
> luck.[40]

The war was reduced to the machinations of the "covetous big powers" that
"depend on certain elements in the region to carry out the plan of subjugat-
ing the Arab nation and controlling the Arab homeland."[41] At the center of
these conspiratorial activities was the United States and the forces of
Zionism. The following analogy by Saddam Hussein draws upon powerful
familial themes to stress U.S. involvement:

> When you are a friend of Mazin and Saddam Hussein for instance, and the
> two quarrel, what is your duty as a friend? It is to come between them and
> settle their dispute, is it not? But if Saddam Hussein sees you unsheathe
> your dagger and give it to Mazin, would not this mean that you are asking
> Mazin to stab Saddam Hussein? The United States has done this more
> than once.[42]

Ba'th Party founder Michel 'Aflaq repeated this theme in April 1987, with

the words: "The United States claims neutrality in the Gulf war and publicly calls for ending it. Then it becomes clear that it is not a neutral party
and that it gives weapons to those who perpetrate terrorism."[43]

Themes of Zionist aggression took a number of twists and turns. At
times the war was presented as an evil distraction from the real task of
fighting Zionist aggression. Iraq had to extricate itself from the battle with
Iran in order to fight the Zionist enemy on its southwestern flank.[44] At
other times, parallels were drawn between "Iranian aggression" and
"Zionist aggression": "Of course, there has been foreign encouragement of
this factor [expansionism]. The Zionists have been the first to encourage it
because they found in it a means to harm the Arab nation," said Hussein in
a 1988 interview.[45] On other occasions direct links were asserted between
Zionism and Iran. "We never, from the very beginning," claimed Iraq's
defense minister, 'Adnan Khayrallah, "had any illusion about the Iranian
regime's links with Zionism."[46] Zionism was accused sometimes of completely controlling the war, as reflected in an *al-Qadisiyah* editorial in
1986: "It became clear the Khomeiniyite war which was imposed on our
triumphant people and great Iraq was masterminded by the Zionist circle
and was given a Khomeinyite facade and for unrealistic, totally irrelevant
reasons, led by the sick dreams of the Khomeinyites who wanted to spread
their hegemony over Iraq, the Arab gulf states, and other Islamic states."[47]
The Zionist motive in the war was presented as counterrevolutionary:
"Zionism sees, observes and realizes that the plan for liberation is found
primarily in Iraq," Hussein was reported to have told his colleagues.[48]
Zionist forces, of course, did not act alone but in the context of a much
broader United States-Zionist-Iranian plot against Iraq and the Arab
nation.[49] In order to strengthen its claims, the regime continually drew links
between war-related events and Israel. Personal links, for example, were
drawn between Khomeini and Zionism. When Khomeini had medical treatment, it was apparently by a "Zionist medical team of five physicians."[50]
The Iran-contra affair provided additional fodder: "After 7 years of the
war," reported the Voice of the Masses in December 1986, "the world
wakes up to discover shameful details about the special and dirty cooperation between U.S. organs and the Zionist entity—a cooperation with those
claiming to be patriotic Muslims and those claiming to seek the Liberation
of Jerusalem. This is their true nature. They could not deceive or dupe
us."[51]

A fourth collection of themes centered around the war as an Islamic
struggle. The Ba'th regime portrayed itself as defender of the Islamic faith.
Islam was presented as the preserve of the Arab nation: "The language of
the Koran, of the angels—the language spoken in paradise—is Arabic and
no other."[52] Iraqi successes in the Faw peninsula in 1988 were attributed to
God, who "asks man to organize and legitimize his endeavours."[53] The
regime also cultivated the importance of martyrdom. Fallen Iraqi soldiers

were described as "righteous martyrs" whose "blood has not gone in vain." Protecting Iraq and "its glories of past and present" was characterized as "the purest and greatest deeds before God."[54] A 1982 speech by Saddam Hussein delved into history:

> Today, our great grandfather, the father of all martyrs, al-Husayn . . . stand[s] as a lofty symbol of heroism, glory and firmness in defending right. This is the vow of Iraqis and the Iraqi army. It became clear to our grandfather al-Husayn that he was facing the enemy's huge army with few men. He was sure that the enemy's army would triumph and he became afraid that history, the kinsfolk and those malicious ones would not be fair to him if he pulled back. Yet, his soul enlightened his way and gave birth to willingness to give and to sacrifice. He moved forward to fight and continued to fight until he fell as a martyr. He preferred to gain the glories of heaven rather than the glories of earth. Since then we have considered this a symbol for all believers and fighters. Now, 1300 years after his martyrdom, al-Husayn remains a symbol for us. We, his grandsons, are proud to be connected with him, we are proud to be tied to him in soul and blood. The army and the people are one and they fight to defend right, justice and the holy land of Iraq which harbours the remains of our grandfather 'Ali, may God brighten his face.[55]

"The martyrs," declared Saddam Hussein, "are God's guests who will live in paradise."[56]

At the same time, the denigration of the Iranian regime was directly linked to the leitmotifs of Iraq's war-populism: "The Iraqis have always been a source of great generosity to mankind. The Arabs have always been a major source of enlightenment and abundance for mankind. On the other hand, the Persians have always been invaders and aggressors, expanding to the detriment of others and destroying other nations' civilizations."[57] The Iranian regime was summed up as the antithesis of Arabism: a form of racist anti-Arabism *shu'ubism* was said to lie at the heart of their motives.[58] The Iranian regime, moreover, was frequently accused of practicing a misguided or ill-informed brand of Islam: "The religion whose ideas Khomeini advocates," declared Saddam Hussein, "is not an Islamic religion. The knowing believers of Iran itself are now saying this."[59] Khomeini was often portrayed as a religious fraud or charlatan: "A man of religion must be truthful. If he is a liar," asserted Saddam Hussein, "then he does not deserve to be a man of religion or claim to be righteous."[60] The regime held that "the path chosen by Khomeyni is not an Islamic path" and that Khomeini "espouses a mistaken, deviant Islamic line." On other occasions Khomeini was described as "a politician working under the guise of religion" or as "a backward man of religion."[61] Iranian "aggression" against Iraq was thus un-Islamic, as evident in Hussein's Open Letter to the Iranian people in 1983:

You are contravening the Islamic faith because you are not only attacking a neighbouring state and violating the Prophet's tenets which say take care of thy neighbour and then of their brother, but also attacking the land of the holy places and the tombs of Imam 'Ali and our lord and grandfather Husayn and the tombs of our great forefathers. This land is not only defended by the Iraqis who are sacrificing their lives for it, but is also defended by the divine will. Almighty God is on the side of right against wrong, against aggressors and on the side of the victims of aggression. God will bless those who defend the holy land and not those who invade it as aggressors.[62]

The Islamic slogans emanating from Iran were presented as a ruse for Zionist activity: "Right from the beginning, we sensed the movement of Zionist fingers behind the aggression coming from the East. We felt that the false Islamic slogans they raised were only a cover, not a true Islamic call."[63]

A fifth—final—analysis of themes draws attention to the creation of a personality cult around Saddam Hussein—a process that was greatly abetted by the war. The war provided a litany of opportunities to hail Saddam Hussein as the father of all Iraqis, guardian of the revolution, historical leader of Islam, and master of the Arab nation. The following excerpt from Sabah Salman's column in *ath-Thawrah* demonstrates this aggrandizing tendency in the context of thinly veiled references to the war:

He is the man of the revolution, the captain of its destiny, and the originator of historical roles and great deeds which require a commander and strong decisionmaking. Saddam Husayn is that strong man and destined originator of strong decisions. . . . I know that Saddam Husayn is stronger than most men because he is in the right. Due to his faith, his greatness is beyond doubt, because to him life without honour is a vast desert, desolate and full of wild beasts. Its bleak hills hold nothing but sand and thorns. For this reason, he believes that he who would remain calm in the heart of the whirlwind must coexist with the unthinkable or he cheats himself of a dreamy peace in the midst of a stormy world.

Salman continues:

He thus soars on the winds to remain above them, with personal honour for the sake of the great culture of Iraq. Saddam Husayn does not wager on the era and its coincidence because today's era is fabricated and not a time to calm the storm. Saddam Husayn is a man of history and the greatest wager is on him, because while the era is the ally of the opportunist who seizes power, history is a record of infinite duration which opens its pages to heroes. My explanation is the absolute truth.[64]

During the war Saddam Hussein could be found sipping tea with Iraqi peasants or gently kissing Iraqi infants. The intended message of the contrived scenarios was unmistakable. The preservation of Saddam was inseparable from the preservation of Iraq and the Arab nation.

Consequently, by using the war, the regime was able to manipulate cultural motifs aimed at counteracting the centrifugal tendencies of contemporary Iraq. To express this conversely, the regime exploited the centripetal forces of patriotism, nationalism, and faith.[65] It could cultivate the spirit of Iraqiness or Arabness and employ it for political gain. "A defensive struggle against an Iran on the offensive," wrote Dilip Hiro, "helped Saddam Hussein to forge national unity to a degree he had not thought possible before."[66] In times of peace, the Iraqi Shi'i from the south of the country might be favorably disposed toward the activities of the Shi'i clerics; in war, this potential was at least momentarily undermined. The Iraqi Shi'i did not defect en masse from the military in the face of the war with Islamic Iran. This factor suggests that "Iraqi Shi'is unambiguously consider themselves Iraqis first and Shi'is second."[67] This is confirmed by Phebe Marr: "As Arab Sunnis and Shi'ah from all parts of Iraq fought in the trenches together, they developed shared experiences, a greater sense of community, and a deeper identity as Iraqis."[68] To précis this, the war helped to foster a transcendent Iraqi spirit that partially overrode the vertical universes of sectarianism and ethnicity and the horizontal universe of class.

As noted earlier, the war provided a further political benefit to the regime, allowing it to expand its social base among Iraq's capitalist class. The privatization drive impelled by the war continually transferred state resources into the hands of businessmen. Many operations expanded, helped by favorable investment conditions and state subsidies. There is evidence to suggest that the privatization drive allowed some individuals to accumulate substantial economic wealth and power.[69] These trends were also well in evidence before the war. The regime was able to enhance the slender social footing it gained among the capitalist class so long as it could maintain the conditions for capital accumulation.[70] The exigencies of the war effort, in other words, continually expanded the regime's capitalist base of support.

Within the Ba'th regime, power unquestionably devolved onto Saddam Hussein. He received a resounding endorsement at the Ba'th Party congress in 1982. Saddam Hussein carefully placed close family members and trustworthy relatives in strategic political positions to help guard against challenges to his rule. An extremely watchful eye was also kept over the military, especially in times of success, and military leaders who sought domestic recognition had their wings quickly clipped. Saddam Hussein also adroitly shunted political figures from post to post in order to preclude the development of countervailing power centers.[71] Thus, as surely as the regime drew political strength out of the costly war, so Saddam Hussein proved adept at minimizing dissent within the ruling coterie and achieving political success for himself. Indeed, the two were increasingly indistinguishable.

The War and Iraq's Political Opposition

For most of the war, the regime faced organized political opposition from at least three sources: the Kurds, in the north, the Iraqi Communist Party, also in the north, and the Shi'i opposition, primarily in the south. The war had the potential to provide the opposition with special opportunities, including the possibility of receiving logistical and financial support from Iran and Syria. It was also a stimulus for them to form a common front.[72] Equally importantly, the operational effectiveness of the Ba'th regime was often taxed to the limit during the war; a situation that created unique windows of opportunity for insurgent forces.

However, Iraq's clandestine opposition, due to factors largely beyond its immediate control, could not translate any of these opportunities into meaningful political gains. To the extent that the war allowed the Ba'th regime to cultivate an Iraqi identity, the opposition factions' chances for widening their bases of support were significantly blunted. The burdens of war, moreover, provided Baghdad with special leverages against its internal foes. The regime easily branded the opposition as traitorous, anti-Arab, and atheistic. This line was even more effective when Iran crossed into Iraqi territory. "The incursion of Iranian troops into Iraq," noted one commentator, "made it appear that the Opposition was siding with the enemy in threatening the country's very soil."[73] In addition to these disadvantages, the war caused further fragmentation among Iraq's opposition forces:

> This problem [differing views on the war] is crucial. Up till now, some parties have insisted that ending the war does not serve the cause of overthrowing the Iraqi regime. They place their hopes on an Iranian military victory to rid them of Saddam. Other forces, notably the Communists, hold the two tasks of ending the war and overthrowing the regime as equally important. In their view, changing the regime is one of the "internal affairs of the Iraqi people," best served through "formulating the most precise program and slogans" around which to mobilize people to fight to end the war and "punish those who waged it."[74]

Even within a single group—the Iraqi Communist Party—the war created intense factionalism and discord.[75] On the whole, attempts to form a politically effective front against the regime were substantially weakened in light of enduring mutual antagonisms and suspicions.

Nonetheless, Iraq's political opposition continued to be a serious concern for the Ba'th regime. This anxiety became evident when the Revolutionary Command Council (RCC) passed Law 840, a law that authorized the death penalty for anyone who publicly insulted the president, the RCC, the Ba'th Party, the National Assembly, or the cabinet.[76] The decree confirmed that if religious or national identities failed to bond the Iraqi people to the Ba'th state, then fear would be the regime's political cement.[77] To this end, the policing apparatus continued to figure prominently in internal affairs, extending its wartime activities to deal with smuggling, forgery, and black-marketeering.[78] Grave human rights abuses were reported throughout the war.[79]

The Iran-Iraq War thus helped to strengthen the Ba'th regime vis-à-vis the opposition. The Ba'th stood at the helm of Iraq's defense against Iran. The war provided Baghdad with a unique opportunity to cultivate and exploit socially unifying and politically levelling themes. The regime could momentarily retard, if not substantially reverse, Iraq's severe class and communal political estrangement. Iran became the primary problem for Iraqis. If support for the regime faltered under the exceptional circumstances of war, then the regime could use Iran's "aggression" to discredit its critics. Failing this, the war provided the Ba'th regime with a blanket pretext to do whatever was necessary to contain its opponents. Understandably, the removal of the war pretext was of serious concern to the Iraqi leadership. As one commentator wrote shortly after the conclusion of the war: "After the ceasefire Saddam Hussein is no longer able to claim he is defending the homeland or use the war as a justification and smoke-screen for mass repression and terror in Iraq."[80]

The War and Iraq's Subaltern Groups

The political strengthening of the Ba'th regime throughout the war entailed profound social costs. The regime was premised upon the denial of the political meaningfulness of Iraq's pronounced social fault lines. The interests of Iraq's underprivileged constituencies were subordinated to Ba'th social and political ideals—ideals increasingly guided by the overriding imperative of regime maintenance. Independent political organization was not permitted by Baghdad. The war did little to enhance the social power of Iraq's Kurdish peoples, its working classes, or Iraqi women. In fact, the Ba'th regime often cited the exigencies of war to justify policies affecting these groups. These policies usually implied a further deterioration in their social condition. An examination of each constituency is beneficial in order to gain insight into the social costs of the war.

The War and Labor

The war contributed to the deteriorating position of the Iraqi working class. Labor was entirely subordinated to wartime imperatives. Workers were pressured to increase and improve their output in order to satisfy the needs of the military effort. High worker productivity was deemed to be equivalent to fighting at the front lines. In an interview in 1983, Saddam Hussein said:

> You know that one gives more under decisive confrontational circumstances, particularly when the issue concerns self-defense and sovereignty, freedom, and independence. This is the case with the Iraqis now. They are exerting efforts in the field of construction on an equal basis with the fighting spirit in the front line trenches in defense of Iraq. Those who are exerting efforts in the field of construction, away from the direct contact lines with the enemy, do this out of patriotism, as we have explained. They feel that those who are confronting the enemy are better than they are because they regard that confrontation as being carried out with weapons; they have to assert their patriotism by being equal to their brothers who are confronting the enemy with their bodies in defense of Iraq. This is the prevalent spirit now in building a new Iraq. Therefore, the job that used to take 6 hours to complete can now be completed in three hours or less.[81]

In the interests of the war effort, workers were frequently forced to accept pay cuts of up to 20 percent or more, work much longer hours, and on holidays, for the same wages, have their pay withheld by the state, waive their vacations, purchase government bonds (equivalent to further slashes in pay), work in increasingly unsafe conditions, and pay special wartime income taxes. Some workers were also subjected to direct repression, including torture and execution.[82] In the period following the guns-*and*-butter campaign, workers' conditions were exacerbated by austerity measures. Consequently, workers faced the dual problem of falling wages combined with rampant inflation: basic commodities were often in short supply, available only on the black market, and prices soared.

Many laborers were forcibly conscripted into the military. The regime partially met the resultant labor shortages by hiring foreign workers, especially Egyptian expatriates. Upwards of two million foreign workers were estimated to be in the labor force during the war.[83] Migrant labor was unable to make demands for better wages or working conditions without being severely punished or sent home. Reports surfaced that migrant workers were often beaten and that Iraqi employers frequently refused to pay them.[84] The use of migrant labor was a worst-case scenario from the perspective of worker disempowerment. Deprived of any means of controlling their work environment, and functioning under extremely vulnerable conditions because of the threat of deportation, expatriate workers were a boon to the Ba'th regime. Their hiring assured the regime of a cheap pool of labor and guaranteed that work disruptions during the war would be kept to a minimum.

Throughout the course of the war, Iraqi workers were afforded no opportunity to empower themselves through collective action. Iraqi labor codes enacted in 1970 and 1987 did not recognize the right to collective bargaining. Strikes were recognized by law but banned in practice. In essence, workers had little power to resist the demands that were placed on them. The Federation of Trade Unions, with direct links to the Ba'th Party, amounted to an instrument of regime control. Even under these austere circumstances, spontaneous strikes occasionally occurred. In order partially to address this problem, the Workers' Democratic Trade Union Movement in the Iraqi Republic was formed. Workers would be organized clandestinely.

Under the forces of privatization, the regime restructured its control of the labor force. In March 1987, it summarily abolished the Federation of Trade Unions and replaced it with the Iraqi General Federation of Trade Unions. Under the new rules, union membership was restricted to workers in private and mixed enterprises. Employees in state enterprises were denied the right to union membership. The labor code of 1970 was abolished. Saddam Hussein declared that workers would henceforth put in twelve-hour-days in the interests of the war effort.[85] These moves were clearly linked to the requirements of the privatization drive. On the one hand, the new Iraqi General Federation of Trade Unions, organically connected to the Ba'th Party, was clearly designed as an instrument of control over a private sector labor force that would inevitably expand with the restructuring of the Iraqi economy. On the other hand, the state denied workers in the state sector any union membership or recourse to labor legislation, thus being free to dispose of its workforce as it saw fit (a process that included layoffs and further efforts to enhance productivity).

The War and Iraqi Women

Prior to the war, the women's movement in Iraq was denied the opportunity to voice freely its concerns and grievances. Authentic women's organizations—that is, organizations acting independently of the Ba'th regime—were not permitted to operate openly. Feminist activists were often incarcerated or expelled from the country. Consequently, as has often been noted, Iraqi women have achieved parity with men only in the areas of detention and torture. The war did little to change this bleak scenario in that—as we have seen—politically it strengthened the regime. The women's movement continued to be artificially enfeebled, and the condition of Iraqi women continued to deteriorate.

The only women's organization allowed to operate was the Ba'th-controlled General Federation of Iraqi Women (GFIW). The GFIW was geared largely to subordinating women to the Ba'th regime. In the war, the GFIW played a key role in mobilizing Iraqi women into the workforce. All indications suggest that these changes did not favor Iraqi women. In 1984, a report out of Kuwait claimed that more that thirty thousand women were working for zero wages.[86] Generally, female workers received only a fraction of the wages that had been paid to men who previously filled the positions. The mobilization of Iraqi women, moreover, was widely viewed as temporary—an exigency of war and little more.[87] In addition, working outside their homes increased the burdens of Iraqi women who single-handedly had to run their households while their spouses were at war.[88]

At the same time as women were being mobilized, the GFIW also figured prominently in efforts to reinforce traditional conceptions of gender. The image of a woman as mother and childrearer was widely extolled. An immediate goal was to increase Iraq's birthrate. In an address to the executive bureau of the GFIW, for example, Saddam Hussein drew direct links between the regime's procreation goals and the war:

> We believe that our motto must be that each family produce five children, boys and girls, as God wishes, and that the family which does not produce at least four children deserves to be harshly reprimanded. We should also express dissatisfaction with this family because history shows that there are many possibilities that trends, jingoism, and other cases may emerge in our Arab east that may pose a threat to Iraq. In any case, our geographic location dictates on us to have a population capable of defending Iraq and enabling Iraqis to live a proud life.[89]

Saddam Hussein explicitly argued that a woman of childbearing age should have children instead of receiving an advanced education:

> Education in Iraq is spreading at the expense of childbirth. . . . If a man comes to me and asks me to allow him to study for his Masters degree or PhD then I would probably let him do so. If, however, a twenty-eight year old women comes to me with the same request then I would have to calculate how long it would take for her to get her doctorate, and I would see that this may take her beyond the age of marriage. . . . I consider the raising of a family to be far more important than getting a PhD. We must unashamedly let this be known to Iraqi women.[90]

Toward the end of the war, slogans—such as "For Saddam the glorious women vow to increase births," or "For your eyes, O Saddam, a million children will be born"—regularly appeared in the state-run media.[91] The GFIW organized meetings to explain the need to procreate and to present gifts to "fertile" women.[92]

Women's traditional roles were occasionally assigned heroic status in the context of the war:

> While the Iraqi people's sacrifices are living evidence of their sincerity, faith, and love for principle, the sacrifices of Iraqi women top all other great and eternal deeds. They have recorded the greatest epics of courage, patience, and faith in the history of our nation. O Iraqi women, your sacrifices and efforts make you an example of courage and generosity. You

have been a *mother,* a *wife,* a *daughter,* and a *sister* to the brave fighters. You have urged them to take initiatives and to make sacrifices; you have alleviated the suffering of soldiers who emerge from the dust of battles and combat. You have encouraged martyrdom.[93]

Despite the rhetoric, women often became direct targets of the regime. Collections of gold jewelry were made forcibly in order to replenish state coffers—a practice that must be considered in the context of the historical importance of jewelry in providing personal security to Iraqi women. Elizabeth Warnock Fernea observed in 1965: "A woman's jewelry is her own insurance against disaster, and the community may take action against men who attempt to seize their women's gold."[94] In another practice that hurt women, the regime sometimes held families hostage as a punitive measure against war defectors. Some Iraqi women were also forced to watch the executions of family members and were prevented from practicing grieving customs when retrieving the bodies of loved ones.

In sum, the war both reinforced conventional conceptions of gender and undermined the chances of their being eroded. It helped to intensify the oppressive cultural code that immures Iraqi women within a narrow range of life options.

The War and the Kurdish Peoples

The Kurdish insurgency had suffered a serious blow as a result of the Algiers Accord of 1975. In the aftermath of the collapse, the Kurdish opposition split into rival factions: the Kurdish Democratic Party (KDP), led by Ma'sud Barazani, and the Patriotic Union of Kurdistan (PUK), led by Jalal Talabani.[95] The Ba'th regime, determined to prevent future uprisings in the region, engaged in a policy aimed at destroying the culture and community-centered life of the Kurdish people. It did this through extensive relocations, Ba'thization, and direct repression.

The onset of the Iran-Iraq War created new possibilities for the Kurdish insurgency by distracting the Ba'th regime and diverting its resources. The KDP seized the opportunity, extending its influence and control in the north of the country. To offset this growing KDP influence, Baghdad entered into negotiations with the PUK. For the Ba'th regime, these negotiations offered a chance to cut into the KDP control; for the PUK, they held out the possibility of gaining greater influence in the region. The negotiations reflected the intense factionalism that plagued the Kurdish opposition.[96] Perhaps more than anything else, the internecine divisions within the Kurdish insurgency restricted its ability to make meaningful gains while Baghdad was preoccupied with the war. The opportunities for cooperation between the two main Kurdish factions increased with the collapse of negotiations between Baghdad and the PUK in January

1985. As relations between the KDP and the PUK warmed toward the end of the war, the strength of the Kurdish resistance increased—a development that alarmed the Ba'th regime.[97]

Overall, however, the war saw a deterioration in the condition of the Kurdish people. Except at politically expedient moments, Baghdad's relationship with the Kurdish population was poor in the extreme. The Ba'th regime aimed at the obliteration of Iraqi Kurdistan, engaging in an aggressive counterinsurgency campaign throughout the war. In August 1983, for example, approximately eight thousand members of the Barzani clan were hauled away. Their fate has yet to be determined.[98] Thousands of Kurds were incarcerated on political grounds. Frequently, detainees were tortured; many were executed. The property of detainees was routinely confiscated and then auctioned. Approximately 75 percent of the villages in Iraqi Kurdistan were destroyed by aerial bombardment. The mass evictions and forced relocations continued throughout the war. The Kurdish region often had economic blockades imposed against it, and basic items such as food, heating oil, and medication frequently failed to reach the civilian population. Throughout these events, the Kurdish legislative assembly amounted to little more than an instrument of the regime. Only Kurdish members of the Ba'th Party were permitted to run for election.[99]

Toward the end of the war, there came a further, horrendous catastrophe. In response to growing Kurdish control, the Ba'th regime resorted to using chemical weapons in areas controlled by insurgent forces.[100] The assault that received most international attention and condemnation occurred in the town of Halabja, along the Iranian border. On 16 and 17 March 1987, the town was attacked with mustard gas and cyanide.[101] The chemical attacks upon Halabja were estimated to have killed five thousand residents. More than fifty thousand were forced to flee the town.[102] Survivors of the Halabja attack were relocated in a new Saddam City of Halabja 15 kilometers away from the old city. The regime encouraged reluctant residents to move by granting them small parcels of land and a subsidy for building a house.[103]

Following the Iran-Iraq War ceasefire of July 1988, the Kurdish situation in many ways resembled the abrupt collapse of 1975. The ceasefire allowed the experienced Iraqi army to turn its attention northward. Within days of the ceasefire, an estimated sixty thousand Iraqi troops, supported by tanks, fighter-bombers, and helicopters, commenced a six-week offensive to recontrol Iraqi Kurdistan.[104] Kurdish insurgent forces, thrown onto the defensive, were limited to small-scale hit-and-run operations. Kurdish civilians, however, once again received the brunt of Baghdad's retaliation. There were widespread reports that the Ba'th regime was regularly using chemical weapons, notwithstanding international reaction to the massacre at Halabja. Relocation programs were intensified as the regime continued to deplete the Kurdish population in the north. More Kurdish villages were razed and their inhabitants moved elsewhere. Human rights abuses, including torture and prolonged detention, persisted.

The chemical weapons attacks on the Kurds, the incarceration and torture of much of the Kurdish population, and the systematic efforts to turn the Kurds into a minority in their own homeland amounted to genocide. Martin van Bruinessen's observations of 1986 that the "news from Kurdistan is sad and grim" rang even truer in the aftermath of the war.[105] Any gains on the part of the Kurdish resistance did not translate into anything meaningful for the Kurdish people: they merely invited harsher reprisals by the Ba'th regime. International outrage over Baghdad's brutal strategy failed to change or improve anything on the ground. Eight years of war and its aftermath at best simply increased the Kurdish hardship.

How the Ba'th Fared

The Ba'th regime was at least as politically strong coming out of the Iran-Iraq War as it was going in—a considerable feat considering the war's steep economic, military, and human tolls. This was owing, in part, to the regime's populist strategies and to the fate of Iraq's opposition forces under wartime circumstances. The social corollary of Baghdad's political consolidation included the continuing decay of Iraq's oppressed groups. The war, in sum, effectively inured the Ba'th regime. Its marginalized social forces were stymied.

Notes

1. See discussion in Frederick W. Axelgard, "War and Oil: Implications for Iraq's Postwar Role in Gulf Security," in *Iraq in Transition: A Political, Economic, and Strategic Perspective,* ed. Frederick W. Axelgard, (Westview Press, 1986), pp. 9–11.

2. The figure is from *Middle East Review,* 1985, p. 110. See discussion about alternative oil outlets and facilities, pp. 110–111.

3. These infrastructural projects are discussed in *Middle East Survey,* 1983, pp. 167–169.

4. Figures extracted from *Arab Oil and Gas,* 16 May 1986.

5. The figures are from *Middle East Review,* 1986, 1988.

6. The price drop in 1986 was ironic for Iraq since by the end of that year it had basically raised exports to its "full export and refining capacity." See *Arab World File,* 23 March 1988, no. 2618.

7. Quoted in *Middle East Review,* 1986, p. 115.

8. These financial arrangements are discussed in detail in *Middle East Review,* 1984, pp. 123–128.

9. Some of the issues involved have been addressed in Basil al-Bustany, "Development Strategy in Iraq and the War Effort: The Dynamics of Challenge," in *The Iran-Iraq War: An Historical, Economic and Political Analysis,* ed. M. S. Azhary, (Croom Helm, 1984) and Jonathan Crusoe, "Economic Outlook: Guns and

Butter, Phase Two?" in *Iraq in Transition: A Political, Economic, and Strategic Perspective,* ed. Frederick W. Axelgard, (Westview Press, 1986).

10. See discussion in Chapter 4.

11. Speech by Saddam Hussein, Baghdad Voice of the Masses, 20 January 1986, *FBIS: Daily Reports,* 21 January 1986.

12. Some commentators have argued that this move reflected the growing influence of Saddam Hussein after the removal of the al-Bakr faction from the ruling coterie. Saddam Hussein, so the argument runs, was ideologically disposed to free-market economy all along. Saddam Hussein, in other words, was a closet capitalist constrained by his colleagues. He could not promote his agenda until his full accession to power in 1979. This argument, however, tends to overemphasize the "socialist" character of the Ba'th regime. A more accurate portrayal would call attention to the shifting emphasis from state-controlled capitalist development to state-encouraged capitalist development under the severe strains of war. The ideological shift—if there was one—was far less profound than suggested. For an outline of the ideological explanation, see *Middle East Contemporary Survey,* 11, (1987), pp. 377–378.

13. See discussion in *Middle East Review,* 1988, pp. 75–76.

14. For a discussion of these trends with respect to the agricultural sector, see Robert Springborg, "*Infitah,* Agrarian Transformation, and Elite Consolidation in Contemporary Iraq," *Middle East Journal,* 40:1, (winter 1986).

15. See discussion in *Middle East Economic Digest,* 15 August 1987.

16. See discussion in Marion Farouk-Sluglett and Peter Sluglett, "Iraq Since 1986: The Strengthening of Saddam," in *Middle East Report,* 20:6, (Nov.–Dec. 1990), p. 22. Also see, for example, *Iraqi Letter,* 4, 1984, pp. 3–5.

17. See discussion in Glen Balfour-Paul, "The Prospects for Peace," in *The Iran-Iraq War,* ed. M. S. El-Azhary, (Croom Helm, 1984).

18. Revolutionary Command Council statement, Baghdad Domestic Radio Service, 22 September 1980, *FBIS: Daily Reports,* 23 September 1980.

19. Baghdad Voice of the Masses, 22 February 1984, *FBIS: Daily Reports,* 22 February 1984.

20. Speech delivered by Iraqi Foreign Minister Hammadi at UN Security Council, 15 October 1980, *FBIS: Daily Reports,* 17 October 1980.

21. Saddam Hussein's address to the Iraqi people, Baghdad Voice of the Masses, 28 September 1980, *FBIS: Daily Reports,* 29 September 1980.

22. Baghdad Domestic Radio Service, 20 June 1982, *FBIS: Daily Reports,* 22 June 1982.

23. Baghdad Domestic Radio Service, 18 October 1987, *FBIS: Daily Reports,* 19 October 1987.

24. Saddam Hussein's address on New Hegira Year, Baghdad INA, 9 November 1980, *FBIS: Daily Reports,* 10 November 1980.

25. Baghdad INA, 10 November 1980, *FBIS: Daily Reports,* 12 November 1980.

26. Interview in Baghdad, Al-Jumhuriyah, 28 January 1988, *FBIS: Daily Reports,* 5 February 1988.

27. *Le Figaro,* 21 December 1982, *FBIS: Daily Reports,* 23 December 1982.

28. Baghdad INA, 21 April 1988, *FBIS: Daily Reports,* 22 April 1988.

29. See discussion in Marion Farouk-Sluglett, Peter Sluglett, and Joe Stork, "Not Quite Armageddon: Impact of the War on Iraq," in *MERIP Middle East Report,* (1984), p. 24.

30. See discussion in Stephen R. Grummon, *The Iran-Iraq War: Islam Embattled,* The Washington Papers, 92, (1982), Chapter 3.

31. Baghdad Domestic Radio Service, 14 March 1981, *FBIS: Daily Reports,* 16 March 1981; Baghdad Voice of the Masses, 6 January 1981, *FBIS: Daily Reports,* 7 January 1981.

32. Baghdad Domestic Radio Service, 29 January 1983, *FBIS: Daily Reports,* 31 January 1983.

33. Baghdad Domestic Radio Service, 8 October 1980, *FBIS: Daily Reports,* 20 October 1980.

34. Saddam Hussein's address on Revolution Day, Baghdad Domestic Radio Service, 16 July 1987, *FBIS: Daily Reports,* 20 July 1987.

35. Baghdad INA, 30 March 1982, *FBIS: Daily Reports,* 31 March 1982.

36. Baghdad Voice of the Masses, 16 July 1984, *FBIS: Daily Reports,* 17 July 1984.

37. Baghdad Voice of the Masses, 6 January 1986, *FBIS: Daily Reports,* 6 January 1986.

38. Baghdad Voice of the Masses, 28 February 1984, *FBIS: Daily Reports,* 28 February 1984.

39. Baghdad Voice of the Masses, 6 January 1982, *FBIS: Daily Reports,* 8 January 1982.

40. Baghdad Domestic Radio Service, 22 March 1987, *FBIS: Daily Reports,* 23 March 1987.

41. Saddam Hussein's 17 July Anniversary Speech, Baghdad Voice of the Masses, 17 July 1983, *FBIS: Daily Reports,* 18 July 1983.

42. Baghdad INA, 2 January 1983, *FBIS: Daily Reports,* 4 January 1983.

43. Baghdad Voice of the Masses, 6 April 1987, *FBIS: Daily Reports,* 8 April 1987.

44. See, for example, address by Na'im Haddad, speaker of the National Assembly, 1 November 1980, *FBIS: Daily Reports,* 3 November 1980.

45. Cairo Al-Ahram's interview with Saddam Hussein, 18 March 1988, *FBIS: Daily Reports,* 22 March 1988.

46. London, *Al-Tadamun,* 20 February 1988, *FBIS: Daily Reports,* 24 February 1988.

47. Baghdad Voice of the Masses, 9 November 1986, *FBIS: Daily Reports,* 10 November 1986.

48. Saddam Hussein's address to the Iraqi cabinet, Baghdad INA, 25 December 1980, *FBIS: Daily Reports,* 29 December 1980.

49. Statement of the regional command of the Ba'th Party, Baghdad INA, 4 April 1984, *FBIS: Daily Reports,* 5 April 1984.

50. See Baghdad INA, 1 November 1987, *FBIS: Daily Reports,* 2 November 1987.

51. Baghdad Voice of the Masses, 1 December 1986, *FBIS: Daily Reports,* 2 December 1986.

52. Madrid, *El Pais,* 27 January 1983, *FBIS: Daily Reports,* 2 February 1983.

53. Saddam Hussein's address, Baghdad Voice of the Masses, 24 April 1988, *FBIS: Daily Reports,* 25 April 1988.

54. Saddam Hussein's address on Iraqi Army Day, Baghdad Voice of the Masses, 6 January 1987, *FBIS: Daily Reports,* 6 January 1987.

55. Baghdad INA, 30 March 1982, *FBIS: Daily Reports,* 31 March 1982.

56. Saddam Hussein's 17 July Anniversary Address, Baghdad Domestic Radio Service, 17 July 1982, *FBIS: Daily Reports,* 20 July 1982.

57. Saddam Hussein's address to the National Assembly, Baghdad Voice of the Masses, 4 November 1980, *FBIS: Daily Reports,* 5 November 1980.

58. For example, see communique 2,789 from the armed forces, which

stressed that air force strikes during August 1987 derived their legitimacy from the merger of shu'bist and Zionist tendencies. Baghdad Voice of the Masses, 29 August 1987, *FBIS: Daily Reports,* 31 August 1987.

59. Baghdad Voice of the Masses, 21 January 1987, *FBIS: Daily Reports,* 22 January 1987.

60. Baghdad Domestic Radio Service, 6 March 1984, *FBIS: Daily Reports,* 7 March 1984.

61. For example, see Baghdad INA, 2 December 1983, *FBIS: Daily Reports,* 5 December 1983.

62. Baghdad Voice of the Masses, 15 February 1983, *FBIS: Daily Reports,* 16 February 1983.

63. Saddam Hussein's address to members of the executive council of the Popular Islamic Conference Organization in Baghdad, Baghdad Voice of the Masses, 21 February 1987, *FBIS: Daily Reports,* 24 February 1987.

64. *ath-Thawrah,* 2 July 1983, *FBIS: Daily Reports,* 1 September 1983.

65. See discussion by Uriel Dann in *Middle East Contemporary Survey,* 9, (1984–1985), p. 174.

66. Dilip Hiro, *The Longest War: The Iran-Iraq Military Conflict,* (Paladin, 1990), p. 257.

67. Marion Farouk-Sluglett, Peter Sluglett, and Joe Stork, "Not Quite Armageddon: Impact of the War on Iraq," *MERIP Reports,* 14:6/7, (July–Sept. 1984), p. 26.

68. Phebe Marr, "The Iran-Iraq War: The Iraqi Experience and its Lessons," (unpublished manuscript).

69. An example: Thirteen of the seventy factories that were privatized by the regime were bought by the al-Bunniyyah family. This family owns thirty-six of the largest private enterprises in Iraq and over forty-five million square meters of land. See discussion in "On the Way to Market: Economic Liberalization and Iraq's Invasion," *Middle East Report,* 21:3, (May/June 1991), p. 18.

70. Some concern about the impact of the war surfaced among Iraq's business class, but this does not nullify the overall political effect for the Ba'th regime—the growth of this class.

71. The most explicit treatment of these tactics is in *Middle East Contemporary Survey,* 9, (1984–1985), pp. 462–464; 10, (1986), pp. 363–368; 11, (1987), pp. 427–431; and 12, (1988), pp. 504–511.

72. See discussion in *Middle East Contemporary Survey,* 5, (1980–1981), p. 585.

73. Ofra Bengio, *Middle East Contemporary Survey,* 7, (1982–1983), p. 572.

74. 'Isam al-Khafaji, "Iraq's Seventh Year: Saddam's Quart d'Heure?" in *Middle East Report,* (March/April 1988), p. 38.

75. See discussion in *Middle East Contemporary Survey,* 11, (1987), pp. 437–438.

76. Ibid., p. 437.

77. The idea that fear is the cement of the Iraqi body politic is the primary theme in Samir al-Khalil, *Republic of Fear: The Politics of Modern Iraq,* (University of California Press, 1989).

78. See discussion in *Middle East Contemporary Survey,* 10, (1986), pp. 368–369.

79. For example, see Amnesty International, *Report and Recommendations to the Government of the Republic of Iraq,* January 1983.

80. Jabr Muhsin et al., "The Gulf War," *Saddam's Iraq: Revolution or Reaction?* ed. CARDRI, (Zed Books, 1989), p. 240.

81. Interview with Cairo al-Ahram, Baghdad INA, 2 December 1983, *FBIS: Daily Reports,* 5 December 1983.

82. Some of these issues are discussed in *Middle East Contemporary Survey,* 7, (1982–1983), p. 567, and 8, (1983–1984), p. 477. Also see various issues of the Iraqi Letter and newsletters of the Committee Against Repression and for Democratic Rights in Iraq (CARDRI, London) over the war period.

83. For a discussion of labor in Iraq, see Sluglett et al, "Not Quite Armageddon," op. cit., pp. 28–29.

84. See "Egyptian Workers are Fleeing Iraq," *New York Times,* 15 November 1989.

85. See discussion in Middle East Watch, *Human Rights in Iraq,* (Yale University Press, 1990), p. 37.

86. *Al-Anba,* 12 April 1984, *FBIS: Daily Reports,* 17 April 1984.

87. A recent study entitled *Gender Inequality in Iraq: 1967–1988* by Lahai A. Mokhif (UMI Dissertation Information Service, 1991) draws attention to the increase in female employment under the Ba'th, especially during the Iran-Iraq War. The study is woefully inadequate, however, in that it fails to address the conditions of the female workforce in the context of gender relations in Iraqi society.

88. On the views of Iraqi women toward work, see the illuminating study by Sana Al-Khayyat entitled *Honour and Shame: Women in Modern Iraq,* (Saqi Books, 1990), pp. 154–155.

89. Baghdad, *al-Jumhuriyah,* 4 May 1986, *FBIS: Daily Reports,* 8 May 1986.

90. See discussion in Celine Whittleton, Jabra Muhsin, and Fran Hazelton, "Whither Iraq?" in *Saddam's Iraq: Revolution or Reaction?* ed. CARDRI, (Zed Books, 1989), p. 248.

91. See discussion by Dehorah Cobbett in *Iraq Solidarity Voice,* 18, Feb. 1988.

92. See discussion in *Middle East Contemporary Survey,* 10, (1986), p. 371.

93. Saddam Hussein's revolution anniversary address, Baghdad Domestic Radio Service, 16 July 1987, *FBIS: Daily Reports,* 20 July 1987. My emphasis.

94. *Guests of the Sheik: An Ethnography of an Iraqi Village,* (Doubleday, 1965), p. 33.

95. The most detailed accounts of the Kurdish struggle can be found in *Middle East Contemporary Survey,* vols. 2 to 12.

96. On the Kurdish alliances with Iran, see Omar Sheikhmous, "The Kurds in the Iraq-Iran War—and Since," paper presented at a colloquium on ethnicity and interstate relations in the Middle East, Berlin, April 20–23, 1989.

97. An interesting account of this growing Kurdish control can be found in "Sons of Devils," *New Yorker,* Nov. 1987.

98. Aspects of these disappearances are well documented in a paper entitled *Eight Thousand Civilian Kurds Have Disappeared in Iraq: What has Happened to Them?* submitted to the Working Group on Enforced or Involuntary Disappearances, Centre for Human Rights, United Nations, 23 May 1988, by a preparatory committee.

99. See discussion in *Middle East Contemporary Survey,* 10, (1986), p. 382.

100. See "Chemicals are not the Kurdish Issue," The Kurdish Program, program update, March 1989.

101. See "The Use of Chemical Weapons: Conducting an Investigation Using Survey Epidemiology," *JAMA,* 262:5, (4 August 1989).

102. See *Christian Science Monitor: Special Report,* December 1988.

103. See discussion in *Human Rights in Iraq,* op. cit., pp. 90–91.

104. See detailed discussion by Ofra Bengio, *Middle East Contemporary Survey,* 12, (1988), 523–525.

105. Martin van Bruinessen, "The Kurds Between Iran and Iraq," in *MERIP Middle East Report,* 16:4, (July–Aug. 1986), p. 14.

7

The Middle East, War, and *Pax Americana*

This study began by contrasting the conventional science of war with the critical science of war. The conventional approach tends to view war as an inevitably destructive and harmful event, and forms implicit parallels with the classical study of theodicy. War and peace are contrasted with each other as comfortably as Saint Augustine would have pitted evil against good. The simple reason for studying war is to eradicate it. The stately idea of securing peace by preparing for war—*si vis pacem para bellum*—has been supplanted by the conviction that peace can be secured by knowing or understanding war. To this end, conventional research has employed a naturalistic model of science derived from the study of biology, chemistry, or physics. War becomes "the thing to be explained." Analysts aspire to provide a nomological portrait of war. This objective portrait can then be employed to suppress or manipulate or coax those causal factors linked with war in order to contain and eliminate it. To use Karl Popper's terms, the cumulative body of scientific knowledge is enlisted in a "piecemeal" fashion in order to "engineer" a better, more peaceful world. Anatol Rapoport's idea of releasing the cold logic of mathematics upon a subject where "passions obscure reason" aptly sums up this research venture. Acknowledgments about the difficulty of following through with this intellectual enterprise have not led to the systematic challenging of its most basic scientific assumptions. The conventional study of war frequently draws upon the study of epidemiology for guidance and inspiration. The inoculation of humanity against social diseases such as war, so the analogy runs, is not unlike the inoculation of an individual against typhoid, yellow fever, polio, and so on.

The conventional enterprise falls firmly within the Enlightenment tradition, resting as it does upon the conviction that scientific knowledge can be used to sculpt a better world. Our purpose here has not been to subject this approach to sustained criticism. It has a firm moral center and clear purpose that demands intellectual care and caution, especially when contrasted with the strategic studies community, a group that views war much more benignly and that is actively plugged directly into the prevailing power blocs of most states. The effort here, rather, has been to contrast the conventional approach with a critical scientific enterprise understood as the contemplation of war in terms of dialectical critiques of social power. The critical study of war rejects the classical liberal conception of society in favor of radical formulations that draw attention to skewed configurations of social power among countervailing social groups (especially socioeconomic classes, racial groups, and gender groups). In this sense, the critical study of war will tend to address its subject matter in terms of race, class, and gender. The critical enterprise is motivated by the preliminary impression that warfare tends to reinforce skewed relations of social power and thereby frustrates or blocks the emancipatory ambitions of subaltern constituencies. Thomas Paine's idea that "wars are the art of conquering at home" assesses the spirit of the critical approach. It seeks to compile theoretical understanding on the relationship between war and the prevailing social relations of power. When it comes down to it, the critical study of war attaches itself to novel premises concerning the relationship between theory and practice; that is, in contrast to instrumentalist views, the critical study of war seeks to transform social oppression by means of self-education and heightened awareness. It aims to provide a clearer picture for oppressed groups, with a view to encouraging less oppressive directions in social practice.

We have applied our critical approach to the Iran-Iraq War. The drift to war between Iran and Iraq began with the disintegration of the old social formations of the Qajar dynasty and the Ottoman Empire. The war began in 1858 with the Ottoman land code, or in 1869 with the opening of the Suez Canal, or at the turn of the century with the growing exposure of Iranian intellectuals to Western ideas, or in 1926 with the full accession of Reza Shah. These dates are pivotal—not because they venture far into the past, but because they mark key points in the socioeconomic transformation of contemporary Iraq and Iran. These changes unleashed and groomed the social forces—especially the modern middle classes, the disaffected traditional middle classes, the working classes, the urban poor, and the peasants—that constituted the heart of the sociopolitical struggles throughout the twentieth century. As these social forces congealed in the post–World War II period, the seemingly inevitable slide to war gathered momentum.

The mounting insecurity between Iran and Iraq in the aftermath of the Islamic Revolution was rooted directly in the broader socioeconomic fields of both countries. Iran's efforts to incite a Shi'i uprising in Iraq were embodied within a theocratic-populist discourse that entered into the intense struggle among the social forces vying for control of the 1979 revolution. In Iraq, the Shi'i struggle reflected the efforts by the ulama to protect themselves from the broad processes of cultural secularization and economic modernization that had drastically eroded their social prestige and material condition. The fact that the Shi'i population was favorably disposed to the clerics was rooted in the changes that had turned the Shi'i tribal members into indigent peasants, many of whom then sought better lives in the city. Ba'th efforts to secure and stabilize oil revenues (a struggle that compelled Baghdad to seize upon Iran's apparent weakness in the aftermath of the Islamic Revolution) were immediately rooted in the regime's efforts to contain the country's subordinate social forces and nurse its developing social base among the emerging capitalist class.

This study has uncovered the social origins of the Iran-Iraq War. It was a war of two societies in crisis. There can be no doubt that it was terribly costly. Its human and material tolls were staggering. The war, however, was also truly suggestive of the above-mentioned idea that "wars are the art of conquering at home." The Iran-Iraq War entrenched repressive political regimes and continually eroded the social power of subordinate constituencies. In this respect the war was a social calamity. It could plausibly be concluded that the working classes, the Kurds, women, and the urban poor of both countries lost the war. Not, to be sure, that the war was fought on behalf of their emancipatory struggles, but rather that the Iran-Iraq War renewed and intensified their oppressive conditions and greatly lessened the chances of them being improved in the foreseeable future.

Our analysis of the Iran-Iraq War establishes a blunt challenge to the field of international relations. International relations has historically been animated by debates that set the terms of reference for subsequent generations of scholarship. The Idealist challenge to Realist thinking and the behaviorialists challenge to the traditionalists constituted the two primary theoretical axes well into the 1970s. More recently, the paradigmatic debate reinvigorated the field and offered a fresh way of approaching the discipline.[1] According to this debate, international relations can be divided into a number of contending paradigms that embody different assumptions regarding the key actors, issues, and dynamics of global politics. The most common division identifies three paradigms: realism, liberalism, and structuralism. This division suggests that research within the field will be more or less commensurate with one of the three. A comparison of standard textbooks within international relations (e.g., Morgenthau's *Politics Among Nations: The Struggle for Power and Peace* or Kal Holsti's *International Politics: A Framework for Analysis* compared with Paul R. Viotti and Mark V. Kauppi's recent *International Relations Theory: Realism, Pluralism, Globalism*)[2] reveals the extended effect of the paradigmatic debate upon the teaching of the discipline.

An engagement with the paradigmatic debate from the perspective of this study is revealing. The thrust here stands in dramatic contrast to analyses that seek to explain war with reference to the distribution of power across the state system. This study helps to disclose the severe limitations of the realist paradigm, as exemplified by Stephen Krasner's recent *Structural Conflict: The Third World Against Global Liberalism.*[3] While states may indeed gaze at each other in a manner befitting gladiators, as Hobbes's famous analogy claims, in order to understand why one particular state becomes a threat to another, or why one state suddenly casts wary glances toward its neighbors, we must look at the dialectics of social power within and across societies. Analysts must consider the manner in which socioeconomic and sociopolitical struggles inside the state come to condition interstate relations. Dynamics of interstate power stand in a relational manner to these social floors. Dynamics of interstate power are not universal; they are entirely contingent; i.e., configurations of interstate power can play themselves out only when allowed to do so by uplifting determinations of the social floor. The practices of realpolitik, so to speak, will matter only if underlying balances among social forces permit them to matter. The very reasons, for example, why in 1980 Iran was a threat to Iraq, as opposed to Kuwait or Turkey or Saudi Arabia, cannot be adequately explained by reference to international power systems or balances of power in the Middle East.

Nonetheless, this study has carefully avoided the ritualistic commination against the dominant realist paradigm. This is due largely to the fact that during the 1980s another challenge has emerged that radically criticizes many of the fundamental precepts of the entire field of international relations, especially its positivist foundations. Any paradigm purporting to offer the definitive account of international relations immediately comes under suspicion. Analysts must recognize that all paradigms secrete a political agenda consonant with a thoroughly contentious set of assumptions. The observations I make in this book could be summarized as the challenge of critical theory. One of the main contributors to this debate has pointed out that "theory is always for someone and for some purpose."[4] The fact that the so-labelled structuralist paradigm is most amenable to the analytical thrust of this study reflects the purposeful nature of the analysis and its underlying presuppositions, and not any claim that this paradigm is closer to some objective or essential truth.

The critical study of war can be significantly extended. A comparative analysis could be undertaken in regions with different colonial experiences. The fractionated colonial history of the twentieth century Middle East, for example, differs radically from the colonial experience in Central America, Southern Africa, or Southeast Asia. Consideration must be given to varying resource wealth: regional conflict and war among the impoverished states in the Horn of Africa may be impelled by different state/society dynamics than those of the oil-rich Gulf states. We should also compare the effects of different regional relationships to the international economy. Areas that supply agricultural products (such as Central or South America) or cheap labor (the Pacific Rim) may experience and create different effects than does the oil-rich Gulf region. Similarly, we would want to compare regions with different cultural traditions, especially those that lack a unifying cultural baseline.

Beyond regional comparisons, the critical analysis of war could also be extended back in time. Paul Kennedy's *The Rise and Fall of the Great Powers: Economic Change and Military Conflict from 1500 to 2000* and David Kaiser's *Politics and War: European Conflict from Philip II to Hitler* are two recent comprehensive examinations of warfare in the modern era.[5] Notwithstanding their respective strengths, both studies reveal the need for a critical survey of warfare in the modern era. What would a critical approach have to say, for example, about the Wars of the Roses, the Thirty Years' War, the wars in the New World, the wars of the Ottoman Empire, King William's War from 1689 to 1713, Queen Anne's War (of Spanish Succession) from 1702 to 1713, King George's War (of Austrian Succession) from 1740 to 1748, the Seven Years' War commencing in 1756, the Napoleonic Wars, the Russo-Persian and the Russo-Turkish wars, and World War I and World War II? We might, to take an example, anticipate that the class nature of warfare during the mercantilist era would be significantly different from the class nature of the two world wars.[6] Again, we might hypothesize that the social nature of regional warfare in the post–World War II period is fundamentally different from the regional nature of warfare prior to 1945.

The critical study of war, moreover, to the extent that it emphasizes previously neglected dynamics, will likely yield a dissenting prognosis on the post–Cold War era, a prognosis contradicting the hubristic celebratory culture of U.S. unipolarism. In short, contrary to the rhetorical euphoria of the post-1989 world, peace does not appear to be at hand. Indeed, the Iran-Iraq War never really ended. Two years after the ceasefire with Iran, Saddam Hussein marched into Kuwait. This time, and in stark contrast to the reception of Baghdad's aggression a decade earlier, the United States reacted with extreme consternation. The Ba'th regime now had something far worse than blood on its hands. Iraq's invasion challenged the U.S. hegemonic order of the Middle East—an order concerned first and foremost with securing Western access to the area's oil riches. Baghdad threatened an understanding that had guided regional affairs throughout the post–World War II period. Challenges to the oil regimes would not be tolerated. In this sense, Baghdad's aggression far exceeded Soviet activity at any time during the Cold War.

And so the neoliberal order rode in on horseback. The second Gulf war did little to lessen the likelihood of future conflict in the Middle East. It was not fought to address the severe social problems that continue to plague the region. It was not fought to democratize Kuwait, Saudi Arabia, Syria, Egypt, or for that matter even Iraq. It was not fought to lessen human rights abuses in the Gulf region. It was not fought on behalf of Middle

Eastern women, or to narrow the gap between the rich and the poor, or to improve labor conditions. It was not fought to arrest the growth of the region's shantytowns. These issues are, at best, incidental to the reaffirmed Pax Americana. They are "problems" to be contained in the interests of interstate balance and stability. Positive social change consonant with the aspirations voiced by the region's indigenous social movements, and change that will inevitably lesson the likelihood of future wars in the Middle East, appears to be little more than a distant hope.

Notes

1. See Michael Banks, "The Inter-Paradigm Debate," in *International Relations: A Handbook of Current Theory,* eds. Margot Light and A. J. R. Groom, (Lynne Rienner Publishers, 1985).
2. Paul R. Viotti and Mark V. Kauppi, *International Relations Theory: Realism, Pluralism, Globalism,* (Macmillan Publishing Company, 1987).
3. Stephen Krasner, *Structural Conflict: The Third World Against Global Liberalism,* (University of California Press, 1985).
4. Robert W. Cox, "Postscript, 1985," in *NeoRealism and its Critics,* (Columbia University Press, 1986).
5. The first was Paul Kennedy's *The Rise and Fall of the Great Powers: Economic Change and Military Conflict from 1500 to 2000,* (Random House, 1987). A more recent study is David Kaiser's *Politics and War: European Conflict from Philip II to Hitler,* (Harvard University Press, 1990).
6. Perry Anderson appears to have been the only writer explicitly to call for a periodization of war. See *Lineages of the Absolutist State,* (Verso, 1979), pp. 31–37.

Index

Abrahamian, E. 36, 41, 50, 119
Aflaq, Michel 151
Algiers Accord 72–73, 81, 87, 89, 161
Anglo-Persian Agreement of 1919: 38
Anglo-Persian Commercial Treaty of 1841: 37
Arab Ba'th Socialist Party 66, 67, 70–71, 155
Arab-Israeli War,1973, 104
'Arid, 'Abd al-Rahman 68
'Arif, 'Abd al-Salam 67
Aron, Raymond 13
Auden, W.H. 11
Augustine, Saint 169
Azarbaijanis 94, 135
Aziz, Tariq 146, 149

Baha'i religion 44
Bahonar, Javad 127
Bakhash, Shaul 121
Baluchis 94, 135
Bani-Sadr, Abolhasson 95, 120–122, 126–127, 128
Barzani, Idris 73
Barzani, Mas'ud 73, 161
Barzani, Mullah Mustafa 71, 73
basiijis (mobilization of the oppressed) 129, 138
Batatu, H. 63, 65, 99, 100
Ba'th regime (Iraq) 2, 54, 67; development policies 105–109; and Kurds 71–74, 161–163; and oil revenues 103–106, 145–146; and political opposition during the war 156–157;

and poverty 79; and Shi'i opposition 77–78, 97–103, 156; state security forces 80; and war populism 148–156; and women 74–77; and working class 157–159;
bazaaris 35, 46–47,
Bazargan, Mehdi 44, 90, 92, 93, 118, 137
Bayat, Assef 137
Beheshti, Muhammad Husseini 92, 125, 127
Bengio, Ofra
Bernard, Luther 6
Bernstein, Richard J. 5
Bill, James 43, 48
Bruinessen, Martin van 163

Carter, Jimmy 44
Choucri, N. 13
Clarke, Robin, 10
Council of Experts 118
Council of Guardians 122, 130
Council of National Resistance 128
critical science of war 2, 3, 11–22, 170; and class 21; costs of war 16–18; definition of war in 14; just war 15–16; and race 21; scientific orientation 18–19, 29*n*.40,*n*.53; and social function of war 14–15; and social oppression 12; society 13–14; theory and practice in 19–20; and women 17–18;

ad-Da'wa party 78, 99
Dulaimi, Naziha 75

175

Kurdish Democratic Party (Iraq) 74,
161–162
Kurds 94, 98, 99; and Algiers Accord
72–73; and Ba'th regime 71–74; during the war in Iran 134–136; during
the war in Iraq 161–163;
Kuwait 147, 172, 173
Kzar, Nadhim 79

labor: during the war in Iran 136–138;
during the war in Iraq 157–159;
Islamic revolution and 50–52
Lors 94

madakhel system 39
Maknoun, Barzin 133
maktabi management 137–138
Manasheri, David 130
Marcuse, Herbert 15
Marr, Phebe 68, 106, 155
Morgenthau, Hans 2, 171
Moss Helms, Christine 72
Mossadeq, Mohammad 35, 50
Mujahedin 91, 118, 127

Nashat, Guity, 132
National Front 44
Nile River 36
North, R. 13

Owen, Roger 60
Owen, Wilfred 4, 15
Ottoman Empire 60–63, 170, 173

Pahlavi monarchy 38–43, 53, 132,
133; bureaucratic reforms 39–40;
class development under 40–41;
educational reforms 40; economic
development 40, 41–2; and fall of
Qajar dynasty 38–39; modern
middle class in 43–46; military
development 39; political development 42–43; poverty in 42; SAVAK
43, 47, 51; traditional middle
class 46–50; working class 50–
52
Paine, Thomas 14, 170
Paris Commune of 1871, 136
Patriotic Union of Kurdistan 74,
161–162
Pipes, Daniel 23

Popper, Karl 9, 169
Portsmouth Treaty 59
positivism 1
post–Cold War era 3
purdah 75

Qajar dynasty 35, 36, 38, 170; class
structure in 37–38
Qasem, 'abd al-Karim 66, 67, 99
Qashqa'i 135
Qatar 147

Rafsanjani, Hashemi, 92, 125
Rajai, Muhammad Ali 127
Rajavi, Mas'ud 127
Rapoport, Anatol 6, 11, 169
Revolutionary Guards *(pasdaran)* 92,
121, 129
Richardson, Lewis Fry 6
Rouleau, Eric 121
Rousseau, Jean-Jacques 10
Russian revolution 136

as-Sadr, Baqir, 96, 99, 102
Salman, Sabah, 154
Sanjabi, Karim 44
Sarraf, Tahmoores 126
Saudia Arabia 146, 147, 173
Schmidt, Herman 18
Shah, Mohammed Reza 41, 42–43, 90,
119, 132; and *bazaaris* 47; and
ulama 47–48
Shah, Reza (Reza Khan) 35, 132; and
Western influence 39
Shari'ati, Ali 127
Shatt al-Arab waterway 23, 88
Shi'i opposition (Iraq) 77–78, 97–103,
156
Simpson, John 133
Sluglett, M.F. 101, 106
Sluglett, P. 101, 106
Snow, Dr. John 10
Soltanpour, Saeed 45
Stork, Joseph 102
Sunni muslims 99
Syria 173

Talabani, Jalal 74, 161
thalweq principle 23
ath-Thawra township 77, 79, 101–
102
theocratic populism 2, 90–97

About the Book and Author

Workman explores the origins of the Iran-Iraq War in terms of the sweeping socioeconomic transformations in both countries as they were drawn into the global economy.

The intense struggles among social forces unleashed by these changes undergirded the slide to war in 1980. Also figuring prominently in the protracted war were the continuing sociopolitical struggles in both states, especially the process of revolutionary consolidation in Iran. In the end, Workman concludes, the Iran-Iraq War significantly strengthened the regimes in Baghdad and Tehran and did little to lessen the oppression of subaltern social constituencies in either country—thus tending to confirm Thomas Paine's axiom that "all wars are the art of conquering at home."

W. Thom Workman is associate director of York University's Centre for International and Strategic Studies.